ROBIN HOOD
OF
KATHIAWAR

ROBIN HOOD
OF
KATHIAWAR

AND OTHER EXTRAORDINARY STORIES FROM

INDIA'S FREEDOM MOVEMENT

THE PAPERCLIP

HARPER

NON-FICTION

An Imprint of HarperCollins *Publishers*

First published in India by Harper Non-Fiction 2026
An imprint of HarperCollins *Publishers*
HarperCollins *Publishers* India, Cyber City,
Building 10-A, Gurugram, Haryana – 122002, India
www.harpercollins.co.in

2 4 6 8 10 9 7 5 3 1

Copyright © The Paperclip 2026

P-ISBN: 978-93-6569-596-0
E-ISBN: 978-93-6569-795-7

Typeset in 10.5 pt/14 Scala Pro
by HarperCollins *Publishers* India Pvt. Ltd

Printed and bound at
Repro India Limited

This book is produced from independently certified FSC® paper to ensure
responsible forest management.

HarperCollins *Publishers*, Macken House, 39/40 Mayor Street Upper, Dublin 1,
D01 C9W8, Ireland

Contents

The detailed notes pertaining to this book are available on the HarperCollins website. Scan this QR code to access the same.

Preface

History may fade from memory, but a story can rekindle it. It can send our grey cells into a tizzy, touch the soul and linger in the mind long after we have read the last word. In a layered country like India, stories about the freedom movement trigger nuanced feelings. Our fight for independence didn't just create a nation; it created a million strange, moving, brilliant stories. There are so many of them—some have been told and retold, some documented, while several others remain untold, or manipulated, reshaped, underappreciated or buried in the far corners of fading memories, away from regular history textbooks. But maybe the best way to keep them alive isn't just through textbooks or monuments. It's by bringing them into our daily lives—through the things we talk about, the food we eat, the films we watch, the fashion we flaunt and the music we listen to. Even the most mundane, everyday objects have a history to them—often hidden from plain sight.

Robin Hood of Kathiawar and Other Extraordinary Stories from India's Freedom Movement is a fresh and creative attempt to rejig memories and shine a gentle light on some of those quieter, hidden corners. Here, you'll find fifty lesser-known stories of courage, wit, conviction and sheer eccentricity that defy narratives. This isn't a retelling of well-worn facts, nor is it an academic chronicle. It's a collection of threads that weave together a picture of India's journey to independence, delightfully packed with trivia, anecdotes and some quirky connections.

You might wonder—why such a title or who is the Robin Hood of Kathiawar?

'Robin Hood of Kathiawar' is only one of the fifty stories in this book. It is about an outlaw—though not the kind you might expect. He did walk the thin line between crime and courage. But one must pick up the book to read more about him. We borrowed this story as it serves as the perfect metaphor for all the others. His story—wild, absurd, and oddly moving—captured the spirit that runs through all the other curated stories. Every tale in this book, in some way, shares that same irreverent heart. From extraordinary freedom fighters to Bollywood magic, sporting icons to revolutionary brands, everyday commodities to secret operations in foreign lands, this anthology aims to walk you through our freedom movement—sometimes in unexpected ways, sometimes through people you've never heard of, and occasionally through things you may have never connected to the freedom movement at all.

This book began as a search for fragments. Our research drew from memoirs, letters, intelligence reports, trial transcripts, forgotten biographies, and oral histories. We do not claim to have written a definitive history—if anything, this book is a reminder that history is rarely definitive. Along the way, we found countless other stories that fascinated, intrigued, or delighted us—stories that could not fit into fifty chapters, but remain with us nonetheless.

For instance, did you know that the legendary Rani Lakshmibai's legal counsel in her battle against the East India Company wasn't an Indian at all? It was an Australian traveller, lawyer and novelist named John George Lang—he travelled India on palanquins and horses. Yes, an Australian! He defended Indians against the British, and launched an anti-government newspaper in Calcutta called *The Mofussilite*. Rani Lakshmibai sent a white elephant to bring him to her palace and requested him to fight a case to stall the annexation of the kingdom of Jhansi. The image of this sunburnt outsider fighting imperial injustice in colonial India is both delightful and deeply symbolic. It is proof that freedom often finds the most unlikely champions.

In many of these tales, India's freedom doesn't appear as a single clarion call but as a patchwork of individual and collective decisions. Some were grand and defiant, like Khudiram Bose's fearless sacrifice at just eighteen. His hanging inspired a generation of students to fight for freedom. Legends quickly grew. Stories of young men wearing dhotis embroidered with his name, and even reports of soda bottles bursting in European clubs that caused panic among the patrons, spread widely—like Goliath not knowing where, when, or how David would strike next. What still stands today is a remote railway station—Khudiram Bose Pusa in Samastipur district, part of the East Central Railway's Sonpur division—carrying forward his legacy.

And then there are those tales that flirt with pop culture—like the curious case of the word 'Bashi-bazouk'. Comic book enthusiasts will instantly recognize it as one of Captain Haddock's many creative expletives in the beloved Tintin series by Hergé—a comical, almost nonsensical insult. But it also has a deeper, darker origin. The term originally described wild and indisciplined soldiers in the Ottoman Empire, known for their cruelty. Interestingly, the same word appears in colonial India as the nickname for a notorious British soldier named John Evans, infamous for his brutality during the 1857 uprising in Delhi. While a comic written by a Belgian cartoonist and India's First War of Independence may seem unrelated, they share a common thread of history. And that says a lot about the strange, stitched-together ways our past continues to live on in modern culture.

There are countless such unusual stories that highlight the unexpected intersections of history and offer a glimpse of everyday lives. Like the story of Boroline—the antiseptic cream in the little green tube that many of us grew up with. Who would have thought that this humble product was once a symbol of the Swadeshi Movement? When Gour Mohun Dutta, its founder, built this brand, he also built a statement. A statement of economic independence, born from the idea that we can create and trust in what is our own. The day India gained freedom, over a lakh tubes of Boroline were distributed to mark the occasion and celebrate self-reliance. The famous Bose speaker might never have been developed if a certain Noni Gopal Bose hadn't been arrested on charges of writing a seditious pamphlet distributed in a protest rally against the British in Calcutta. He escaped with other freedom fighters when they were rescued from a prison van, and eventually made his way to America. His son, Amar Gopal Bose, founded the Bose Corporation in Massachusetts years later.

And then there are those whose stories remained hidden for decades. There was a Dalit man named Mangu Ram who was caught in Indonesia when smuggling arms to Punjab. He miraculously escaped just hours before his execution and eventually went into hiding in the Philippines, moving from one island to another to avoid a British death warrant. All the while, his family believed he was dead. And yet, these are the stories that make the freedom movement feel real, messy and human. Shaheed Udham Singh acted in Hollywood movies. Netaji organized Durga Puja celebrations inside a prison in Burma. A little boy from Benares (now Banaras or Varanasi), orphaned by the Great Indian Rebellion of 1857, went on to score a goal in the prestigious FA Cup final. The stories keep unfolding.

History is not always linear. It zigzags across continents and shows up in strange places. What connects these stories is not just their strangeness or their obscurity, but the deep human values at their core—resistance, resilience, humour and hope. Take Mahatma Gandhi, for example. He is everywhere. We met a group of dancers during the Carnival in Salvador, Brazil. Dressed in white, the men moved to the deep rhythm of Afro-Brazilian percussion. They called themselves Filhos de Gandhy—Sons of Gandhi. The story goes that it all began a year after Gandhi's assassination. A small group of dockworkers in one of Salvador's poorest neighbourhoods gathered under a tree. Inspired by India's struggle for freedom and Gandhi's message of peace and resistance, they formed a group in his name. Gandhi never visited Brazil. Yet, his ideas found a home there. A century later, Gandhi's reputation remains so universally iconic that in a Russian prison scene in the Netflix hit series Stranger Things (Season 4 Episode 3), a prison guard sarcastically name-drops him as the moral opposite of a crooked smuggler. That's Gandhi—crossing borders, genres and generations, with quiet power.

If you're an Apple user, you might be surprised to know that Steve Jobs, who reshaped the modern world with Apple, changed his style after being fired from the company. He chose a pair of simple, round, wire-rimmed glasses, inspired by Gandhi's iconic appearance. Jobs carried Gandhi's photo in his wallet and there was no one he admired more than the Mahatma. He came to India in 1974 seeking meaning, and found resonance in Gandhi's belief that change doesn't always need to be loud or violent—it can be graceful, moral, even quiet, and still be revolutionary.

In fact, it's this very spirit of quiet revolution that inspired this book. Each chapter in this book takes you through such mini-revolutions—moments, people and symbols that may not feature in our school history books but deserve their own place in our collective consciousness. The chapters are short, readable and full of fascinating digressions—designed not just to inform, but to entertain and connect.

This book does not aim to glorify or exaggerate. It simply aims to remember. To bring back to life the lesser-known stories of our freedom movement, to spark conversations around bonfires, and enlighten curious kids through simple storytelling. At Paperclip, that's what we always aim to do—tell a good story. Stories shape minds more than arguments ever can.

This curated collection of stories aligns with our belief that stories like these remind us that truth is often multi-coloured, complex and full of delightful contradictions. They also remind us that history is not just something to be studied—it is something to be felt. This isn't a history lesson or a scholarly journal. This is a book of curiosity and discovery, where history isn't a monologue. The stories in this book come from a wide mix of backgrounds. It is a lively blend of places, people, objects, courage, humour, brands, fashion, films and everything in between. If you've followed The Paperclip before, you probably know how much joy we take in finding the little things—whether it's by reading, travelling, watching an old TV show, or trying a new cocktail.

We've been fortunate to travel a lot over the years and lucky to meet some truly fascinating people along the way. Some were friends, some were experts, and some were complete strangers—but each of them helped us learn and see things differently. You'll find many of those encounters scattered across the chapters of this book. These experiences shaped how we've put this together. Everything we learned, whether through long conversations or unexpected moments, found its way into these pages.

There was that wild night watching lucha libre in Mexico City, after which we stumbled into a nightclub that was once the home of a Bengali nationalist. A spicy dinner in the Caribbean led us to an unlikely connection with the 1857 rebellion. We searched for the old address of a Ghadar Party hideout, just a few kilometres from where Lionel Messi grew up. One time, it was just going to Tokyo and finding a bakery that serves a chicken curry recipe passed down from an Indian rebel in disguise. Back home, we passed by a local football ground and later learned it had witnessed an assassination that shook the British Empire. We made several trips to libraries in Kolkata, Delhi and even Chicago, poring over books, old magazines and archives to piece things together. All these stories are tucked into different chapters in this book, offering a fresh and unexpected way to look at the history of the freedom movement.

We spent weeks, even months, reading through books, journals and memoirs to connect the dots. We're not historians, and we don't pretend to be. But we've made an honest effort to share how we've seen and felt the story of India's freedom—in a way that's curious, welcoming, and human.

We are deeply indebted to the authors of all the fascinating books, journals, scholarly articles, and references we've cited. We are especially grateful to the historians and the journalists who have tirelessly documented India's long and complex journey to freedom. This book would not have been possible without their work. We also want to acknowledge everyone we spoke to—those who generously shared sources, offered unforgettable anecdotes, and joined us along the way. Thank you to each and every one of you who made this work possible.

Each story has been carefully crafted. Sometimes we took detours, got sidetracked or followed a hunch—and often those moments led us to something even more interesting than what we were originally looking for. That's how this book has been—a bit whimsical, a little unpredictable. In today's world of WhatsApp forwards and post-truth noise, we tried to approach history without making it a burden. We hope each story in this book will make you step back and wonder, smile, even amaze you a little and, most importantly, feel a little more connected to the rich and quirky patchwork of our past.

Because freedom, like storytelling, is never truly about just one voice.

It's about all of us.

007
VOTE FOR GHOSE
CHICAGO RADIO
Symbol of
Freedom

1

The Quiet Legacy of the Nehru Jacket

Since 1942, Archie comics have entertained readers with stories of high school drama, friendship and fun. Growing up, these comics were a staple for many urban English-speaking children in India. It was, quite possibly, one of the few portals for Indian young adults to experience American high school culture. Archie is the classic all-American teenager with a knack for getting into trouble. And, of course, he also juggles his love for Betty and Veronica.

In the February 1969 issue of *Betty and Me*, a popular Archie comics series, Archie made an unexpected style statement. He appeared wearing something that many Indians could instantly recognize: a purple Nehru jacket. For fans of the beloved red-haired high schooler, this was a surprising departure from his usual casual attire. We love to find stories around us. Comic books are no exception. But why would a certain Nehru jacket, which is inherently Indian, appear in a teenage comic from 1960s America? It's something we weren't prepared for.

When we started exploring deeper, it became clear to us that it wasn't just an abrupt fashion choice. At Kolkata Comic Con, 2025, we had an unexpected encounter with Bill Golliher, the legendary artist behind Archie comics for the past thirty years. Of course, Bill started writing the comics after the swinging sixties. But, we couldn't help but ask about the Nehru jacket in the Archies. Bill graciously responded, 'Yes, the Nehru jacket craze in 1960s America was very real, so it's not very surprising that it made it into the comic book.' Bill wasn't exaggerating. The Nehru jacket, named after Jawaharlal Nehru, India's first Prime Minister, was once a symbol that fascinated America and the West. And it was no accident.

The Nehru jacket has its roots in traditional Indian clothing, specifically in the bandhgala and achkan. For those who don't know, an achkan is a buttoned coat that is knee-length and usually worn to formal events. It is perfectly designed to fit India's subtropical environment and blends style with functionality.

This traditional clothing was adapted by Jawaharlal Nehru to fit his political beliefs and personal style. Nehru, in fact, wore a smarter and more manageable version of the classic achkan. In keeping with his personality, he got the length shortened and tailored to fit. The mandarin collar, with its high, banded neckline, was what distinguished the Nehru jacket from Western blazers.

Nehru's outfit became an essential part of his persona, along with a red rose in the buttonhole and a white kurta-pyjama. This was definitely not by chance. He was clearly aware of the significance of symbolism. His clothing represented a new India that was sophisticated yet deeply rooted in its culture. The idea of a country that could embrace development without losing its cultural character was mirrored in it.

Back in 2013, the *Wall Street Journal* interviewed P.K. Vaish, Nehru's favourite tailor from south Delhi. Vaish, trained in London, began making achkans for the Prime Minister in the early 1960s. 'Nehru was very cautious about his dress. He was a royal man,' says Vaish, who was seventy-one at the time of the interview. He remembers Nehru's strict colour palette. 'He wore only black, white, cream and grey,' recalls Vaish. Nehru also loved bamboo fabric, a material that has since faded out of fashion.

Elegance in motion: Jawaharlal Nehru on horseback, dressed in a gorgeous achkan, circa 1950. (Photo author unknown. Public Domain via Wikimedia Commons.)

When the style was the message

Nehru believed fashion had a political dimension. For a figure like him, it was never just about appearance. The Nehru jacket carried this idea forward. By wearing it as his signature style, Nehru sent a subtle yet strong message to the world. India was ready, and Indians were not going to hide their cultural pride and political independence.

The Nehru jacket's global journey began in the 1950s and 1960s. It was a period of rapid cultural exchange and globalization. As India emerged as a key player in the post-colonial world, Nehru became one of its most prominent faces. He himself said on the eve of India's independence on 15 August 1947, 'Those dreams are for India, but they are also for the world.' The 1950s was the time when India was about to knock on the doors of destiny. In that brave new world, his diplomacy and charisma brought him into the international spotlight. His style, epitomized by his eponymous jacket, added a touch of pizzazz.

> ### Similar but so different: The Mao jacket
>
> The Nehru jacket was not the only item that made waves across cultures at the time. The Mao jacket, part of the costume known as the 'Mao suit', had strong political implications. The Mao jacket was named after Chinese Communist leader Mao Zedong to imitate his style. Michael Alexander Langkjær, in his article 'From Cool to Un-cool to Re-cool: Nehru and Mao Tunics in the Sixties and Post-Sixties West', explored in detail the differences between the two jackets named after these towering statesmen. The Mao jacket looks quite similar, the only difference being its turndown collar and four flapped pockets.
>
> Aesthetically, the Mao jacket would make you think of structure and uniformity, which were frequently associated with the rigidity of Communist dictatorship. In contrast, the Nehru jacket had its modern universal appeal that resonated well beyond its origins.

Nehru's unique style soon caught the attention of Western designers who were looking for new ideas. Minimalist aesthetics were becoming popular in Europe and America. French designer Pierre Cardin was one of the first to introduce the mandarin collar to Western audiences. His Cylinder suit became a signature of 1960s fashion. And, it was quite clearly inspired by the Nehru jacket.

When talking about fashion, one name cannot be left out: Johnny Carson, the king of Late Night. In 1968, Johnny Carson walked onto *The Tonight Show* wearing a Nehru jacket. It was designed by the famous Oleg Cassini.

Cassini was already famous as Jacqueline Kennedy's preferred designer when she was First Lady. He recalled, 'I liked the clean, uncluttered simplicity of it.' He said his fascination with the Nehru jacket came from seeing Indian maharajas in achkans and then Nehru wearing his personalized version when he visited the White House.

When Carson entered the stage wearing the Nehru jacket, it caused a cultural ripple effect of epic proportions. It was almost an overnight mania. That night, thousands of people called to ask about the jacket. After all, it was Johnny Carson. Soon, the Nehru jacket quietly made its way into movies, television and high-profile events.

Pandit Jawaharlal Nehru, Prime Minister of India, arriving at Valkenburg Airport, Netherlands, in his signature Nehru jacket, circa 1957. (Photographer: J.D. Noske/ ANEFO. Public Domain via Wikimedia Commons.)

Everybody wants the Nehru cool!

The first James Bond movie, *Dr. No* (1962), featured the Nehru jacket on the big screen for the first time. Perhaps, there isn't a better movie than a James Bond one to capture the trend. Joseph Wiseman played the role of the brilliant mad scientist, Dr Julius No, in this Bond classic. He is often seen wearing a beige tunic with a mandarin collar. It was a well-thought-out style statement to blend the Western and Eastern worlds.

In fact, James Bond himself, played by Sean Connery, also wore a Nehru-style jacket in the same film. To put it mildly, it was an outstanding debut. The jacket frequently appeared in other Hollywood movies in the coming years. It became quite a sensation. From Frank Sinatra to Sammy Davis Jr—the who's who of Page 3 celebrities were all seen sporting a Nehru jacket.

Designers instinctively adopted the Nehru jacket into their collections. Nehru jackets for men and boys were widely accessible during the 1960s and early 1970s. Women also embraced a variant of the style, which included a flared Nehru jacket and matching pants or a skirt.

Hollywood certainly brought the Nehru jacket into mainstream fashion. However, it really gained cultural momentum a few years later. The Beatles played a big role in this. The year was 1965, and Shea Stadium in Queens, New York, was ready to host the milestone event. This concert, one of their biggest during the tour, would mark the beginning of the mania for stadium rock concerts. Incidentally, it was on 15 August. The atmosphere was electric. At exactly 9.02 p.m., the Fab Four stepped onto the stage. They were all wearing beige Nehru-inspired jackets in front of their audience of 50,000 screaming and clapping fans.

It's said that George Harrison was in love with Indian music and spirituality, and he was the one who suggested the idea of the Nehru jacket as the band's attire. It meant something special to their fans.

For the youth of the 1960s, the Beatles stood as a break from tradition and conformity. They were true icons of counterculture. Soon, the Nehru jacket became very popular among American youth. This was also the time of the Vietnam War protests. American youth clearly did not want the war. Students united in the belief that the Vietnam War was wrong. They rejected, on moral grounds, the idea of old-world dominance. They believed Vietnam should be for the Vietnamese. The freedom movement of India was seen as a quiet symbol of anti-colonialism and social democracy. Nehru's minimalist style resonated with the generation. It became a way to show solidarity with global anti-imperialist struggles.

Let's circle back to the Archie comics. Actually, the Nehru jacket made it into the comic books not once, but twice in consecutive months. First, it was in January 1969, in the story 'Ding-A-Ling', where Veronica Lodge is seen swooning over Archie's slick competitor, Reggie Mantle, who is wearing a Nehru jacket. Of course, Veronica thought it was cool. Just a month later, Archie himself adopted the style in 'A Stitch in Time', which appeared in *Betty and Me* (February 1969). It was a gift from Veronica. She wanted to surprise Archie with a purple Nehru jacket for their supposed anniversary. Archie loved the surprise and was elated. After all, who wouldn't like a classic Nehru jacket?

By the 1970s, the Nehru jacket gradually lost popularity in the West, until its worldwide revival in this century. Nehru likely never imagined that his sartorial choices would inspire a global phenomenon. For him, the jacket was a practical, elegant garment— one that symbolized India's identity and aspirations. It was likely India's finest fashion export after Independence. It was possibly the best symbol that preserved the political and cultural significance of India's freedom movement, second only to the Gandhi cap. Is there anything else quite like it?

2

Chicago Radio: Voice of Freedom

One scene from the 2022 Hindi-language biographical crime drama *Gangubai Kathiawadi*, directed by Sanjay Leela Bhansali, truly captivated us. In this scene, Alia Bhatt, who plays the charismatic character of Gangubai, gives an impressive speech in front of a packed crowd at Azad Maidan. The scene went quite viral. She looks imposing in a white saree and retro sunglasses. Here, we must credit the creators for their attention to one simple but important detail. It wasn't just Alia Bhatt's powerful performance that grabbed our attention—it was also the public address system in front of her: Chicago Radio.

But what's the story behind it? It's one you definitely don't want to miss.

Let's take a trip back to the late nineteenth century, to the heart of Sindh, where a young Gianchand Motwane set off on an extraordinary journey that would shape his destiny.

Gianchand was just twelve years old when tragedy struck. His father, Diwan Chandumal Motwane, a respected lawyer in the city of Larkana, Sindh (now part of Pakistan), passed away at the young age of forty-five. Despite Diwan's successful career, the family was left nearly penniless. His generous heart had led him to spend almost every penny on charity, dedicating himself to the service of the needy and the sick.

To help support his family's modest means, Gianchand tried his hand at a variety of ventures. He bound books, made rubber stamps and crafted kites. Though he had to abandon his formal education before completing matriculation, Gianchand's natural knack for all things technical drove him to teach himself telegraphy. This skill opened the doors to a job as a signaller with the railways, where his talent quickly shone through. Before long, he was promoted to the position of inspecting telegraph master in the Post & Telegraph department of the North-Western Railway.

But his true spark came when he took a leap of faith and started his own electrical equipment company, Eastern Electric & Trading Co. in Sukkur (Sindh), with a capital of Rs 300 generated from his earnings.

Gianchand's entrepreneurial journey began with importing flashlights from Germany, but he didn't stop there. He expanded his business to include mobile power plants, providing electricity and telephones. A true visionary, he was an early believer in the power of advertising, famously saying, 'Nothing but a mint can make money like advertising can.' His belief paid off—soon, over 200 agents were selling his flashlights across undivided India. In just three years, his business had grown so rapidly that he relocated his operations to Karachi and closed his Sukkur office.

A disaster made into an opportunity

When World War I broke out in 1914, Gianchand's business faced a setback, as imports from Germany came to a halt. But he was undeterred. Quickly adapting, he began importing what he needed from the United States and Great Britain instead. As the years passed, his business continued to grow, and in 1919, he reached another significant milestone. That April, he made the bold decision to move his company's headquarters to Bombay (now Mumbai). This move marked the beginning of a new chapter for his business.

Gianchand secured a contract with the Chicago Telephone Supply Company in India and, with their permission, went on to establish his own firm under the same name. In 1926, he took another bold step, rebranding the company as Chicago Telephone and Radio Co., setting the stage for even greater success.

The newly established company soon made a name for itself, providing and installing telephone systems for a wide range of private businesses and government agencies. With each successful installation, its reputation grew, becoming a trusted partner in the ever-expanding world of communication.

Driven by his deep passion for technological innovation, he took matters into his own hands by setting up his own radio transmitter. Broadcasting under the call sign '2-KC' through the Bombay Presidency Radio Club Ltd, an organization he had helped establish, he became a pioneer in the field. Before long, his fascination with radio evolved into a business venture, as he began importing radio receivers and selling them to eager customers, bringing the magic of wireless communication into homes across the city.

Ten years after giving his company a new name, he took it a step further, transforming it into a limited liability company. Meanwhile, his other business was also evolving. As he ventured into the world of heavy electrical and mechanical engineering, he rebranded it as Eastern Electric & Engineering Co. in 1928, marking a bold new chapter in his entrepreneurial journey.

Amplify the call for freedom

By this time, Gianchand's son Nanik Motwane joined him to support the growing family business. Nanik was a volunteer in the Indian National Congress (INC). In 1929, Nanik watched as Gandhiji moved tirelessly from one platform to another, his powerful words often lost in the noise of the crowds. He knew that India's greatest voice against British imperialism needed to be heard—loud and clear. Determined to amplify the call for freedom, Nanik found the perfect solution: Chicago Radio loudspeakers.

As a document from the company archives aptly noted, it was only fitting that a firm that had pioneered radios in India would be the one to conceive, refine and bring to life the use of loudspeakers to amplify the human voice.

The true test for these loudspeakers came in 1931 at the Congress session in Karachi. It was here that the Congress Party would make a defining statement, passing the Karachi Resolution that outlined for the first time a vision of fundamental rights and duties under Purna Swaraj or complete independence. Before the session, Sardar Vallabhbhai Patel had asked Nanik to take 'personal charge of the loudspeaker arrangements'.

Dr B.R. Ambedkar addressing a gathering in Nashik with a Chicago Radio microphone, circa 1935. (Photo author unknown. Public Domain via Wikimedia Commons.)

Chicago Radio quickly gained the trust of Congress, and almost all the eminent leaders of India's independence movement addressed the masses through Chicago Radio loudspeakers and public address systems. And when the historic 'Tryst with Destiny' speech of Nehru echoed across the land on the eve of India's independence, Chicago Radio stood as a silent witness and helper.

The voice of the leaders of India's freedom movement became stronger and louder, and most importantly, the masses could clearly hear their beloved leaders without any distortion.

Swadeshi: The seeds for 'Make in India'

Chicago Radio became a symbol of reliability nationwide. Gandhi, Nehru, Sardar Patel, and Rajendra Prasad—all had addressed the nation using Chicago Radio speakers and warmly praised the quality of the apparatus. Gandhiji stated:

> The cheers that punctuated my remarks on some of the most important amendments showed that the listeners were following my exposition with the utmost attention. All this was possible because of the perfect Chicago Radio loudspeaker arrangements that were made for the Subjects Committee as well as for the Open Sessions.

'Your loudspeakers did most excellent work and the arrangements were very much appreciated by all,' said Pandit Nehru.

The girl who ran a rebel radio

Usha Mehta's story is well known today. As a young girl she ran a secret radio station called Congress Radio during the Quit India Movement. In 2024, the movie *Ae Watan Mere Watan* was released, where Sara Ali Khan played her role.

What many people don't know is that after Usha Mehta was arrested, the CID continued investigating the source of the radio transmitters used in the underground operations. According to the *Maharashtra State Gazetteers: Greater Bombay District (Volume I)*, published in 1986, 'An important question arises as to from where did the Radio Transmitter come in those difficult times. It was Mr Nanak [*sic*] Motwane, the patriotic proprietor of the Chicago Radio Telephone Company, Bombay, who had provided the equipment for the cause of the nation.' Six days later, Nanik Motwane was arrested as well.

On 28 January 1950, an advertisement for Chicago Radio appeared in the *Times of India* (Delhi), featuring none other than India's first Prime Minister, Jawaharlal Nehru, as its endorser. By then, Gianchand Motwane's dream had become a reality—his brand had earned the approval of the nation's most prominent leader. However, in hindsight, some might find it rather unusual, even controversial, for a sitting Prime Minister to publicly endorse a commercial product. If there's anyone to hold accountable for this unexpected twist, it would have to be Nehru himself. On the other hand, there was a tradition from before, of leaders endorsing swadeshi products (Chapter 4). It was the dawn of the age of 'Make in India'.

Of course, there were some controversies. *Filmindia* magazine, in its November 1945 issue, published an exchange of letters between Ambalal J. Patel, chief of the Central Camera Company, and Nanik Motwane. A few days after the All-India Congress Committee session in Bombay, Mr Patel accused the Congress of giving a monopoly on recording the session to only one company. He also claimed that Motwane's policy of distributing free loudspeakers was a way to create a monopoly and gain free promotion by displaying the Chicago Radio banners everywhere.

It is true that Chicago Radio was believed to be very close to the Congress party. However, it was also true that they had earned their place in the spotlight by always supporting India's freedom movement, even in the most difficult times.

A legacy of national pride

The company still stands strong today, and over the years, Chicago Radio speakers have been a steadfast companion to many of India's historic moments. One such milestone unfolded in 1960, when millions of spectators gathered along Mumbai's iconic Marine Drive to witness the grand celebration of the Indian Air Force's 27th anniversary. As fighter jets roared across the sky, the crowd listened in rapt attention to the live commentary—every word crisp and clear, carried through the powerful speakers of Chicago Radio.

Mahatma Gandhi addressing the Asian Relations Conference in Delhi, April 1947, via a Chicago Radio microphone. (Photo author unknown. Public Domain via Wikimedia Commons.)

The iconic patriotic song '*Ae mere watan ke logon*' was penned by the legendary poet Kavi Pradeep and composed by C. Ramchandra as a tribute to the brave Indian soldiers who laid down their lives during the 1962 Sino–Indian War. Two months later, on Republic Day—26 January 1963—Lata Mangeshkar's soulful voice filled the National Stadium in New Delhi as she performed the song live before President Sarvepalli Radhakrishnan and Prime Minister Jawaharlal Nehru.

Among the lasting images of that moment is one of Lata Mangeshkar singing into a Chicago Radio loudspeaker—a testament to the enduring legacy of Gianchand Motwane. Chicago Radio wasn't just a brand that amplified sound; it became the voice of a nation, forever etched in history as the one that broadcasted the sound of freedom.

3

The Three Wise Monkeys

As we stood admiring the sculpture inside the Sabarmati Ashram, a man walked up to us and asked: 'Do you know what they are called?'

'The three wise monkeys?' we said.

'Yes! But they also have names of their own,' the man said with a quick smile.

'Mizaru is the one who doesn't see, Kikazaru is the one who doesn't hear, and Iwazaru is the one who does not speak. However, time has obscured the original versions of the names, especially the last two. Though their Indian versions exist, they are hardly used,' he informed us, his eyes lighting up in excitement as he dispensed the knowledge.

'Quite interesting, right? Japanese macaques at the heart of Gandhi's ashram,' our new friend said, and then asked, 'Why do we have three Japanese monkeys at the heart of Gandhian philosophy?'

Contrary to popular belief, the three monkeys transcend Gandhi's time and many before him, for that matter. But strangely enough, they have been smuggled into our collective consciousness through different media.

In 1968, a scene from the Hollywood movie, *The Planet of the Apes*, directed by Oscar-winning director Franklin J. Schaffner, depicts three apes mimicking the three wise monkeys. Schaffner may have wanted to allude to different concepts of power and censorship, subjects which were at the time boiling points of debate. Over the years the concept has been used in other films though the influence is more subtle than visual.

The monkeys: Origins, migration and naturalization

The origins of the monkeys are a bit mysterious. Nikkō, a small city in the Kanto region of Japan, is home to one of the country's most revered shrines, called the Nikkō Tōshō-gū. It is dedicated to Tokugawa Ieyasu, founder of the shogunate rule in Japan and its first shogun. Here at the shrine, carved over a door of a stable, stand eight panels, and one of the panels depicts the three wise monkeys. The carvings are believed to be the first depiction of the mystical monkeys and their philosophy. There is the strange thing in Japanese folklore, especially influenced by Taoism—they don't mention evil, as the saying goes, mizaru, kikazaru, iwazaru: 'see not, hear not, speak not'. However, there are disagreements on the original saying.

But how does Gandhi fit into all this?

In the beginning of 1933, Gandhi was in Yerawada Central Jail in Poona for several months, but he was released due to ill health. While he continued to fight for equal rights for Harijans for most of that year, he also had a run-in with a mysterious Japanese monk at Sabarmati Ashram.

In May, residents of the ashram mention a Japanese monk arriving in Sabarmati. A visitor at the ashram, Duncan Greenlees, noted: 'A Japanese Buddhist priest came with his drum and strange chantings in the night, and worked among the villagers with tireless energy.' Records show the monk was Nichidatsu Fujii. Soon, the ashram and its residents shifted to Wardha, where it is believed that Fujii met Gandhi and impressed him. Gandhi speaks of him in a letter to Vallabhbhai Patel on 27 October 1933:

'This monk is a jewel. He is extremely frank, humble, cheerful and courteous. He is learning Hindi and spins on the charkha and the takli. He observes all the [ashram] rules scrupulously.'

Two years before that in 1931, Nichidatsu Fujii landed in Calcutta, and went around the city beating the drum and chanting daimoku—

Nam-myoho-renge-kyo—which is the central tenet of Nichiren Buddhism. A quiet testament to Fujii's influence stands along the tranquil edge of Rabindra Sarobar Lake. A modest, pagoda-style temple, its presence easily overlooked, offers a sanctuary of peace. This two-storeyed structure, a mere three kilometres from the ancient Kalighat temple, embodies the Nipponzan Myōhōji form of Buddhism, a path forged by Fujii in Japan in 1918.

The Nipponzan Myōhōji Temple, founded by the Japanese monk Nichidatsu Fujii, is located at the eastern end of Kolkata's Rabindra Sarobar. Established as part of Fujii's global mission of peace and non-violence, the temple continues to serve as a tranquil retreat for reflection and prayer.

Nichidatsu Fujii spent several years in India, during which time he visited the ashrams at Sabarmati and Wardha and met with Gandhi multiple times. Gandhi even included Fujii's prayer, the daimoku, at his Sevagram Ashram. In one of his visits, Fujii is believed to have gifted Gandhi a figurine of the three wise monkeys and explained their philosophy to him. Gandhi, who despised all material things and strictly adhered to a lifestyle of non-possession, made an exception for this and became quite fond of them. Perhaps because he saw them as an extension of his values.

The statue made of china clay was handed over to the ashram. Gandhi named the monkeys Bapu, Ketan and Bandar. As the years went by the three monkeys became inseparable from Gandhian philosophy, becoming associated with his commitment to truth, non-violence and self-discipline, which were core principles of his approach to social and political change.

Nichidatsu Fujii: Contradictions that slowly melted

Nichidatsu Fujii seems to have visited Gandhi on multiple occasions, strengthening his knowledge about non-violence. His views on India's independence movement stood somewhat in conflict with his views on Japanese imperialism. Fujii and the Nichiren Buddhism order he founded, Nipponzan Myōhōji, were active in Japanese-occupied China and Manchuria throughout the Sino–Japanese War. Yet they seemed to have been oblivious to the horrific crimes, especially the looting and killing that went on in Nanjing. But 1945 changed everything. When Hiroshima and Nagasaki were completely obliterated by atomic bombs, for Fujii this became a time of reckoning. After the war ended, Fujii started teaching ways of non-violence and building peace pagodas. Among the first that came up were in Hiroshima and Nagasaki. Nipponzan Myōhōji helped build multiple places of worship all over Japan and the world. Fujii threw himself into the forefront of anti-war rhetoric and nuclear disarmament. By the time of his death in 1985, almost seventy peace pagodas across Asia, North America and Europe were built by Nipponzan Myōhōji.

Gandhi's Non-Cooperation Movement invoked the silent wisdom of the three wise monkeys. He urged passive defiance, a refusal to 'see' and 'hear' the dictates of the Raj, thus rendering them impotent without resorting to violence. Yet the monkeys' stoic silence served as a double-edged sword. It can be interpreted not only as a shield against evil, but also as a veil of wilful ignorance. Regardless of the nuanced readings, the monkeys, and the philosophy they embody, have etched themselves deeply into the Indian soul, a potent emblem of non-violent resistance with an enduring influence.

4

Netaji in Every Pocket

It was 1944, and the air was heavy with the scent of gunpowder. Deep in Burma (present-day Myanmar), a good distance inland from Rangoon, there was a small village by the Sittaung River. It was a moonlit night when a group of ten men arrived. The villagers came out to greet them. They were curious but welcoming. For a moment, it felt like the war had taken a pause. They were no ordinary visitors—these were doctors, unmistakably Bengali in their appearance. They belonged to the Azad Hind Fauj, Subhas Chandra Bose's army, stationed deep in the interiors of Burma, far from the chaos of Rangoon.

The next morning brought a sense of celebration. The group met beside the riverbank to enjoy a rare moment of leisure. The calm flow of the Sittaung River provided an ideal environment for a casual picnic. Fresh fish from the river sizzled on makeshift grills, infusing the air with a wonderful smoky aroma. Nearby, one man was happily preparing his special spicy chicken. Everyone called him Colonel Goswami. It was a moment of friendship and peace. For a short time, surrounded by laughter and the tempting smell of food, they forgot about the harsh reality of war.

This story comes from a remarkable memoir we found in the archives of *Desh Magazine*, published in 1946. Dr Satyendranath Basu, a doctor in the Azad Hind Fauj, wrote a series of articles about his experiences. His writings described army life in detail. They spoke of sacrifices, friendship, struggles and their deep loyalty to Netaji.

The stories, as fascinating as fiction, were deeply rooted in truth. They provide rare insights into the extraordinary journey of the Azad Hind Fauj.

A bidi packet stood for hope

Out of all the fascinating accounts, one story particularly stood out—a small, almost fleeting anecdote that captured the essence of their humanity and the deep emotional connection these men had to their leader, Netaji. It was a reference to a bundle of bidis. Now, most of us are familiar with them—a bidi is a slender cigarette or cigar originating from the Indian subcontinent. It's made by hand-rolling tobacco flakes in a leaf and securing it with either a string or adhesive. During the darkest days of the Azad Hind Fauj, a packet of bidis with Netaji's image on them became an unlikely symbol of hope and inspiration for the weary soldiers.

Now, returning to the group of doctors near the Sittaung River. The village wasn't their home. They all came from the nearby town of Zeyawaddy, where the INA regiment was encamped, about 215 kilometres north of Rangoon. The doctors were usually busy tending to the injured in its makeshift hospital. There were about 3,000 people in the camp, which had a close connection with the local Indian villagers who had settled in Burma. It had become a refuge for injured soldiers and civilians, with doctors like Dr Basu, along with 500 other nursing comrades, working tirelessly to treat nearly 1,000 patients. Sometimes they were assisted with rations; other times, the soldiers helped protect the villagers from both British and Japanese persecution, who were both unkind masters in their own ways.

Zeyawaddy was already a hub for Indian settlers. It had its own share of interesting history—during British rule, a small slice of India was established when the British brought over Indian settlers and granted them land. The Dewan of Dumraon State and his son took a group of Bihari labourers to clear thousands of acres of land. It was heavily forested, but the workers, incentivized by land grants, cleared it and began growing sugarcane and paddy. And thus, Zeyawaddy became a little India in the distant land of Burma.

But in 1944, the air in Zeyawaddy was thick with tension. As the war tilted against the Japanese, the British began advancing. Not far from Zeyawaddy lay the town of Phyu, where battles between the British and Japanese were at their peak. Japanese forces and the INA retreated as the British forces advanced. The British air strikes on Japanese positions were frequent, and slowly, they made their way towards Zeyawaddy. It was only a matter of time before Zeyawaddy, too, would fall.

The INA camp at Zeyawaddy braced for the inevitable. The situation was dire. The choice was simple: fight and face certain death, or surrender. Eventually, Netaji gave the order to surrender, knowing that their survival would allow them to contribute to the cause later. On 24 April 1944, the British army, armed with tanks and supported by fighter planes overhead, entered Zeyawaddy. The camp was filled with sorrow, but the doctors continued their work, treating patients. They became prisoners for the first time. Gradually, the soldiers were sent back to India, while the critically ill patients were transferred to other hospitals. The doctors, nurses and hospital guards were the last to leave the camp.

After nearly two months at Zeyawaddy, Dr Basu and the remaining hospital staff were transferred to Pegu prison. Pegu, a small and isolated spot nestled between the Pegu Mountains and the Sittaung River, had earned a different kind of fame, as well. It is home to a legendary Victorian-style British gentlemen's club from the colonial era, and cocktail aficionados worldwide recognize it for a drink that bears its name—the Pegu Club cocktail. (If you're a connoisseur of cocktails, you might be familiar with this gin-based concoction, made with gin, orange curaçao, lime juice, and Angostura bitters, traditionally served in a coupe glass.) Yet, for the doctors, Pegu was a very different experience. The prison, located in this isolated town, was small, cramped and had very limited amenities for prisoners.

Soon, the group was transferred to Rangoon's notorious Insein Prison. The doctors were housed in barracks guarded by armed soldiers. Life continued to be harsh, but they endured. The days passed slowly, with uncertainty hanging in the air. Then, in August, the British decided to send 200 prisoners of war, including Dr Basu and six other doctors, back to India. The journey back from Rangoon dock to Calcutta was a gruelling one. The prisoners were placed in the lower deck of a ship, hot and suffocating. The conditions were unbearable. Days passed in that lower deck, and the smell of sweat and fear hung in the air. Eventually, the ship reached Calcutta's Kidderpore dock.

From there, the group was taken by train to the Jhikargacha camp in present-day Bangladesh. The camp was nothing more than another prison. They were again subjected to rigorous questioning. After ten days of intense interrogation, it was decided that the doctors and nurses would be released. They could finally return home.

But there is one event, one minor but essential detail, that Dr Basu describes in his memoirs. It was already late in the evening. The group was at the Jhikargacha railway station, quietly preparing to board the train that would take them closer to home. The train was scheduled to depart at 2 a.m. They were exhausted and drained by then. A few hours of rest would be good. But just as they lay on the platform, something drew their attention. A small tobacco and betel shop was still open, quite late in the night. As they passed by, they noticed something that brought a rush of emotions.

The shopkeeper was selling bidis—a brand of bidi with a picture of Netaji on the pack.

It wasn't a unique or unheard-of phenomenon. After Mahatma Gandhi's call for the boycott of foreign goods, many swadeshi products began to appear in the market. Many of these swadeshi products began using patriotic imagery, endorsing nationalism. From big manufacturing companies to small bidi-making houses, the images of Gandhi, Nehru and Netaji appeared on everything from soap wrappers to hair oils to matchboxes. Rabindranath Tagore endorsed many handmade swadeshi goods. Netaji himself endorsed the Shree Ghee brand from Bengal. The list goes on.

The resurgence of the bidi industry was also a remarkable phenomenon in the 1930s. As cigarettes were mostly foreign products, young people began boycotting them and started using bidis more often than before. Acharya Prafulla Chandra Roy strongly wrote:

> If smoking is inevitable, then give up foreign cigarettes and instead smoke indigenous bidis. They are truly Swadeshi—made with local tobacco, local leaves, and by the hands of local people. On the other hand, the tobacco in foreign cigarettes comes from abroad, rolled in foreign paper, and manufactured in foreign machines. By consuming these, you end up sending two crore rupees annually into the pockets of foreigners. I once visited a few small bidi manufacturing units in the Gondia region. I observed that in that barren and underdeveloped area of Central India, nearly 50,000 men, women and children were rolling bidis, earning daily wages ranging from one anna to two annas. In this way, this small-scale cottage industry is sustaining nearly half a lakh people by providing them with the means to feed themselves.

This shift led to the formation of numerous companies dedicated to making and selling bidis. The names of Gandhi, Nehru and Netaji were frequently used on these products, adding a patriotic touch that resonated deeply with the masses.

The shopkeeper's bidi brand, named after Netaji, was one of them. As Dr Basu recalls, most members of the Azad Hind Fauj carried a small picture of Netaji along with their personal belongings, often alongside a Geeta or Quran. These were frequently confiscated by the British. When the men saw the image of Netaji on a bidi pack, it stirred something deep within them. Without a moment's hesitation, the entire group began purchasing every packet in sight. Within minutes, the shopkeeper's stock was completely sold out.

The shopkeeper, who was Bengali, mentioned to Dr Basu that many people bought the bidi simply for the picture of Netaji. 'Some even worship him,' he added. Dr Basu explained, 'It's the same for these men—they are soldiers of Netaji's Azad Hind Fauj, and they revere Netaji like a god. Today, they don't have any photo of him with them, and this bidi pack is their way of holding on to his image.'

And why wouldn't they love Netaji? Major General Shahnawaz Khan, in his book *My Memories of I.N.A. and Its Netaji*, recounted the sacred relationship Netaji had with his soldiers. He wrote:

> Netaji dearly loved his soldiers and was always most concerned about their welfare. He used to go and inspect their kitchens and would frequently have meals with them. He had issued strict orders that the food cooked for him should be exactly the same as that given to his soldiers. He was always a frequent visitor to hospitals, where he would send special sweets prepared for them in his own house.

It's small moments like these, seemingly insignificant, that make up the true fabric of history. The kind of history that is often overlooked or forgotten. The journey of the Azad Hind Fauj was about to end. But in that moment, they felt the pulse of freedom once again.

Acknowledgement: The story is based on the memoir of Dr Satyendranath Basu, published in multiple segments as a weekly series in Desh Magazine in 1946. We are grateful to the author for providing such a detailed and vivid account of that time.

5

Kappalottiya Thamizhan: The Tamilian Who Sailed Ships

Almost eight decades after India gained independence, a troubling trend has appeared recently. A few prominent Indian entrepreneurs and executives are asking working-class citizens to work exhausting seventy- to ninety-hour weeks. They say this hard work is the key to success. But are we really creating growth, or are we just creating a new kind of slavery?

A century ago, a different kind of entrepreneur graced Indian shores. V.O. Chidambaram Pillai, affectionately called VOC, stood shoulder-to-shoulder with the exploited workers of the Thoothukudi Coral Mill, battling the oppressive A. & F. Harvey firm. With fiery conviction, VOC declared, 'If the coolies stood out for extra wages, European mills in India would cease to exist.'[1] Their demands were radical for the time: fair wages, weekly rest and other essential benefits.

In a nation still under colonial rule, these demands seemed outrageous. But inspired by VOC, the mill workers went on a nine-day strike. They refused to give up until their demands were met. This historic struggle reminds us of the sacrifices our ancestors made in their fight for dignity and fair treatment. However, beyond this act of defiance, VOC's journey also teaches valuable lessons for modern entrepreneurs.

VOC was a man of many facets—a skilled orator, a successful lawyer, a revered politician and a freedom fighter. But of all the feathers in his cap, one that stood out was his grit as an entrepreneur. He was neither innovative nor a visionary in his line of business, and he was unsuccessful in his venture—and yet he made history. How?

A.R. Venkatachalapathy meticulously documented VOC's journey in his book *Swadeshi Steam: V.O. Chidambaram Pillai and the Battle against the British Maritime Empire*. His story started at the port of Tuticorin (now known as Thoothukudi) on the southern coast of present Tamil Nadu. In his autobiography, VOC mentioned the place with great pride, referring to it as 'the town of the sacred chant'.[2] In the early 1800s, European travellers travelling to south India would normally get off in Colombo before making the risky overnight passage over the stormy Bay of Bengal. When they landed in Tuticorin, it was rather underwhelming. However, the fate of this small town was linked to the expanding British Empire, which was driven by the uncompromising rise of British naval power.

In the early part of the nineteenth century, British merchants were growing increasingly frustrated. Trading with India, a promising country, was slowed by the excruciatingly slow pace of sea transit. Because of its insatiable desire for new markets and raw materials, the British economy demanded a faster response to demand. The pressure mounted. Powerful mercantile houses in London, joined by influential firms in Calcutta, Madras and Bombay, clamoured for change. They demanded the Empire embrace the revolutionary power of steam navigation. Their ambition was realized by the 1870s. Steamships, once a distant dream, were now unquestionably the dominant force on the oceans.

A marine monopoly

When the Suez Canal opened in 1869, it changed worldwide trade by creating a single, interconnected market that allowed goods to travel freely to even the most remote parts of the world. In less than ten years, the Peninsular and Oriental Steam Navigation Company (P&O) became the undisputed monarch of the sea lanes by seizing this unprecedented opportunity and quickly establishing dominance over Indian Ocean trade. British maritime control in the region was reinforced when the British India Steam Navigation Company (B.I.S.N.Co. or B.I.) joined the race.

B.I. was one of the world's largest shipping corporations at the time.[3] The firm played an important role in the tumultuous events of 1857, transporting troops to quell the rebellion. Throughout both World Wars, this strategic alliance with the imperial state was maintained, ensuring B.I.'s function as a weapon of British dominance. B.I. relentlessly crushed any competition by using its strong links to colonial power, leaving a trail of bankruptcies in its wake. B.I. ruled the Indian Ocean after systematically destroying opponents who attempted to challenge its naval power.

William Mackinnon,[4] the visionary behind B.I., dreamed of a fleet of steamships forging a rapid and reliable link between Britain and India. In his ambitious plan, London would be routinely connected to major ports like Calcutta, Madras and Colombo. Most crucially, Mackinnon recognized the strategic importance of Colombo as a hub for access to Tuticorin and the Malabar coast. Tuticorin, once a relatively unknown harbour, would quickly become firmly inscribed on the maritime map as a result of this foresight.

As British shipping expanded with money looted from Indian shores, a simmering resentment swelled within the country. The fiery speeches of Indian National Congress (INC) leaders Bal Gangadhar Tilak, Lala Lajpat Rai and Bipin Chandra Pal inspired the Indian Nationalist Movement, which erupted across the country in the late nineteenth and early twentieth centuries. When this revolutionary wave swept over India, the British responded brutally. On 20 July 1905, Lord Curzon, the viceroy of India, declared the partition of Bengal in an attempt to undermine Indian unity. This proclamation meant to divide Bengal into two parts: Hindu-dominated West Bengal and Muslim-dominated East Bengal. However, it sparked a violent response, uniting Indians in a shared rage rather than hurting the nationalist movement.

VOC until then hadn't taken part in active politics. But all that changed when he met Swami Ramakrishnananda, a direct disciple of the ascetic saint Ramakrishna Paramahansa. VOC in his own account said it was Swami Ramakrishnananda who 'sowed the seed of Swadeshism in my heart'.[5]

This was the era when the vibrant voices of the INC leaders kept the country united and energized. It didn't take long for Bal Gangadhar Tilak to notice the young Tamil firebrand. Tilak quickly took VOC under his wing. He knew he had found a gem. He became VOC's mentor in the art of political agitation.[6]

A minnow against the sharks

Fuelled by Tilak's revolutionary zeal, VOC dared to dream the impossible. He challenged the mighty British, the undisputed rulers of the seas, by launching his own shipping company—the Swadeshi Steam Navigation Company (SSNCo) in October 1906.

It was more of a political project than a business venture. His biggest shareholders were Haji Mohammed Rowther Sait, a merchant, and Pandithurai Thevar, a zamindar. He relied on them and his strong supporters to run the company. Recognizing the power of the people, he strategically priced shares at a modest Rs 25,[7] making ownership accessible to the common man. This populist move, coupled with VOC himself actively distributing application forms, and widespread media coverage in Indian newspapers, ignited a wave of public enthusiasm.

Despite strong public support, SSNCo struggled to raise enough funds at first. But VOC did not give up. He travelled across the country, urging people to invest. His passionate speeches stirred patriotism and brought in the support SSNCo needed to survive and grow. However, there was a big challenge. SSNCo did not have its own ships. They relied entirely on leased vessels from the Shah Steam Navigation Company, another Indian venture, led by Essaji Tajbhoy.[8] Tajbhoy had started his own venture by purchasing old steamers from P&O. Fearing competition, B.I. resorted to underhand tactics. They threatened to cancel the lease for the Shah Steam Navigation Company. When that didn't quite scare Tajbhoy, they launched a ferocious price war, decimating Tajbhoy's customer base. Faced with mounting financial losses, Tajbhoy was ultimately forced to sell his company to B.I.

The Raj, smug in their belief that they had finally silenced the fiery Tamil, were sorely mistaken. VOC's wife was heavily pregnant with their second child, and their firstborn was seriously ill. Yet, he refused to back down. With fearless determination, he set out on a journey to Bombay. For nearly five months, he worked tirelessly in the complex world of finance, persuading investors in Bombay and Colombo.

During his stay in Bombay, one of his letters written to a fellow Tuticorin-based businessman took everyone by surprise. He wrote:

> Be sure that I will return with two beautiful new steamers of twenty knots speed ... You need not be anxious where I will get money for the purchase of two steamers simultaneously & other such matters. God has promised to give me whatever money I require for the cause of the country.[9]

The SSNCo now had their own ships—the SS *Gallia*, a steel twin-screw steamer registered at Colombo and built in Nantes, France, by the Compagnie Française de Navigation et de Construction Navale, and a second one, the *Lawoe*, an iron screw steamer, larger than the *Gallia*, built by R. Dixon and Company of Middlesbrough, England.

The move surprised even the mighty B.I. In response, they reduced the fare to one rupee per passenger. Despite the huge debts for acquiring the steamers, the SSNCo responded in kind to the B.I. by reducing their fare price to half a rupee or eight annas per passenger. In a desperate attempt to regain market share, B.I. announced free trips to its passengers along with complimentary umbrellas as a token of goodwill. But the Indian public, tired of B.I.'s past exploitative practices, saw through this desperate ploy. They chose to pay for SSNCo's service, showing their full support for the new Swadeshi company and their wish to break free from colonial rule. In just a year, SSNCo emerged as tough competition to the undisputed king of the sea, B.I. Despite the heavy cost of maintenance, VOC did not give up and kept seeking public support.

A heavy price paid

By early 1908, VOC had already become an important political figure. His excellent oratory skills made him a growing threat to the British administration. They repeatedly warned him to stay in his home district and steer clear of political activism, but VOC paid no heed to that. He delivered a fiery speech in Tirunelveli on 9 March 1908, celebrating the release of Bipin Chandra Pal, one of the architects of the Swadeshi Movement. This defiance proved to be his undoing. Three days later, he was arrested and sent to prison. This sparked fury across Tirunelveli.

The town exploded in protest. People vandalized police stations, municipal courts and other public properties. The streets ran red with the blood of four innocent people killed by the police. Hundreds were arrested. A general strike was declared in Tirunelveli, which is widely seen as India's first political strike.

The Raj, however, had achieved its objective. V.O. Chidambaram Pillai, the thorn in their side, was convicted of double sedition and sentenced to two life imprisonments, effectively a forty-year sentence. However, according to a Press Information Bureau (PIB) release,[10] the Madras High Court reduced his sentence and released him on 24 December 1912.

In the interim, without VOC's hand at the helm, the SSNCo had floundered and ultimately, within three years of VOC going to jail, the company was liquidated. Upon his release from prison, VOC was plunged into abject poverty. He moved to Chennai with his family and ran a small shop. But that didn't deter him from his nationalistic activities. He had a long correspondence with Gandhiji even before he became the Mahatma. He spent his last years heavily in debt, selling off his law books to survive. VOC breathed his last at the Indian National Congress office in Tuticorin on 18 November 1936 'as was his last wish'. It was a peaceful end for a patriot considered a forerunner to the Mahatma.

6

Kirloskar and the Engines of Freedom

In 1904, the plans for building India's first industrial township were set in motion in a village called Sakchi, deep in the Chota Nagpur plateau. Rich in minerals, the site would become what we now know as Jamshedpur, also known as Tatanagar or Steel City. However, what is not known is that in 1910, India's second industrial town was built 200 kilometres from Poona near a small town called Kundal. The architect of this new township was a colour-blind painter who once ran a bicycle repair shop—Laxmanrao Kirloskar.

Fondly known as Lakaki, Laxmanrao had a pretty exceptional life. He was fascinated by machines from a young age. At the age of twenty, he joined the J.J. School of Art in Bombay (now Mumbai) against his father's wishes, as he was passionate about painting. However, after two years, his dreams were shattered when he discovered that he was colour-blind. Despite realizing his ambition of becoming an artist was over, Laxmanrao was not ready to give up. He stayed on at the institute and pursued mechanical drawing. It helped Laxmanrao land a job as an assistant teacher for a princely salary of Rs 45 per month, at the Victoria Jubilee Technical Institute (VJTI), now known as Veermata Jijabai Technological Institute, in Bombay. At the institute, Laxmanrao was discriminated against and allegedly even denied a promotion that went in favour of an Anglo-Indian.

The first steps

Sometime in the early 1890s, Laxmanrao left his job in Bombay and landed in Belgaum where he opened a bicycle-repair shop in Raviwar Peth in Central Belgaum, a road now named Kirloskar Road. Within a few years, he had designed and fabricated an iron plough. The seed of his industrial empire was planted. But Kirloskar found it hard to sell his iron plough, as farmers believed that it would poison their land.

While Laxmanrao was going around trying to persuade farmers to buy his plough, the town's municipality annexed his shop and land for constructing a suburb. This was just after a plague hit Belgaum in 1897, as it had Poona and Bombay,[1] and people fleeing into the countryside needed housing.

Laxmanrao was desperately looking for another place to live and work. At this point, an unexpected ally emerged—the raja of Aundh. Having had previous dealings with Aundh, Kirloskar turned to the raja for help. Without hesitation, the raja of Aundh extended his support, offering him an interest-free loan and a small tract of land to establish his venture—laying the foundation for a new industrial chapter in India's history. The land was near a small town called Kundal. Kirloskar named his new home and workplace Kirloskarwadi.

He assembled a team of twenty-five workers and their families, and in 1910, he established Kirloskarwadi's first factory. The new community was equipped with all the necessary living amenities.

He started again on his iron ploughs. Initially, there was hesitation around using iron ploughs, but demand gradually picked up. When World War I broke out, disrupting imports of British-made ploughs, Kirloskar's ploughs became the only ones available in the market. Despite the surge in demand, there was no compromise on quality— Kirloskar's ploughs were on par with, if not superior to, their British counterparts. After the success of the ploughs, Kirloskar developed a series of other agrarian products. The plant and the little village of Kirloskarwadi were at the heart of this revolution that forever transformed India's agrarian sector.

Kirloskar believed his village and factory couldn't prosper without progressive thinking. He inspired factory workers to do away with several traditional customs, such as untouchability, even facilitating intercaste weddings. His trust in humanity made him accept two former convicts, the dacoits Tukaram Ramoshi and Pirya Mang, and appoint them as night guards in the factory. Discrimination had no place in Kirloskarwadi. Industry, for him, was India's new religion. Children from every caste, including ex-prisoners' children and those from the backward castes, went to the same school as everyone else.

Gandhi's call echoes in Kirloskarwadi

While Kirloskarwadi was growing at a steady pace, the rest of the country was intensifying its struggle against British rule. The wave of resistance and nationalist fervour sweeping across India inevitably washed over Kirloskarwadi. The underground movement and armed revolutionaries used Kirloskarwadi as a safe haven and a meeting place to discuss strategies and clandestine activities.

In 1942, when Mahatma Gandhi gave the clarion call of 'Do or Die', and the Quit India Movement erupted across the country, the factory workers of Kirloskarwadi also plunged into the movement. There is a lovely photograph where a number of women from Kirloskarwadi are seen spinning the charkha[2] to support the Gandhian movement. At the forefront of the photograph, there is an elegant woman with a determined gaze spinning the wheel. She was none other than Radhabai, Lakaki's wife, leading the Satyagraha.

In the adjoining city of Satara, however, peaceful marches and protests soon turned violent, especially in Vaduj and Islampur. Leading the march in Islampur was Umashankar Pandya, a mechanical engineer at the Kirloskar factory and Sadashiv Pendharkar. As the police opened fire on the protesters, both Pandya and Pendharkar were killed. A memorial was later set up to honour them in Kirloskarwadi.

Shoots of hope

Meanwhile, Kirloskar continued his industrial innovation at the factory. It manufactured lathe machines, pumps, engines, groundnut-shellers and sugarcane crushers. His unwavering belief that Indian products could not only compete with but even surpass their Western counterparts drove every innovation. By maintaining the highest standards, Kirloskar ensured that Indian industry stood at par with the best in the world.

When Pandit Nehru visited Kirloskarwadi in July 1940, he was so impressed by their signature iron plough that he remarked, 'How I would love to be a farmer.' This pioneering industrial hub would go on to play a crucial role in shaping India's industrial revolution in the post-Independence era.

In the 1970s, Kirloskar made its foray into Egypt and quickly made a name for itself. In a span of five decades Kirloskar machines have been installed at fifty pumping stations which have helped transform approximately 150,000 hectares of desert into arable land, significantly boosting agricultural productivity. They are also a leader in the market in the Middle East region. Some are surprised to learn that Kirloskar is an Indian company. But they shouldn't be—after all, they were one of the original pioneers of 'Make in India'.

7

A Freedom Forged in Natural Calamities

'Blessed is the man who remains steadfast under trial.'
—James 1:12

In 1942, in a severe trial, the people of Midnapore (what is today Purba [East] Medinipur) district of West Bengal faced a triple crisis—a deadly famine, a devastating cyclone and an oppressive ruler. That was when heroes—most of them faceless and nameless—rose from the unlikeliest of places and scripted a golden chapter in our freedom struggle. Unfortunately, time has nearly erased this incredible tale of valour, determination and patriotism from the pages of history. In this chapter, we shall try to bring those forgotten heroes back to life.

On 8 August 1942, Mahatma Gandhi uttered the battle cry of 'British Quit India', marking the formal start of the Quit India Movement—a final thrust for independence. The Raj hit back brutally, arresting practically the entire Congress leadership and throwing them behind bars. Yet, even this drastic action could not quell the fires burning in the heart of the common Indian.

War, famine, revolt

Many parts of the Bengal Presidency were then reeling under the onset of a severe famine that would ravage the land in the coming years. While the famine affected the eastern part of Bengal more, in western Bengal, Midnapore was one of the pockets where the famine had already put lives in severe distress. A big cause for the famine was the diversion of food grains to Europe to sustain Allied war efforts. The rampant black market in food grains made the famine worse but the British administration had turned a blind eye to it. Moreover, with Rangoon having already fallen and large parts of Burma under Japanese control, there were strong rumours of a seashore invasion by the Imperial Japanese Navy. The British decided on a scorched-earth policy to slow down potential enemy movement. Fishing boats were forcibly seized and sunk or burnt.

With Midnapore having a sizable coastal stretch, the British policies worsened matters, as coastal residents, already reeling under the failure of crops, had their source of subsistence from the sea snatched from them. There was palpable anger on the ground against the British rulers. Against this backdrop came Gandhiji's clarion call. For a populace already at the end of their tether, it was like putting a match to a powder keg. But the British administration possibly had little idea of the force that was about to hit them.

The district of Midnapore had been a problematic one for the British for many years. The armed resistance movement reached its peak here in the late 1920s and early 1930s, with a particular crescendo when three district magistrates were gunned down between 1931 and 1933. Matters came to such a point that no young British ICS officer was willing to take a posting in Midnapore. We shall talk about this story later in the book (Chapter 44). By the mid-1930s, however, with the non-violence approach espoused by Gandhiji prevailing, the armed revolution movement had nearly died down. But the people of Midnapore had not lost their rebellious streak and soon, it would erupt again.

At the start of 1942, anti-British sentiment was at an all-time high. Processions, rallies, hartals, student strikes and mass agitations were rampant. Post Gandhiji's call of '*Angrezon Bharat Chhodo*' (British Quit India), the protests found a new life. While many of the local INC leaders had been arrested, a few like Satis Chandra Samanta,

Ajoy Mukherjee and Sushil Kumar Dhara had successfully evaded the British police. They took refuge in the villages and started spreading the word by moving from village to village and trying to get the villagers to join the protests. It was a smart move in more ways than one: the famine had affected rural areas more, so there was a lot of anguish to be tapped into. Moreover, it was more difficult for the police to quell protests in village after village, as compared to the towns where the advantage was with the administration. This ploy would soon pay rich dividends.

By September, the famine only got worse but the administration was arrogantly indifferent. In the first week of September, locals got wind of a rice mill smuggling its output for export in collusion with the administration. When they tried to stop this, police resorted to firing on an unarmed crowd, killing three villagers. Although they did stop the export, this incident sent temperatures soaring.

The people take over

On the intervening night of 28–29 September, the revolutionary movement blocked all the major high roads of the area by digging up pits, felling trees and blowing up all the culverts. They also disrupted communication links by cutting telephone and telegraph lines across forty-four kilometres. Ferry boats on the rivers were sunk or stolen. The idea was to isolate the Tamluk subdivision and stop news from going out and prevent or at least delay the arrival of reinforcements from Calcutta or elsewhere.

Village resistance teams had already been organized. Sectors were created and teams were allocated defence of individual sectors. Although the local administration immediately got into the act of trying to restore road and communication links, the progress was slow, as local villagers did not cooperate. At 2 p.m. on 29 September, huge processions—consisting of men, women and children, both old and young, and Hindus and Muslims alike—started converging on Tamluk town from different parts of the subdivision, shouting anti-British slogans. Five such processions started marching towards Tamluk police station. The government forces responded by firing indiscriminately. Ten people died instantly. First among them was Matangini Hazra—who was lovingly called 'Gandhi Buri'. Cradling the Tiranga (tricolour—the Indian flag), she kept shouting 'Vande Mataram' even as she was riddled with bullets. Until her last breath, Matangini did not relinquish the tricolour from her hands—keeping it upright.

But demonstrations and rallies weren't the only plan. Simultaneously, the resistance movement captured multiple police stations in the subdivisions. The leadership in this daring adventure was given by the 'Vidyut Bahini', a trained paramilitary wing of the movement under the leadership of Sushil Kumar Dhara. Local zamindars provided their personal forces to support some of the police stations. But this came to nought against the zeal of the Vidyut Bahini who were reinforced by common men and women, mainly peasants, who had been abused beyond their endurance by cruel landlords and now joined the fray with whatever weapons or implements they could lay their hands on.

The speed and precision with which the plan unfolded took the British administration by surprise. It was truly 'shock and awe'. After taking control of the police stations, possession was taken of various government bodies like the Union Board, Debt Settlement Board, and Rent Collection Centres. In a large swathe of the Tamluk division, British control had effectively ended and it was truly Swaraj.

In October 1942, a devastating cyclone hit the area. The British administration in Calcutta refused to provide relief and tried to suppress news of the calamity through press censorship. Policemen started looting the villagers and set fire to the houses. Faced with this predicament, the resistance leadership decided to form an administration of their own to restore peace and order to the area.

A government that really worked

On 17 December 1942, the Tamralipta Jatiya Sarkar (literally, Tamralipta Community Government—also translated as Tamralipta

National Government) took oath with Satis Chandra Samanta as the 'Sarbadhinayak' (supreme leader). At a lower level, Thana (police station) Jatiya Sarkars were formed in Mahishadal, Sutahata, Nandigram and Tamluk police stations to administer areas under each station. The heads of the Thana Jatiya Sarkars were called 'Adhinayak' (captains). The Vidyut Bahini was declared the formal military force of the Tamralipta Jatiya Sarkar. A subsidiary force called the 'Bhagini Sena' (Sister Army), comprising female volunteers, was also raised. Tamralipta, according to legend, was an ancient port city located where Tamluk stands.

Individual ministers were appointed under Satis Chandra Samanta, with Ajoy Mukherjee assuming charge of home and finance, and Sushil Dhara entrusted with defence. Besides the ministers, an advisory council of experienced workers was also formed to guide the government on policy matters.

The Tamralipta Jatiya Sarkar functioned from 17 December 1942 to 1 September 1944. It was successful in restoring law and order in the area, providing relief for those stricken by the cyclone, and ensuring a sense of safety and security in the people. The Tamralipta Jatiya Sarkar also took steps to provide succour against the devastating famine by forcing large landowners to share their hoarded stocks of grain with the poor villagers.

Incidentally, the leaders of the Tamralipta Jatiya Sarkar were all Congressmen and followers of Gandhi. Yet, the resistance movement could not always stick to the path of non-violence preached by the Mahatma. On 9 January 1943, government forces surrounded three villages, detained the men and then proceeded to commit unspeakable horrors, raping forty-nine women brutally. The Jatiya Sarkar hit back with vengeance for this horrible crime. The intelligence department identified the local agents who aided the government forces and the Vidyut Bahini volunteers avenged the traitors' treachery and brutality by executing all of them.

In May 1943, Sarbadhinayak Satis Samanta was arrested in Calcutta. His trusted lieutenant Ajoy Mukherjee assumed office as the new Sarbadhinayak. Despite two subsequent changes in the office of Sarbadhinayak, the Tamralipta Jatiya Sarkar continued to function smoothly, and large parts of Tamluk and Contai subdivisions of Midnapore district remained outside British control and free from subjugation for nearly two years.

Voluntary shutdown

Unfortunately, the end of this glorious resistance was rather abject. On 6 May 1944, Gandhiji was released from prison. He decided to call off the Quit India Movement shortly afterwards and advised all Congressmen, in hiding or otherwise, to publicly surrender themselves. Barada Kanti Kulti, the Sarbadhinayak at the time, thus ordered the suspension of the Tamralipta Jatiya Sarkar's activities on 8 August 1944 and courted arrest. Following his lead, around 150 workers who were wanted by the police also surrendered. A big dampener for the Jatiyo Sarkar was the defeat of Netaji Subhas Chandra Bose's Indian National Army and the Japanese army in Imphal and Kohima. The original plan was for the Vidyut Bahini to link up and provide support to Netaji's forces as they marched into Bengal through Assam. With that hope also dashed, the Tamralipta Jatiya Sarkar was formally dissolved on 1 September 1944.

Incidentally, in December 1943, Netaji Subhas, supported by the Imperial Japan forces had 'liberated' the British colony of Andaman and Nicobar Islands, and named the two islands 'Shaheed' and 'Swaraj'. It is an event that is rightfully remembered and celebrated today.

Ironically, on the Indian mainland, barely 100 kilometres from Calcutta, a densely populated area was liberated, without outside help, from British control and kept free for nearly two years. It was done by ordinary men and women who became greater than the sum of their parts during adversity. Their achievement surely deserves to be remembered better. They were the flagbearers of independence, and their two-year government a symbol of the power and capability of the common Indian.

In the words of the defence minister of Tamralipta Jatiya Sarkar, Sushil Kumar Dhara:

তোমার পতাকা যারে দাও,
তারে বহিবারে দাও শকতি।
তোমার সেবার মহৎ প্রয়াস
সহিবারে দাও ভকতি।

(To the one you have entrusted your flag
Give him also the strength to bear the responsibility
And the faith to sustain
The noble aim to serve you.)

8

An Iconic Indian Brand Inspired by Gandhi

If you are into social media memes, you must have come across the one featuring actor Akshaye Khanna from the movie *Taal*. From Narayana Murthy to Virat Kohli, everyone has been put into this meme template that's quite the rage of late on Instagram and other social media platforms.

The thing that stands out in the image is Akshaye Khanna's blue raincoat, shielding him from the downpour. Our focus is on the raincoat, which is the highlight of the story we unfold here. We shall roll back time to a 100 years ago, when a raincoat, or rather a company manufacturing raincoats, became a major voice of the Swadeshi Movement.

The year was 1920. A young man had recently returned from the United States of America where he had been educated in the best of institutions such as Berkeley and Stanford. The India he returned to was one of turmoil. In a new century, the Indian mind had finally fully awakened and had begun a determined fight to break the century-and-a-half-old shackles of foreign rule. The face of the movement was a charismatic man: Mohandas Karamchand Gandhi, whose simple practices and value-driven approach was already proving to be a formidable opponent for the mighty colonial administration.

In particular, Gandhiji's call to boycott foreign and imported goods found a lot of resonance. The British had systematically discouraged the growth of Indian entrepreneurship, and actively dumped British-made products in India. Gandhiji encouraged people to use more swadeshi, i.e., Indian-made, products to counter the influx of British-made goods, several of poor quality, but which were forced upon Indian buyers at high prices.

A clarion call and compassion

Gandhiji's clarion call inspired many—one of them being Surendra Mohan Bose, the protagonist of our story. There was another thing that had been bothering Surendra Mohan. While in the United States and even after coming back, he had read accounts of the miseries of Indian soldiers on the frontlines in the Great War, who were not even issued raincoats or gumboots for the muddy terrain of the battlefield and suffered greatly as a result. As the war ended, returning Indian soldiers carried with them these stories and the lack of waterproof gear was a recurring tale. Surendra Mohan was moved by reading these accounts and decided to address it. As a student of chemical engineering, he had learnt waterproofing techniques and believed he could make a difference.

According to some accounts, Surendra Mohan had become actively involved in the freedom movement and while taking part in a rally in the United Provinces, he was detained. It was while he was in a British prison in Hamirpur that his dream took shape. Surendra Mohan decided to launch his own brand of waterproof gear—one that would fulfil Gandhiji's call for swadeshi brands while also protecting his countrymen—whether soldier or farmer—from India's incessant downpours in the monsoon. Thus began the journey of one of India's most iconic brands.

Surendra Mohan's business kicked off as a sole proprietorship from his ancestral home at Nazar Ali Lane in the Beck Bagan area of Calcutta. For the name of the brand, Surendra Mohan resorted to the classic English idiom 'like water off a duck's back', and named his brand 'Duckback', the name an implicit declaration of the product's superior quality. From the beginning, Surendra Mohan was clear on one thing: while Duckback was a fully commercial venture, the profit motive would never overtake his supreme goal—to provide high-quality yet affordable rain-protection wear to his countrymen.

Pre-Independence start-up success story

In 1932, Surendra Mohan was joined by his three brothers in the business venture. The product portfolio by this time was quite diversified: apart from raincoats and gumboots, Duckback also made waterproof railway-travel 'holdalls', air pillows for train journeys, dak bags for use by postal agents, waterproof headwear, hot water bottles, anti-bedsore sheets and oil cloth. Over the years they added more niche items such as rubber heels, shoe covers for protecting shoes from mud and grime, tennis-racket and gun covers, cyclist caps and mining boots. Surendra Mohan had also acquired a 22-acre plot in Panihati on the outskirts of Calcutta to set up a large manufacturing plant.

A Duckback advertisement from the pre-Independence era, published in *Desh* magazine, Year 12; Issue 32 (দেশ পত্রিকা বর্ষ ১২; সংখ্যা ৩২), dated 16 June 1945, promoting 'India's favourite raincoat' and evoking the nostalgia of monsoon. (Source and courtesy: *Desh* magazine / দেশ পত্রিকা)

In 1940, with business booming, it was incorporated as a limited company: Bengal Waterproof Limited. It is said that there was hardly a household across the entire undivided Bengal which did not have at least one Duckback product. As India stepped out of nearly two centuries of British rule and embraced independence on 15 August 1947, did Surendra Mohan Bose shed a silent tear or two of joy? We shall never know, but the man who had taken to commerce as a means to fight against colonial rule must have been overjoyed as he and his company were now both part of a free nation.

In 1948, Surendra Mohan Bose passed away suddenly. However, the company was left in able hands. Debabrata—Surendra Mohan's eldest son, who, like his father had pursued higher education abroad, returned to take over the helm. Over the coming decades, under Debabrata's inspired leadership, Duckback went from strength to strength, at one point even manufacturing G-suits worn by pilots of the Indian Air Force! It was Debabrata who gave the brand its iconic logo—the one with four droplets, designed by artist Ranen Ayan Dutt in the 1960s.

From Rs 40.42 lakh in 1940, gross sales hit Rs 1.18 crore in 1968. But that was only the financial angle. Long before Onida made the slogan 'Neighbour's envy. Owner's pride.' popular, Duckback lived it with Duckback bags and raincoats eliciting envious glances at schools. It would seem unbelievable today, but with practically no extra focus on marketing, Duckback became a truly aspirational brand—one that consumers, especially in Bengal, swore by.

It was a tribute to both the efficiency of Duckback's operations and the equity of the brand that even through the turbulence of the 1970s and labour troubles of the 1980s in Bengal, the brand remained in the pink of financial health with turnover hitting Rs 51 crore in 1995. But eventually, as the economy opened up, the Indian consumer was exposed to newer and better alternatives. The trolley bag replaced the holdall, Chinese raincoats offered cheaper alternatives and Duckback's halcyon days were over.

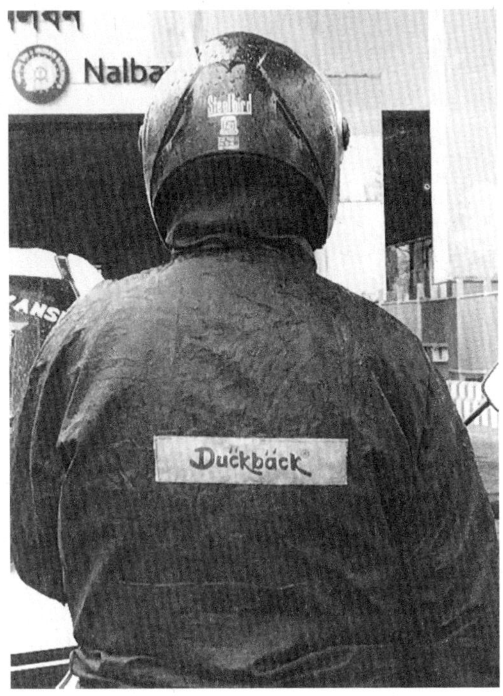

Even today, a Duckback raincoat is a common sight during monsoons on the streets of Kolkata.

Even though Duckback no longer enjoys the same prestige and market presence as it did in the glory days, for multiple generations it remains a nostalgic association, a personal connection—and an iconic brand born from the Swadeshi Movement.

007
CHICAGO RADIO
VOTE FOR GHOSE
Lights,
Camera,
Azadi

9

Bollywood, Tagore and the National Poet

If you love Bollywood movies, you probably remember the grand spectacle of *Goliyon Ki Raasleela Ram-Leela*. Yes, the one starring Deepika Padukone and Ranveer Singh, directed by the master of opulence, Sanjay Leela Bhansali. This Indian adaptation of Shakespeare's 'Romeo and Juliet' is set in the Gujarati hinterland. Interestingly, the film's original title had to be changed due to protests from various communities. Given its intense themes of passion and violence, Bhansali could have just as easily named it *Guns & Roses*.

From the very first scene, the film pulls you into its world. It opens with the folk song '*Mor bani thanghat kare*' (My heart dances like a peacock), a joyous tune celebrating the season's first rain.

A poetic contrast, isn't it? Love and longing woven into a story filled with guns and bloodshed. Perhaps that's exactly what Bhansali wanted to capture—the beauty of love in a world of violence.

An old poet behind a new hit song

But here's something most people missed. Just before the film starts, in a blink-and-you-miss-it moment, a black-and-white photograph of a man appears on the screen as a tribute. His name is credited as the creator of '*Mor bani thanghat kare*'. The screen also mentions that he was a Gujarati poet—so influential that Mahatma Gandhi called him

Rashtra Kavi, the National Poet of India. And most importantly, he was also a freedom fighter.

So, who was this freedom fighter to whom Bhansali paid tribute in his magnum opus? The answer is Jhaverchand Meghani. And to know his story, let's rewind to 1938.

In Rajkot, a literary gathering is being held for the Charan (pronounced Chaaran) community.[1] But in an unusual turn, a forty-one-year-old man from the Bania community, Jhaverchand Meghani, is invited to the dais to speak.

For the next ninety minutes, Meghani captivates the audience with his words. His speech is not just eloquent but deeply moving, holding in rapt attention an audience filled with established Charan poets, court writers and literary stalwarts.

As Meghani completes his address, Shankardan Detha, the Rajkavi[2] of Limbdi, gets up on his feet, approaches Meghani, hugs him affectionately, and says, 'Meghani! Kaljug (Kaliyug), they say, has already set in. I now feel convinced it indeed has. How come, otherwise, could this happen: A Vaaniyo (Bania) goes unfolding and interpreting Charanee literature, quoting from it copiously and extempore for one-and-a-half hours; and we, hundreds of Charans, called Deviputras (sons of the goddess), sit listening to him, silent and sheeplike, hypnotized, so much so that we forget to rekindle our extinguished hookahs in between!'

It prompts a hearty laugh from everyone present.

Meghani's reply is, 'I am just a postman.' A messenger.

Jhaverchand Meghani's discourse that day in Rajkot cemented his legacy as a poet deeply rooted in Gujarat's folk traditions (Chapter 26).

Decades later, his influence would quietly surface in Bollywood. In 2013, a connection between Bhansali and Tagore emerged— through the medium of music. The song '*Mor bani thanghat kare*' from *Goliyon Ki Raasleela Ram-Leela* tied Bhansali's work to Tagore's world, bridging literature, history and cinema in a fascinating way. The lyrics of the song are similar to a Bengali song by Tagore. This connection entails a story.

Meghani's long journey to Tagore

Born in Chotila in Saurashtra in 1897, Meghani started writing poems at the age of twelve as Vilapi, a pen name he would often use. At the age of nineteen, he got his BA degree. India at the time was moving through the gears, as the momentum picked up for its independence movement. Muhammad Ali Jinnah and Bal Gangadhar Tilak had put together the Lucknow Pact, which was adopted by the Congress in its Lucknow session in December 1916. Then there was Gandhi who had plunged headlong into the freedom movement, having returned to India just a year before. Meghani as a student was active in the Swadeshi Movement and other social activities as well.

The tryst with Tagore started when Meghani landed a job at an aluminium utensil factory in Belur near Calcutta in 1918. He was quick to learn the Bengali language and imbibe the culture, and was fondly called Pagdi Babu by his colleagues and the factory workers. For three years Meghani stayed in Calcutta, and his knowledge of literature compounded as he read the works of Bankim Chandra, Dinesh Chandra and Tagore, which left a profound impact on him. He even translated Tagore's *Katha O Kahini* (*Stories and Tales*) into Gujarati. He returned home in 1922 and joined the editorial board of the weekly, *Saurashtra*.

Over the next few years, apart from gathering and documenting Gujarati folk culture and songs, Meghani would try his hand at almost every form of writing, from novels, short stories and poems to composing songs that would stir emotions, often arousing an unbounded sense of patriotism.

In 1928, Meghani came out with one of his finest works, the poem 'Charan Kanya', a tribute to the courage of a young girl from the Charan community. A couple of years later, Gandhi was on his march from Sabarmati to Dandi on Gujarat's southern coast to defy the British with a pinch of salt. Meghani, seeing this unfold first-hand, would release a collection of fifteen songs commentating on the Dholera Satyagraha, which included the Salt Satyagraha or Dandi

March. The book *Sindhudo*, not surprisingly, was banned by the authorities and most of its copies were confiscated.

In 1930, Jhaverchand Meghani—who would give a rousing oration in Rajkot eight years later—was in jail. British authorities were making arrests left, right and centre; anyone even remotely associated with the freedom movement was seen as a threat, and that included writers and poets, who some could argue were more seditious and dangerous than the people carrying guns and bombs. Meghani was tried for making an inflammatory public speech, an offence he, in fact, had not committed. Regardless, Meghani declared that he was more than happy to lay down his life for his country.

The British authorities had reason to be afraid of this man—a stroke from Meghani's pen could arouse a thousand young boys and girls to rise up and try to snatch back from the clutches of an ungodly imperial force what was rightfully theirs—freedom.

By this time, Meghani had earned quite a name for himself. His works catapulted him from his place as a writer and poet to that of a ringing voice of dissent. In 1931, just before Gandhi was to head off to England for the Second Round Table Conference, he received a poem by Meghani. It was titled 'Chello Katoro' (The Last Cup). After reading it, Gandhi observed, 'The poet, it seems, has entered my heart and mind, and read my thoughts'; he then gave Meghani the title of Rashtra Kavi or National Poet.

It was not until 1933 that Meghani finally got a chance to meet Tagore in Bombay, thanks to Nandalal Bose, the notable Indian artist. Bose had encountered Meghani's work when he observed Gandhi's Salt March up close. The meeting, which was supposed to last for half an hour, went on for four hours. Tagore was so impressed, he invited Meghani to Shantiniketan and urged him to stay there for some time. Meghani happily obliged and delivered his lectures to packed audiences during his visit in 1941.

Shortly after this visit, in 1944, Meghani released a Gujarati translation of Tagore's songs and poems in an anthology titled *Ravindra-Veena*. It included Tagore's poem 'Naba-Barsha' (New

Rain), which he translated in the style of Charan poetry. It was titled 'Navivarsha', later known as '*Mor bani thanghat kare*'. Later on, a modern version was composed by Hemu Gadhvi and that was the one used by Bhansali for his film.

And that's how one song from Bhansali's film weaves together Tagore, Gandhi, Satyagraha and the timeless folk poet of Gujarat, Jhaverchand Meghani. Perhaps he deserves more than just a fleeting tribute—maybe a place in our collective memory, where his words continue to inspire generations, just as they did during the Satyagraha days.

> ### Fighting words, in verse
>
> In his poem 'Virat Darshan' (Magnificent Vision), Meghani urged people of the world to rise in rebellion against oppression.
>
> *The drum roars across the horizon,*
> *The infinite steps thunder ahead.*
> *Look ahead, O blind ones! A dark storm rises,*
> *From lands far and wide, men and women,*
> *Holding their heads high,*
> *Come marching in unity.*

On 5 March 1947, Jhaverchand Meghani passed away, just a few months before India's independence. He was just fifty years old at the time.

Meghani captured the essence of the struggle for freedom like few poets of his time, his words cutting through hearts and minds like a dagger. His work has not only stood the test of time but is a testament to the country's diverse and multicultural richness.

But Meghani was more than just a poet—he was a composer, a singer, a friend and, above all, a hero.

10

When a Hindi Film Song Said 'Quit India'

In August 1942, Mahatma Gandhi launched the Quit India Movement. The movement called for an immediate end to British rule in India. Gandhi's famous 'Do or Die' speech urged Indians to engage in non-violent resistance against British colonial rule. The movement led to widespread protests, strikes and acts of civil disobedience across India. Despite being repressed by the British authorities, the movement marked a significant turning point in India's struggle for independence.

On 9 January 1943, a Hindi film premiered at Roxy Talkies in Bombay. The film went on to become the first all-India blockbuster, celebrating golden and silver jubilees in multiple cities of undivided India. The film also set a record of running for 187 continuous weeks at Roxy Cinema in Kolkata. The film was *Kismet*, directed by Gyan Mukherjee. Starring Ashok Kumar and Mumtaz Shanti in leading roles, *Kismet* has a dramatic plot containing crime, romance and redemption in a series of complicated twists in the tale. It also introduced somewhat shocking new themes such as an antihero and an unwed pregnant woman. The film's success at the box office and its enduring popularity have cemented its place in the history of Indian cinema.

Kismet is also known for its iconic music composed by Anil Biswas who had introduced the concept of a 'full chorus' for the first time in a Hindi film song. The full chorus song in the film sparked the nation's patriotic fervour during the independence movement and also left the British authorities in a state of helpless rage, because the song came in a brilliant disguise.

The riveting track '*Duur hato ai duniya waalon, Hindustan hamara hai*' (Back off foreigners, Hindustan belongs to us), sung by Amirbai Karnataki, Khan Mastana and other singers (the chorus), clearly got its inspiration from Gandhi's Quit India Movement. Kavi Pradeep wrote the stirring lyrics. He was a revolutionary at heart, who took part in the Quit India Movement. He realized that films were a powerful tool for spreading the message of Indian nationalism.

Back then, the British Empire, clinging to its last vestiges of power, was eager to crush any perceived threats. Kavi Pradeep wrote the song during the Quit India Movement, when most Indian leaders were imprisoned. So, how did this song manage to pass the gates of the censor board? The answer lies in the brilliance of its lyrics.

Cleverly crafted lyrics

Film historian and our friend, Pavan Jha, described the song as a 'follow up' of Gandhi's Quit India call. He shared the recording of his Allahabad Music Club discourse, 'Songs of Nation Building and Bonding', during our conversation with him. Kavi Pradeep's genius shone from the first line of the song '*Duur hato ai duniya waalon, Hindustan hamara hai*' as well as the line '*Shuru hua hai jang tumhara, jaag utho Hindustani*' (Your war has begun, wake up all Indians) and the war cry intensifies in the second stanza's line, '*Tum na kisi ke aagey jhukna, jarman ho ya jaapaani*' (Don't you bow down to anyone, be it Germans or Japanese). This clever reference, dressed as a warning to the Axis powers during World War II, masked the song's intent and allowed it to be passed by British censors.

Our friend Balaji Vittal, a national-award-winning author, mentions in his book, *Pure Evil: The Bad Men of Bollywood*, that the unfamiliarity of the British with the Hindi language helped these songs get overlooked by the censor board.

The song spread like wildfire across the country and became a rallying cry for India's long-awaited freedom. Everywhere one went, the song was being hummed or sung by ordinary people. Pavan, in his talk, also mentioned that freedom fighters who were being imprisoned sang this song while going to prison.

Kavi Pradeep (1915–98), poet and celebrated lyricist known for his profound patriotic songs. (Photo courtesy: *Filmindia* Magazine. Public Domain via Wikimedia Commons.)

Kismet caused a stir at the box office and the song became an instant smash hit. Theatres all over the country were jam-packed with eager crowds who wanted to hear it over and over again. The song had to be rewound several times, as the audience chanted 'encore' after each screening.

The effect of the song did not go unnoticed by the British authorities. They attempted to ban the film and issued a warrant for the song's writer, Kavi Pradeep, who had to go underground to avoid arrest.

Despite the threats, '*Duur hato ai duniya waalon*' continued to inspire. It became an anthem for independence movement rallies and a symbol of the country's tenacity and determination.

Songs of India's soul

Pavan Jha, film historian, mentioned two other songs—the brilliant C. Ramchandra composition, again penned by Kavi Pradeep,
'*Ai merey watan ke logon,*
Zara aankh mein bhar lo paani.
Jo shaheed hue hain unki
Zara yaad karo qurbani'
and
'*Kar chale ham fidaa jaan-o-tan saathiyon,*
Ab tumhaare hawaale watan saathiyo',
written during the Sino–Indian War of 1962 by Kaifi Azmi and composed by Madan Mohan. The latter song was used at the end of the film *Haqeeqat* (1964) as a tribute to all the Indian soldiers who fought the battle of Rezang La, a battle which was considered the only part of the Sino–Indian War in which India emerged victorious.

The British may have tried to suppress *Kismet* and '*Duur hato ai duniya waalon*', but they could not muffle the power of music or the indomitable spirit of freedom fighters. We concur with Pavan in his concluding thoughts that as we look at the history and social and political commentary of building the nation India, we must acknowledge the contribution and intellect of the creators of these songs. They gave us a legacy that lives on to this day, a testament to the power of art and the nation's unbreakable spirit.

11

The Cinemawallah

'The copy was just sitting in some film laboratory,' said Arnab, his tone hinting at his displeasure. In 1995, Arnab Jan Deka, an Assamese author, actor, screenwriter and documentary film director, was in Bombay (now Mumbai) attending a programme at the Chhatrapati Shivaji Stadium celebrating 100 years of world cinema. Many dignitaries graced the stage, including M. Saravanan, the owner of AVM Productions, one of the oldest film studios in the country, established in Madras (present-day Chennai) in the 1930s. During his speech, Saravanan claimed that Tamil cinema brought dubbing technology to India for the first time in the year 1937—a claim that, according to Arnab, was audaciously false. But to his surprise, neither Bhupen Hazarika nor Biju Phukan, stalwarts of Assamese cinema at the time who were at the ceremony, uttered a word of protest. Arnab says an Assamese movie *Joymoti* pioneered dubbing technology in India two years before AVM Productions did.

Precious print resurfaces

The original print of the movie had been left behind in a studio in Lahore after Partition and thought to be lost, but then it mysteriously found its way back to Bombay one fine day. Arnab recovered it in 1995, and reported it to the Assam government and the newspapers.

Joymoti was a pioneering film for various reasons. Based on the eponymous play by Laxminath Bezbarua, it was the first film to come out of Assam and, through its lens, we get a rare glimpse into its maker, a firebrand freedom fighter.

Deep into India's freedom struggle, as a war raged in multiple corners of the world, the Bombay Session of the Indian National Congress in 1942 passed the resolution of Quit India; 'Do or Die' became the cry. The British authorities were quick to act by placing all the frontline leaders of the INC, including Gandhi, Jawaharlal Nehru, Maulana Azad and Sardar Patel, behind bars, but the movement wasn't going to easily fade away.

Nationalism blossoms in Assam

The Assam branch of the Congress had already set things in motion. It was as if the people of Assam had prepped for this for years. A key proponent behind this was a man named Jyoti Prasad Agarwala. It was under his direction that they planned to hoist the tricolour in all the police stations across the state. On 20 September 1942, a huge crowd had gathered near the police station in Dhekiajuli in the Sonitpur district. As the crowd led by Manbar Nath, a resident of Dhekiajuli and active INC member, attempted to enter the police station holding the national flag and chanting slogans of Vande Mataram, they were met with lathis and a subsequent volley of bullets. Manbar Nath and many of the group lost their lives that day. On the same day at Darrang, two young women, eighteen-year-old Kanaklata Barua accompanied by twenty-three-year-old Mukunda Kakati, both independence activists in the Mrityu Bahini, led a big unarmed procession to the Gohpur police station carrying the tricolour. Both Kanaklata and Mukunda were shot dead as they attempted to bring down the Union Jack.

While in Sootea the movement was a success, the authorities were now on the lookout for the main conspirators. While many were arrested, they never managed to capture Jyoti Prasad Agarwala. He fled and went underground, from where he continued to assert influence on the movement.

Jyoti Prasad was a man of many talents. He dived into the freedom movement at the tender age of seventeen, after Gandhiji visited his home in Tezpur in 1921. His family had migrated in the nineteenth century to Tezpur from Churu in present-day Rajasthan. The Agarwala family home, fondly named Poki, was the source of considerable influence over Tezpur and Assam's sociopolitical landscape, shaping key movements and fostering local engagement in the broader struggle for independence. It was from Poki that the nationalist movement spread through all of Assam.

Berlin detour, then back home to fight

Jyoti Prasad hoped to follow in the footsteps of his grandfather, Haribilash, father, Paramananda, and uncle, Chandra Kumar Agarwala. Chandra Kumar Agarwala wrote the first Assamese romantic poem 'Bon Kunwari'. Together with Lakshminath Bezbarua and Hemchandra Goswami the trio is considered the 'Trimurti (triumvirate) of Assamese Literature'. Needless to say, Jyoti Prasad was deeply influenced by his family's cultural background, but his encounters with Gandhi and several prominent figures from the worlds of art and culture further shaped his early views. He penned his first play, *Sonit Kunwari*, at the age of fourteen, which was later staged in 1925 at the Ban Theatre in Tezpur. In 1926, he went to Edinburgh to study economics, but left in 1930 before finishing the course. On his way home, Jyoti Prasad stopped for seven months in Berlin to learn filmmaking at Universum Film AG (UFA).[1] He submitted an English translation of *Sonit Kunwari* at UFA in 1930.

> ### When Germany touched Indian films
>
> The German association with Indian filmmakers is rich and multifaceted. A few years before Jyoti Prasad arrived in Berlin, a young man from Calcutta, Himanshu Rai, travelled to Germany and formed close ties with several German directors, some of whom were affiliated with UFA. This collaboration marked the beginning of a long-standing relationship, with figures like Franz Osten[2] going on to direct several films with Himanshu Rai and his Bombay Talkies.

Jyoti Prasad's writings, such as the lines, 'To die for our country / the young men and women in our village / do not fall behind', often evoked deep emotions and inspired the masses to join the struggle for the country's independence. In April 1931, he led a large group of workers and volunteers, marching through the night while singing patriotic songs that he had composed, to participate in the peasant assembly held at Biswanath. Soon after, in 1932 he was imprisoned and held by the authorities for fifteen months due to his active involvement in the freedom movement.

An ancient legend in a modern world

It was only after his release in 1933 that he began working on *Joymoti*. The film portrays the heroic sacrifice of Joymoti, an Ahom princess who endured torture and was ultimately killed by the Ahom king, Borphukan, for refusing to betray her husband, Prince Gadapani, by revealing his whereabouts. It was not only the first film to come out of Assam but also one of the earliest in the country to portray a female character in the lead role. The filming was done in Chitraban Studios, which Jyoti Prasad had established at his family's Bholaguri Tea Estate.

The film is unique in more ways than one. Jyoti Prasad portrayed Joymoti's tale in a contemporary style. Many now consider it to be a pioneering work in depicting realism in Indian cinema. Apart from the film having serious nationalistic undertones, all the characters portrayed in the film including the three main female characters were rooted in realism. Realism was still a relatively new idea; before its emergence, characters, particularly women, were often rendered as figures drawn from fable or myth. Through the film Jyoti Prasad tried his best to give the audience a sense of its connection with the wider struggle for freedom in the country at the time.

However, bringing that kind of realism from paper to the screen was not going to be an easy job. Seventeenth-century costumes were partly designed by Jyoti Prasad himself; he also taught his actors how to develop, process and edit, and recognize the difference between mixed shot, fade out and zoom. Filming was completed later in 1934, and Jyoti Prasad himself did all the editing in Lahore, but there was a problem—for the first half of the film, there was no recorded sound. Since he could not call the actors back, Jyoti Prasad hired a sound studio there and dubbed the voices of both the male and female actors in the film. It was eventually released in 1935. This explains why the original copy of the film was in Lahore in 1947.

After *Joymoti*, Jyoti Prasad made another film, *Indramalati*, and went on to record several songs, author books and experiment with his creativity. His staunch beliefs in Gandhian non-violence continued to serve him until his last days.

His birth anniversary, 17 January, is now celebrated as Silpi Divas, to commemorate his pioneering work in the field of arts and culture. In Assam, Jyoti Prasad is fondly known as Rupkonwar, meaning 'prince of beauty', a fitting moniker.

Acknowledgement: We sincerely thank Arnab Jan Deka for his valuable insights and the work he has put in to make Jyoti Prasad Agarwala and his work relevant again.

12

A Play Named *Meerut*

'**M**urder! Murder! MURDER! MURDER!'
The shouts rang out near the dock gates on Trafford Road in Salford. An odd bunch of ruffians, barely twenty years old, seemed to be enacting something on what looked like a makeshift stage. A crowd had gathered, mostly lascars and labourers working the morning shift at the docks. The year was 1931. In happier times the chatter among the crowd may have been about football and how the local team Manchester United was relegated to the second division, but this was not the time for fun and games. Given the high unemployment rate, there was resentment all over Britain, and mass protests were erupting. It was hard to gauge the mood of the crowd, and indeed some of them may have thought that the youngsters were crazy, but they stayed on anyway.

One of the ruffians said: 'The average wage for all workers and peasants is less than a shilling a day in India—the brightest jewel in Britain's crown.'

The rest of them replied: 'Must we not revolt?'

Theatre of rebellion

The world was still reeling from the Wall Street crisis of 1929 and in Britain it was no different. In these turbulent times, a few boys and girls chose to voice their opinion, using theatre as a medium. One of them was James Henry Miller, a teenager who was heavily influenced by the Bolsheviks and their ideas of revolution. Miller was an impressionist mimicking famous people, and though a novice, his talents were noticed by a member of the theatre group Clarion Players, part of the working-class movement initiated by English socialist Robert Blatchford. Miller would have been hardly sixteen or seventeen at the time.

In London, the workers' theatre movement had already carved a niche, and Miller and his fellow mates sought to amplify it in Manchester. In early 1931, the Clarion Players broke up and formed a new group, called the Red Megaphones, and Miller became its producer and main scriptwriter. The group was, as Miller liked to call it, agitprop[1]—a mobile, exhortative revolutionary theatre created for quick outdoor performances, flexible enough to suit different locations, audiences and casts, and designed to take advantage of the sights and acoustics of outdoor spaces. A far cry from normal theatre, it had its history rooted in the October Revolution and its architect, Vladimir Lenin.

On Trafford Road, the Red Megaphones continued to entertain the audience.

A boy went up and said: 'The police shot at them, their brothers in the Indian army were forced to shoot them. Your brothers, your husbands, your sons were sent from England to shoot them, to massacre them, to break their strike.'

The others went: 'The Tsar failed—and they too will fail.'

The crowd dispersed as the performance on Trafford Road ended. The ruffians came out shouting, 'Comrades! Comrades! Comrades! Comrades—smash the bars!' It was the Red Megaphones' second such performance; the first one took place on May Day 1931 in Platt Fields, Manchester.

But for Miller the second one was special; it was called *Meerut*.

Meerut—revolt and resolution

The original idea was from a theatre group in London, which Miller later improvised. He wanted his work to mean something, to speak to his audience in a manner that would arouse empathy and awareness.

But what was so special about *Meerut*? Why was a theatre group in Salford talking about a town in the United Provinces of British India at the time?

Meerut was no stranger to rebellion—this city in western Uttar Pradesh (called United Provinces at the time) never bowed to tyranny and had stood tall and proud through history. While the stories from the 1857 War of Independence (Chapter 27) are deeply etched in our minds, Meerut is also the place where, still in the future at the time of our story, the last session of Congress would be held before India became independent. The Congress passed its final resolution on that day on a motion by Acharya Narendra Deo. The resolution reaffirmed the Congress's commitment to an independent sovereign republic on the eve of the Constituent Assembly's summoning.

But between these two landmark events, something else also happened in Meerut.

Searching for clues

Our curiosity led us to the National Library in Kolkata. 'What kind of information do you need? The year and the month would be helpful,' said the clerk on the second floor of the new building. The old building has been undergoing renovation for a very long time and is closed to the public. The new wing looks modern, though it could do with a fresh coat of paint. They say the old building is haunted by colonial-era ghosts. Some say it is Lady Metcalfe, the mysterious woman who roams the estate at night. Some say it is Warren Hastings himself.

The ghosts of the National Library

Lady Metcalfe would usually make her presence felt if you were alone or had not kept things in their proper place—she was known to be quite strict about order and tidiness.

Governor-General Warren Hastings upbraided his political nemesis Philip Francis, a member of the Bengal Supreme

Council, for his adulterous affair with Mrs Catherine Grand, wife of an officer and a celebrated beauty. It was a matter of honour, so Francis had to call Hastings out to a duel on the grounds of Belvedere House (now the National Library). Neither was a good shot. Francis missed but Hastings managed to hit him—and was horrified. In an act of chivalry, Hastings called for his own palki to carry the wounded Francis to medical aid. Legend has it that, even after two centuries, on nights of the full moon, a spectral palki can still be seen gliding across the grounds. The place where the duel took place is now known as Duel Avenue.

'We need some information on the Meerut Conspiracy Case—that would be March 1929,' we said.

'I see, please take a seat. I will have to check.'

India in 1929 was a hotbed of anti-colonial activities—conspiracies, robberies, protests. However, what happened in Meerut was partly owing to the fall of the Russian Empire in 1917 and the creation of the Communist International, or the Comintern in 1919.

The clerk came back with a month's collection of newspapers which was quite bulky. Pieces of the fragile paper were disintegrating, crumbling like fine dust, although for the most part it looked fine. We were told to handle it with care.

The headline on 20 March 1929 read: 'Round up of communist leaders in Bombay'.

Among the ones arrested were S.A. Dange and Shaukat Usmani. On the same day, the CID branch of the Calcutta Police raided several secret hideouts and about forty other known places and arrested, among others, Philip Spratt, Muzaffar Ahmed, Asutosh Roy and Bankim Mukherjee. The premises of the newspaper *Anandabazar Patrika* were raided. Kishorilal Ghose, the assistant editor of another daily, *Amrita Bazar Patrika*, was among those arrested. Raids were also conducted in Lucknow and Allahabad. They even arrested a

British citizen, B.F. Bradley, from Grant Road Bridge in Bombay. A total of thirty-one people were arrested and charged under Section 121-A of the Indian Penal Code, for conspiring against the crown and undermining the sovereignty of British India—or sedition in simple terms.

But how did it come to this? By the mid-1920s communist ideals had penetrated deep into the Indian psyche, particularly in the trade unions. One of the founders of the All India Trade Union Congress (AITUC), Chaman Lal, was also a member of the Workers' Welfare League of India in London, which served as a proxy for the Communist Party. Mill workers and railwaymen gradually came under the influence of these trade unions.

To fuel the movement, a couple of British communists made their way to India, Philip Spratt from Camberwell in South London and Benjamin Francis Bradley, also from London. Bradley and Spratt were quick to get into action. They became members of the Workers' and Peasants' Party and held a meeting in Meerut. The authorities, alarmed at the movements of Bradley and Spratt, and the continuing worker protests, decided to step in.

In a letter to the governor of Bengal dated 1 January 1929, Viceroy Lord Irwin wrote: 'We have ... at present reasonably good hopes of being able to run a comprehensive conspiracy case against these men. If we could do this, it would, in our opinion, deal a more severe blow to the Indian Communist movement than anything.'

The Meerut Trial bites back

The choice of Meerut as the venue for the trial was a strange one. Normally such a big case would have gone to either Calcutta or Bombay, but the authorities wanted to avoid trial by jury. Jawaharlal Nehru, who volunteered to defend the accused, appealed to the British Trades Union Congress (TUC) for support, claiming that the trial was an attempt to suppress trade unionism in India.

The trial that went on for four years led to the conviction of twenty-seven men. However, most of them were released or had their sentences reduced either upon appeals made to the High Court of Allahabad or because part of the sentence had already been served. The trial evoked solidarity from all over the world. Members of the British press sympathized with the movement and demanded the release of the prisoners.

The trial had adverse effects for the British authorities, much to their dismay. It publicized the work of the communists and within the nationalist circles, the accused, such as Dange and Ahmed, became noteworthy figures. But to have made enough of an impact to have a bunch of kids dedicate a play halfway across the world was truly unique. For Miller and his Red Megaphones, the play named *Meerut* was special. It was no Shakespearean drama, of course, but the hushed attention of the audience was proof that the cause was not lost and that the world was watching an imperial power conducting an unjust trial on its subjects.

13

The Unlikely Pioneer of Bhojpuri Cinema

Long before Bhojpuri cinema found its modern stars in the likes of Manoj Tiwari, Ravi Kishan or Dinesh Lal Yadav, one man left an indelible mark on this industry, right from its inception. That man was Nazir Hussain. Mainstream audiences may not instantly recognize him, but his contribution to shaping Bhojpuri cinema remains unparalleled. He was not just an actor. He gave Bhojpuri-speaking people their own cinema. He helped build an industry that grew for decades.

Most might recognize him from Hindi films, but not for any standout roles. He was often the warm peripheral character in classics like *Devdas*, *Do Bigha Zamin* and *Naya Daur*. He played the priest in *Amar Akbar Anthony*, the police commissioner in *Jewel Thief* and countless other supporting roles. Filmgoers often amusingly labelled him the melodramatic, teary-eyed father of Bollywood. His face was familiar, yet his impact was rarely discussed.

But behind these minor on-screen characters was a man whose real life was larger than any role he ever played. His journey took him through war, imprisonment, revolution and theatre, before he made history by creating a brand-new cinematic tradition. And above all else, Nazir Hussain was a freedom fighter—a man who fought for India's independence before he fought for the recognition of Bhojpuri cinema.

Modest beginnings

Born in Usia, a small village in the United Provinces (modern day Uttar Pradesh), British India, Nazir Hussain grew up in a modest household. In his book, *Cinema Bhojpuri*, Avijit Ghosh provides a thorough account of Nazir Hussain's life. His father worked as a railway guard, ensuring the family had a stable, though simple, life. The young Nazir, too, followed in his father's footsteps and found himself working in the Indian Railways as a fireman. At this stage, there was nothing in his life that hinted at the cinematic legacy he would one day create. He was an ordinary man with ordinary struggles.

War—what is patriotism?

As the world plunged into the chaos of World War II, young men across British India were recruited into the British Indian Army, and Nazir was no exception. He joined the army and was soon deployed to Southeast Asia, where the war was raging in full force. His battalion saw action in Burma, Malaya and Singapore, as part of Britain's efforts to counter the advancing Japanese forces.

But then came a turning point—one that would alter the course of his life forever. It was in 1942, after Singapore fell, when Indian prisoners languished in camps facing an uncertain future. Mohan Singh and the Japanese began recruiting them for the Indian National Army (INA), blending appeals to nationalism with promises of better treatment, and Subhas Chandra Bose soon ignited the fire with his call to arms. The INA eventually grew from a band of scattered prisoners into the Azad Hind Fauj. When the Japanese forces overran British positions in the region, Nazir was among the many Indian soldiers taken prisoner. As a prisoner of war, he found himself face to face with a larger ideological battle—one that was far more personal than Britain's fight against Japan. It was the question of India's own freedom.

Nazir had always opposed British rule. His time in prison made his feelings even stronger. He realized how Indian soldiers were being used by the British. They were forced to fight wars that were not their own. In the Japanese prison camps, he found a new path. This path was the fight for India's freedom. He was inspired by the powerful speeches of Subhas Chandra Bose. Nazir decided to join the INA under General Mohan Singh.

The INA sought to liberate India from British rule through armed resistance, aligning itself with the Axis powers in the hope that Japan's victories in Asia would pave the way for an independent India. Nazir Hussain fought in the brutal Burma campaign, where INA soldiers battled both British and Indian troops loyal to the Raj. But as the tides of war turned against Japan and the Axis, the INA's dream crumbled. Bose's army was defeated, and its soldiers—including Nazir—were once again taken captive, this time by the British.

Leap into a new life

When India gained independence in 1947, many INA soldiers found themselves in a strange situation. They had fought for India's freedom, but most were not integrated into the Indian army, which chose to remain apolitical, whereas the INA was deeply political. Possibly, the Indian army was uncomfortable with the more complex nature of their role in the war against the British. Nazir Hussain was one of the soldiers who faced discrimination. In the years that followed, he had trouble finding work. He was stranded with no clear future. And for someone like him, who had actually fought in a war, the idea of a regular civilian job was not so easy. During these uncertain times, he turned to something that had always interested him—something he had also done during his time with the INA. He started performing in theatres.

Seeking new opportunities, Nazir moved to Calcutta, which had a thriving theatre scene at the time. In Calcutta, he met the legendary filmmaker Bimal Roy.

Roy was working on a film about the INA and Subhas Chandra Bose, and he wanted to cast real-life INA soldiers for authenticity. Nazir's deep voice, intense expressiveness and natural presence caught his attention. Though Nazir had no prior film experience, Bimal Roy took a chance on him and cast him in *Pehla Aadmi* (1950).

The film's plot revolves around Dr Vijay Kumar, played by Nazir Hussain, a doctor residing in Pegu, Burma. Dr Kumar lives with his son Kumar (played by Balraj Vij), who is in love with their next-door neighbour, Lata (played by Smriti Biswas). As their lives unfold, the news arrives that Netaji Subhas Chandra Bose has reached Burma, sparking a fire of hope and urgency among the nationalists.

A scene from the movie *Pehla Aadmi* (1950), where Dr Vijay Kumar, played by Nazir Hussain, holds a copy of *New Times of Burma*, featuring Netaji's image and his stirring slogan. (Source: Screenshot from *Pehla Aadmi* [1950], via Gold Movies YouTube channel. Fair use for scholarly commentary.)

Dr Vijay Kumar, deeply moved by the arrival of Netaji and his revolutionary ideals, is determined to push his reluctant son Kumar to join the Indian National Army, despite his hesitations. Although the film was far from Roy's best works, it effectively blends historical reality with fictional storytelling, using real footage of Netaji, the war, and the INA, which brings an undeniable authenticity to the narrative. Among the many memorable frames in the film, one stands out—Nazir Hussain holding a newspaper, *New Times of Burma*, in which the iconic image of Netaji appears with his famous slogan: 'You give me blood, I will give you freedom.'

One of the most striking aspects of the film is its portrayal of life in the soldiers' camp, which gives viewers a glimpse of the hardship, sacrifice and resolve of the fighters. This part of the film, with its vivid depiction of the soldiers' lives, was likely influenced by Nazir Hussain's own experiences as a member of the INA.

The film marked Nazir's entry into Bollywood, and what followed was a career that would span over four decades. Nazir quickly established himself as a dependable character actor, known for his realistic performances and deep emotional range. Whether playing the supportive father, the wise village elder or the morally upright police officer, he brought an authenticity that made his characters unforgettable. He became a favourite of top filmmakers like Bimal Roy and Mehboob Khan, appearing in *Do Bigha Zamin*, *Devdas*, *Naya Daur*, *Ganga Jamuna* and many other films.

But despite his success in Bollywood, there was a part of Nazir that longed for something more—something that would connect him to his own roots. That longing led him to his greatest achievement: the birth of Bhojpuri cinema.

Return to roots—and a new path

Though Nazir was deeply immersed in Bollywood, he never forgot his Bhojpuri heritage. At a time when regional languages were still struggling for representation in mainstream cinema, he envisioned a film industry that would cater specifically to Bhojpuri-speaking audiences.

His biggest breakthrough came when he approached President Rajendra Prasad, who was himself a Bhojpuri speaker. Dr Rajendra Prasad, the first President of India, had a deep affection for his mother tongue, Bhojpuri. Despite his distinguished position in the country, he never let go of his roots. He would converse in Bhojpuri with his relatives and even wrote letters to his wife in Bhojpuri, when he was away. His love for the language was not just personal but also cultural, a bond that connected him to his homeland.

> ### The humble earth grows great jewels
>
> There is a poem by Bhikhari Thakur, the celebrated Bhojpuri poet, that beautifully reflects Rajendra Babu's roots in Chhapra, Bihar, and his rise to become India's 'crown jewel'—the first President of independent India.
>
> छपरा रहत राजेंद्र बाबू, जीरादेई मकान।
> हिन्दुस्तान के मुकुटमनी, दिल्ली तकथ महान॥
>
> (From Chhapra town comes Rajendra Babu, his home in Jiradei;
> The crown jewel of India, in the great seat Delhi.)

Nazir Sahib passionately argued for the need to create cinema in Bhojpuri, a language spoken by millions but ignored by the film industry. The President, recognizing the cultural significance of the idea, encouraged him to write a script.

Nazir already had a script that delicately explored societal struggles.

It was a story of a rich boy who falls in love with a poor girl. Defying his moneylender father's demand for dowry, he leaves his home. The girl, however, is forced into an unwanted marriage, endures tragedy, survives, and eventually becomes a dancing girl. Fate brings the two lovers back together, but not without pain and hardship.

But there was a catch. While working as Bimal Roy's assistant, Hussain had already given this script to Roy who was known for his expertise in women-centric films. But deep inside, Hussain wanted to tell this story himself. He wanted to make it in a way that reflected his own culture. When Hussain approached Bimal Roy to reclaim his script, Roy was taken aback. Surprised, Roy questioned the significance of Bhojpuri as a language of cinema. Hussain replied confidently, 'It is the language of the President.'

That moment defined his mission. Determined to preserve and celebrate his linguistic heritage, he took back the script and turned it into a historic cinematic milestone—the first-ever Bhojpuri film, *Ganga Maiyya Tohe Piyari Chadhaibo*. Despite the industry's initial scepticism, the film didn't just do well at the box office—it became a symbol of Bhojpuri culture. It proved that Bhojpuri cinema had a place in Indian film culture, paving the way for an entire industry.

It was first shown at Prakash Theatre in Varanasi in February 1962. But the real excitement began when the film was released at Veena Talkies in Patna. The streets were filled with bullock carts as people lined up to watch it. Many had to stay overnight in Patna if they couldn't get tickets and would head back to their villages the next day after watching the film.

We had the privilege of speaking to M.W. Ansari, who comes from the same village, Usia, where Nazir Hussain was born. Ansariji, now settled in Bhopal, is a charming gentleman. He was patient enough to share many stories and newspaper articles he had written in the past.

Ansariji told us, 'In fact, my father, Haji Ahmed Ali, who was a great freedom fighter, was Nazir Hussain's senior in Azad Hind Fauj. They travelled together to Java, Sumatra, Malaya and Rangoon. They spent days together.' He affectionately recalled many stories. He shared how, in his younger days, Nazir Hussain was a good dancer and played the flute and dhol very well. Sometimes, he would visit the nearby village, Vasuka, which was known as the village of tawaifs or courtesans, where he would dance and play the dhol. His father, a strict and respectable man, often reprimanded Nazir for such misadventures.

All these stories remain undocumented and live on only in memories. Ansariji was kind enough to invite us to his ancestral village. He offered to show us Nazir Hussain's ancestral house and several film shooting locations from his first film.

Today, Bhojpuri cinema is often criticized for its association with obscenity, but that was never the vision when Nazir Hussain began his journey. His love for the country went far beyond his fight in Netaji's army. His first film tackled serious issues like widow remarriage, and throughout his career, he focused on social messages and the importance of women's education.

Perhaps society doesn't really need superstars or mega stars. What it truly needs is an artist like Nazir Sahib.

14

A Photographer against the Raj

When India's fight for independence was gaining momentum in the early twentieth century, resistance was not limited to just speeches or protests on the streets. The camera was one of them. Photojournalism, silent but powerful, has often captured unadulterated stories and become an extremely effective means to narrate stories of struggles. Nora Ephron, the American journalist and writer of *When Harry Met Sally*, has rightly said in her groundbreaking essay 'Boston Photographs' for *Esquire*, 'That they [the photographs] disturb readers is exactly as it should be: that's why photojournalism is often more powerful than written journalism.'

At the heart of the early days of this visual rebellion in India was one Narayan Vinayak Virkar. He was a fantastic photographer who immortalized some of the most pivotal moments of India's nationalist movement. His camera did not just capture India's freedom movement—it practically became a part of it. Above all, his photographs accomplished something remarkable that has never been highlighted enough. He investigated what was arguably British India's most brutal crime scene.

Turning their tools against them

Photography was never only about art or documentation. It was also a tool for imperial power. Colonial rulers used it to control the story they wanted to tell. The British, like other European colonizers, used the camera to show their dominance. They photographed different races, customs and professions, often portraying native people as inferior.

Photography had been employed as a tool to help cement the ideological basis for European or white superiority by portraying Africans as inferior, satisfying the white gaze. Colonial archives used photos to present India as a land needing civilization. British rule was shown as a benevolent force saving an ancient land from decay. Architectural ruins were often photographed before British-led restorations, creating the myth that India could not preserve its own heritage. Ethnographic photography was also used to classify and stereotype Indian communities by race and caste. This reinforced European ideas of superiority.

In her article, 'Photography as a Tool of Power and Subjugation: How the Camera Was Used to Justify Black Racial Inferiority', Zara Chowdhury explains three ways photography was used for imperial control. The first was ethnographic photography, which focused on physical features to support racial classification. The second type showed colonizers standing next to the colonized, highlighting their dominance. The third category included staged studio portraits. This is where subjects wore traditional clothes or posed in their work settings against artificial backgrounds. The first type supported pseudoscientific racial theories, while the other two fed European curiosity about the 'exotic' and justified colonial rule. Although her study focuses on Africa, these methods were also used in India and other colonized countries.

For example, while visiting the iconic Das Studio in Darjeeling, we spotted an evocative photograph hanging on the wall. It was taken in 1903. The image captures an elderly woman, over 100 years old, sitting by the roadside near Darjeeling. The title of the photograph reads *Witch of Ghoom*. Several different photographs of this woman exist on postcards and cigarette cards from around 1900, all similarly identifying her as the *Witch of Ghoom*. But if one checks with the locals, they have no memory of any such woman being called a witch. This raises an uncomfortable question—why would the British photographer label her that way? The answer likely lies in the audience the photograph was meant for. It fed into colonial stereotypes by turning an ordinary elderly woman into an exotic spectacle for Western consumption. Without belittling their artistic and intellectual significance, these photographs were always taken by the British, for a British audience.

However, the colonized nations didn't just remain subjects of the imperialist gaze—they embraced the technology for themselves, starting from the early twentieth century. In India, despite the dominance of the colonial perspective, the photography industry saw participation from a diverse range of people. Commercial studios sprang up across the country, and a new generation of Indian photographers began to emerge.

Narayan Vinayak Virkar was one of them.

Learning a craft

Born in 1890 in the rugged terrain of Ratnagiri, Maharashtra, Virkar's journey was shaped by an early fascination with capturing reality. His introduction to photography came through the legendary Shripad Damodar Satwalekar. He was a man of many talents—artist, nationalist and scholar of the Vedas. Under Satwalekar's mentorship in Lahore, Virkar honed his craft.

His next destination was Bombay, the vibrant heart of colonial India. On Satwalekar's advice, Virkar moved to the metropolis and soon found himself navigating the city's elite circles. Virkar's trajectory changed when he took up a job as an X-ray photographer aboard the hospital ship HS *Madras* during World War I. HS *Madras* proved itself a distinguished World War I vessel. Among its crew was Narayan Vinayak Virkar, serving in the radiology unit. The experience gave him a broader perspective on life, death, and the impact of war.

> ### A peek at a WWI hospital ship
>
> As we discovered in one of the letters from one of the ship's officers to the editor of the *Indian Medical Gazette*, the Madras War Fund took over B.I.S.N.Co.'s ship, SS *Tanda*, made for transporting Japanese emigrants, and refitted it as a hospital ship for the British Indian Army in East Africa. The hull was painted white, while the upper works gleamed in yellow. A scarlet band was painted along the side, with the Geneva Cross, also in scarlet on white, in the centre. This was brightly lit with electric lights at night so enemy ships knew this was a hospital ship and left it alone. The name HS *Madras* was prominently displayed in large brass letters at the fore and aft. The ship proudly flew the white flag bearing a scarlet Geneva Cross (precursor to the Red Cross) at the mainmast. The HS *Madras* carried food, medical supplies, operating theatres, a radiology unit, a bacteriological lab, surgeons, doctors, nurses and attendants specifically for sepoys.

Upon returning home, Virkar established his own photography studios in Girgaum, Bombay, gaining fame for his masterful portraits. As documented in Thacker's Indian Directory in 1931, N.V. Virkar & Co. had its office in Mohon Building, a landmark Art Deco structure in what is now Mumbai's Girgaon area. Established in 1904, this iconic building holds a special place in the city's history. Today's Mumbaikars might recognize it as the home of the century-old Panshikar shop, famous for its modaks, shrikhand and other classic Maharashtrian snacks.

In this Bombay studio, his clientele included local aristocrats and their loved ones. His fame spread far and wide, but Virkar was destined for greater things. He increasingly aligned himself with the Indian nationalist movement. His mentor, Shripad Damodar Satwalekar, was closely associated with the nationalist movement.

Satwalekar admired Tilak and Gandhi and supported the Ghadar and Home Rule movements, which led to his Lahore studio coming under British surveillance. It's undeniable that Satwalekar had a profound influence on Virkar, shaping both his personal and professional journey.

Chronicles of freedom and reality

Virkar gradually became the de facto chronicler of Congress events. Unlike the colonial photographers who carefully curated images to reinforce British narratives, Virkar documented the movement with an insider's empathy. He followed nationalist leaders, carrying heavy photographic equipment across the country, and, despite no significant financial incentives, continued to cover political events tirelessly. His work became possibly the most vibrant archive of the Indian independence movement.

In his seminal book *The Coming of Photography in India*, Christopher Pinney noted, 'His numerous portraits of nationalist leaders (such as Bal Gangadhar Tilak, Chittaranjan Das, Subhas Chandra Bose, and M.K. Gandhi—but also many, many others) place them in the opulence and comfort of a bourgeois European photographic studio.' This was important—Virkar thus moved Indians from the stereotypical Orientalist settings to sharing the ordinary backdrops of the British, making them equals and each other's counterparts. His portraits of these icons did more than just depict their physical likeness; they conveyed their determination, their weariness and their defiance.

Malavika Karlekar, in her essay 'Photographer's Dilemma—Making Stylistic Choices' published in the *Telegraph* on 2 September 2012, noted that Virkar often travelled long distances to cities like Lucknow, Calcutta, Delhi, Amritsar and Agra, carrying heavy photographic equipment. However, his primary focus remained Bombay, where it was rare for a major political event in the early twentieth century to take place without accommodating Virkar, his team, and their essential gear.

The date 13 April 1919 remains one of the darkest days in Indian history: the day of the Jallianwala Bagh massacre, in which British troops under General Reginald Dyer fired upon unarmed civilians. In its aftermath, the British government scrambled to control the narrative. The official photographs of the site, taken by colonial authorities, were chilling in their emptiness. They depicted desolate grounds, devoid of the hundreds of bodies that had once lain there. The absence of people in these images was deliberate, a means of downplaying the scale of the atrocity.

But Narayan Vinayak Virkar had a different vision. Arriving in Amritsar a few days after the massacre, he did what no one else dared to do—he documented the aftermath. His photographs captured the bloodstained walls, the infamous bullet marks circled in chalk, and survivors pointing to where the bodies had fallen. Unlike the British images that sought to erase evidence, Virkar's lens bore witness. In *Photography's Orientalism: New Essays on Colonial Representation*, Christopher Pinney documented Virkar's striking images of Jallianwala Bagh. The photographs capture survivors pointing to bullet-riddled walls, marking the very spot where countless protesters were killed. Two similar photographs were later published anonymously in the Indian National Congress's 'Punjab Inquiry Report' (1920), one captioned, 'Western walls in Jalleanwala [sic] Bagh showing holes caused by bullets even six inches deep'. The report also showed haunting images of survivors' injuries. One image was of a young boy sitting with his left arm amputated near the shoulder. Later, these photographs were published in London. They caused severe public outrage in both Britain and India. Virkar's photographs told a story of loss, resilience and unhealed wounds—not just physical ones.

We were determined to see those photographs, so one gentle February afternoon, we walked into the Nehru Museum and Library in New Delhi. This museum and library, located within the Teen Murti House complex, is a leading resource centre on Nehru and Gandhi. We were eager to see the original photographs of the

Jallianwala Bagh massacre by Virkar. However, even the curators were not very familiar with his name.

Treasure trove

We were sent from the museum to the library, and then to the photography section. Mr Vikas Kumar from the Library and Information department assisted us in searching through the archives. After some time, we got lucky.

The photography section has over 200,000 photos, mostly scanned and digitized. The library had purchased fifty-eight photos from N.V. Virkar in 1968, in two lots—forty and eighteen photos. We saw portraits of Lala Lajpat Rai and Bipin Chandra Pal at the Calcutta Congress (1918–19), Bal Gangadhar Tilak at the Amritsar Congress (1919), and Sarojini Naidu at the Bombay Chowpatty in 1920. Among these, we found those haunting photos from Jallianwala Bagh— images of the bullet-marked walls and the survivors. We were looking at history, and the work of a man seldom remembered.

On that fateful day, people had peacefully gathered (admittedly against Dyer's orders) to celebrate Baisakhi and discuss non-violent responses to recent events connected to the infamous Rowlatt Act. Dyer arrived with his troops, and without issuing any warning to the crowd to disperse, he ordered the soldiers to block the main exits and open fire on the densest parts of the crowd. The shooting lasted for about ten minutes, with 1,650 rounds fired. Unarmed civilians— men, women, the elderly, and children—were brutally killed. According to the Indian National Congress report, around 1,000 people lost their lives. Without Virkar's photographs documenting the scene of the massacre, General Reginald Dyer might never have been held accountable for his heinous crime.

Narayan Vinayak Virkar made an invaluable contribution to India's history. But his name or his photographs are not as famous as those of later Indian photojournalists. His work stands alongside the great documentarians of history—who made a choice to speak up when silence was the easier option.

While on the subject of photography and the freedom struggle, one of our colleagues has a personal connection to this history. Kishori Mohan Roy (the grandfather of one of our co-authors Srinwantu) was part of the armed resistance in Bengal. Even during those turbulent times, he had a deep love for photography.

Some photographs of film personalities taken by Kishori Mohan Roy, a 'Tamrapatra' awardee and freedom fighter who later became a photographer in the Tollygunge film industry, from the author's family archive. Roy also played a key role in founding a school, a library and an orphanage in his native village. (Photo courtesy: Mitra De, daughter of Kishori Mohan Roy.)

After Independence, he found his way into the world of professional photography, working in Kolkata's Tollygunge film industry. We've seen his old portraits of actresses, tucked away in his family home—remnants of a life that took an unexpected turn. He worked at Radha Studio in Calcutta, but his career was short-lived. Years of living in exile, hiding from the British police in remote areas and surviving on whatever food he could find, had taken a major toll on his health. He couldn't continue for long. And yet, in his brief time behind the camera, he left behind a fascinating contradiction—perhaps the only freedom fighter we know of who later became a fashion and glamour photographer.

Stories like his, much like Virkar's, have faded from collective memory. But they deserve to be told.

007
CHICAGO RADIO
VOTE FOR GHOSE
The Fury
Road

15

From Paris with an Explosive Trunk

'A lot can happen over coffee.' Clichéd though it sounds as a tagline for a coffee chain, it proved to be true during a casual chat with a friend and colleague, Ashmita Lahiri. We had met over coffee and were discussing our love for spy thrillers. The Mossad famously used a book-bomb in its failed attempt to assassinate Saddam Hussein in the 1970s, believing it to be a ground-breaking tactic.

Ashmita, however, had a surprising revelation. Her paternal great-grandfather, Narendranath Bakshi, was one of the revolutionaries implicated in the infamous Alipore Bomb Case. Through conversations with her father, she had learned about Bakshi's fellow revolutionary, Hemchandra Kanungo, who had pioneered this method of assassination decades before the Mossad.

Initially sceptical, we were quickly intrigued by Ashmita's firsthand accounts. The stories her father shared, the notes he had preserved—all pointed to Kanungo as a true innovator in revolutionary warfare. As we delved deeper into researching Kanungo, his obscurity was striking. How could such a significant figure be so overlooked in our history books?

His character, as fascinating as his innovation, took centre stage in India's struggle for independence in the early years of the twentieth century when the British were dismissive of the Indian revolutionaries' abilities; Kanungo despised the path of non-violence and came knocking louder than ever at the doors of His Majesty's army.

Early attempt: A railway bomb

On the night of 6 December 1907,[1] a special train was coming from present-day Odisha, headed for Kharagpur. Amongst the passengers, surrounded by several guards and a few British officials, was the then lieutenant-governor of Bengal, Sir Andrew Henderson Leith Fraser.

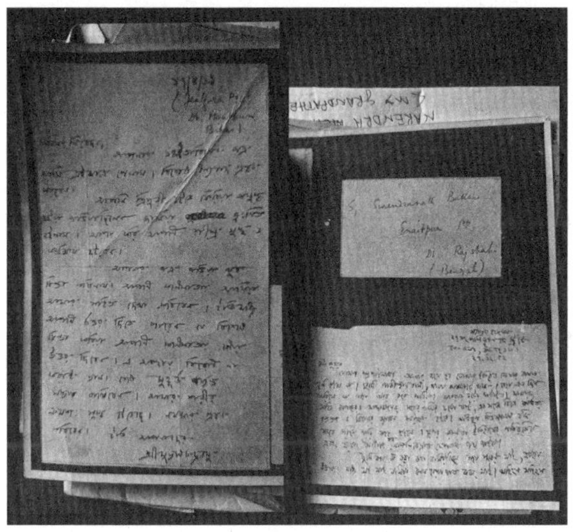

Rare letters from Netaji Subhas Chandra Bose and Barin Ghose (respectively from left to right) to Surendranath Bakshi (brother of revolutionary Narendranath Bakshi), sourced from the private archive of Ashmita Lahiri.

Fraser was amongst the closest confidants of the viceroy of India, Lord Curzon, and earned his notorious reputation by co-creating the plan that partitioned Bengal into two religion-based divisions. It wasn't a secret anymore that he was one of the top targets for assassination amongst the agitated Indian nationalists. Hence, his scheduled visit to Kharagpur was planned for the dead of the night.

When the train was about nineteen kilometres from its destination, a tremendous explosion under the railway carriages halted the journey. The engine and a couple of carriages at the front were heavily damaged but Fraser remained unscathed—a narrow escape from certain death. For the imperialist government, it was just another failed plot. Little did they know that the echoes of the explosion would reverberate beyond the initial blast. A new weapon had entered the field in the Bengali resistance movement, and in the coming time, its main architect would be Hemchandra Kanungo, who was learning to master this new weapon 8,000 kilometres away in Paris.

Simmering anger can explode

During the early 1900s, the growing sense of Indian identity amongst the middle class fed the rising tide of nationalistic sentiments. It was at a time when the need for radical and violent movements against the British Raj collectively led to the formation of secret societies across the entire Bengal Presidency from Calcutta to Dacca, as well as in parts of northern India.

Hemchandra Kanungo, one of the cofounders of a secret society in Midnapore, believed that centuries of dominance by foreign powers had created a slave mentality amongst Indians and it was time to break free from that. In his book, *Account of the Revolutionary Movement in Bengal*, he had said: 'We feel diffidence or disinclination to do something without precedence. The Italians, who were a slave nation like ours, have recently secured their freedom through the medium of secret society. By similar methods Russia has been enlarging her rights and privileges and entertaining the hope of securing her absolute freedom.'

These secret societies became the breeding ground for building strategies of political resistance to overthrow the imperialist government in years to come, which later caused Kanungo to undertake a perilous journey across continents.

It was necessary to make the British hear the roars of 'Azadi'. A new kind of weapon was required to terrorize even the mightiest—a bomb. But, back then, bombs, unlike guns, were not available in the market, legal or illegal, anywhere in the world. They had to be made and for that, a specific skill set and knowledge was required. Bombs wouldn't only be used for killing; they could be used to intimidate as well. It became the most sought-after weapon for the revolutionaries.

In his book *Account of the Revolutionary Movement in Bengal*, Kanungo stated: 'The purpose of the bomb is usually to destroy the body. The bomb is also "modern" not only in the sense of mobility but also in its randomness and amplitude. It is the violent analogue of amplification, the expansion of what a single voice or a single body is able to do. In this sense body and bomb are connected: the bomb is the super-body.'[2]

Anushilan Samiti is born

Kanungo's desire to destroy the Raj brought him closer to Aurobindo Ghose, another charismatic leader, who with his brother, Barindra Ghose, led the Anushilan Samiti, ostensibly a bodybuilding institute, but operating as a secret society in Calcutta.

In the early 1900s, the Ghose brothers had ignited a wave of militant nationalism among the youth in Bengal through their publications, *Bande Mataram* and *Jugantar Patrika*. They inspired the youth, emphasizing on physical fitness and combat training, and created the Anushilan Samiti, which served as a clandestine hub for revolutionary activities, laying the groundwork to fight British colonial rule in India.

When Aurobindo inducted Kanungo into the Anushilan Samiti, he was asked to follow a quasi-religious ritual, taking a sword in one hand, the Gita in the other, and reciting a verse in Sanskrit.[3] Kanungo followed the instructions, but he chose to recite the verse in Bengali instead of Sanskrit. For him, the most important thing was to commit to the moral of the verse—that he would do everything in his power to defeat the British rule and protect his fellow comrades and his motherland.

Despite the common goal of overthrowing the ruling imperialist government, Kanungo had differences of opinion with the Anushilan

Samiti, especially about their religious and spiritual practices, which had become a norm amongst the society members. Kanungo believed that it would further strengthen the very evil they were fighting against. The ideological differences grew so great that Kanungo planned to leave Anushilan Samiti and create his own party. However, for various reasons, that didn't happen.

One might wonder how someone who opposed some of the fundamental practices of a secret society became the chosen one to bring the magic weapon. The answer lies in Kanungo's past. His brief attempt at medical studies at the Campbell Medical Hospital (later known as the Nil Ratan Sircar Medical College and Hospital[4]) in Calcutta made him the only one from the group who had some elementary knowledge of chemistry. Kanungo was best fit for the mission. Also, a significant amount of money was required for such a long journey that had no certain date of return. The Samiti could not furnish those funds. This led Kanungo to sell off his ancestral properties and board the ship to Marseilles in July 1906.

A lot of historical accounts suggest that Hemchandra Kanungo was the first Indian revolutionary to travel to Europe for militant training. Kanungo himself never claimed this as a fact in any of his journals.

In search of a bomb school

When Kanungo made up his mind to travel abroad, his initial choice was the United States of America, but the expense compared to Europe forced him to change his mind. However, the journey to France was far from easy. Upon reaching Paris, he discovered that no country would admit him to their military academy without an approval letter from the British Indian government. Having no other option, he decided to learn the science and technology of making explosives from the rebellious underground societies. But making contact with these revolutionaries and persuading them to teach him bomb-making was a bigger challenge than he had imagined.

Back home in India, Anushilan Samiti members were trying to come up with solutions without him. Ullaskar Dutta, a fellow revolutionary from the same society, was running his own experiments to make bombs, but his amateurish skills weren't producing the desired result. A failed test had already killed a comrade.

Time wasn't on Kanungo's side. The first five months in France went in trying to secure any reliable contacts, travelling back and forth between London and Paris—but every time he returned empty-handed. A turning point came when he met P.M. Bapat, a student studying in Edinburgh. The growing Indian freedom movement resonated with Bapat, prompting him to relocate to London, and eventually Paris, where he came to pursue the study of explosive chemistry in the cause of Indian independence.

Kanungo and Bapat soon met Madam Bhikaji Cama, the founding member of the Paris Indian Society. Madam Cama was immensely impressed by Kanungo's vision and ideology. The flag of Indian independence she unfurled in Stuttgart, Germany, was derived from the 'flag of Calcutta', credited to have been designed by Kanungo and Sachindra Prasad Bose. Madam Cama eventually became the key to his goal. She introduced Kanungo to Emma Goldman, an American anarchist, who led him to a mysterious man known as 'PhD'[5] whose real identity remains elusive to this day.

PhD informed Kanungo that in order to get into a secret society in Paris and learn the techniques of bomb-making, one must have an active membership of the Socialist Party. Additionally, he would require recommendation letters from at least three socialist members to even be considered for such a training. Just when things had started to look bright, Kanungo could sense a cloud of uncertainty looming over him, as this could bring a premature end to his bold endeavours.

But lady luck was about to smile on him. PhD agreed to plead for him and arrange financial support to fund his training and journey back home. Kanungo and Bapat were finally inducted into the secret society where an old exiled Russian revolutionary, Nicholas Safranski,[6] was appointed to train them.

The language barrier made the training extremely difficult. To start with, Kanungo and Bapat had to study socialist literature—

history, geography, economics, socialism and communism—before they were considered fit to be taught the subjects they had come to learn: explosive chemistry and revolutionary organization. Even then, it was hard work. They had to make exhaustive notes, and often made mistakes from misunderstanding the language or the concept. Safranski would correct the notes after classes. The drawings and the pictures were so elaborate in Safranski's huge manuscript that Kanungo had to spend a fortune to have them lithographed. But his journal on bomb-making was coming together.

A trunk full of future bombs

By January 1908, Kanungo's training was over. It was time for him to go home. In late January, when he got off the train in Calcutta, Hemchandra Kanungo was carrying a trunk. Under the usual, innocuous clothes and travel items was hidden a seventy-page journal. It was about to alter the history of Indian nationalism dramatically.

With Kanungo back in the team, Barindra Ghose couldn't resist the opportunity to start an all-out war. The kill list had been prepared for some time now and the first name was of the then French mayor of Chandernagore. The long intercontinental voyage and the exhaustive training had taken a toll on Kanungo's health. Besides, the time and equipment required to build a fully functional bomb was barely available at the Garden House (32, Muraripukur Road, in Manicktolla, was a secret bomb-making factory of the Anushilan Samiti). Nevertheless, Kanungo agreed to help the cause, only to see their efforts go to waste as the bomb didn't explode at the scene.

The failed attempt alerted the British police and they ran a widespread search to take out all the underground society offices and their arsenals. The margin of error was becoming slimmer for Kanungo with every passing day, but he was determined to show off his freshly learnt skills. He found a new address at 15, Gopi Mohan Dutt Lane, near his own residence and took Kanailal Dutta, Indu Bhusan Ray, Nirapada Ray and Sushil Sen with him to set up a new bomb-making factory under his supervision. The product that came out of it was ingenious—a book bomb for Douglas H. Kingsford, then the chief presidency magistrate of Calcutta.

Ingenious book bomb

Kanungo procured a copy of a 1,075-page book, titled *A Commentary on the Common Law: Designed as Introductory to Its Study*, by Herbert Broom, and cut a cylindrical hole deep inside the pages. He then placed a Cadbury cocoa tin containing picric acid, a detonator and a trigger device in the cut-out space.[7] An envelope was kept inside the book in a way that a small portion of it would be visible from the outside. However, the book was tied with a tape so that the envelope could not be taken out without untying the tape. As soon as the book was opened, a trigger would activate the bomb. The book was then wrapped in brown paper. The British Indian Police back then didn't have the slightest idea that such a weapon could even exist, or that it could be made by an Indian revolutionary.

But as fate would have it, Kingsford lived to see another day. Although the book was delivered to him through a parcel, he never cared to open it. Had he opened it, Kanungo wouldn't have had to manufacture another bomb for Kingsford. The new bomb was to be thrown into Kingsford's carriage.

Mistaken murders: The Alipore Bomb Case

The volunteers, Prafulla Chaki and Khudiram Bose, made an error and threw this bomb into the wrong carriage, where it took two innocent lives—the wife and daughter of barrister Pringle Kennedy. Chaki shot himself before being arrested from the Mokama railway station platform the next day and eighteen-year-old Khudiram was tried, convicted and executed, becoming one of the youngest martyrs in India's history of freedom struggle.

The subsequent trial, known as the 'Emperor vs Aurobindo Ghose' (aka the 'Alipore Bomb Case'), went on for almost a full year with forty-nine people accused, 206 witnesses, 400 documents and more than 5,000 exhibits produced in court.[8] Kanungo was sentenced to transportation for life at the Cellular Jail in the Andaman and Nicobar Islands and forfeiture of all his properties. Kanungo remained in Cellular Jail until he was freed in 1921.

The greatest rebel poet of undivided India, Kazi Nazrul Islam, wrote a song where he referred to Kanungo as 'Dronacharya—the lord of weapons'. (Despite talking to several 'Nazrul Geeti' experts, we couldn't find the title or the lyrics of the actual song.) The Hindu epic Mahabharata, from where the comparison was taken, never lauded Dronacharya very highly compared to his students, and neither did the history of Indian freedom struggle applaud its Dronacharya. Hemchandra Kanungo remained an overshadowed figure in Indian history but his impact in the nationalistic movement became a nightmare for the Raj. Kanungo was captured, but ever since, no British officer ever felt safe again. Behind every loud sound, they saw the shadow of the impeccable anarchist Hemchandra Kanungo.

Acknowledgement: We would like to thank Mr Abhijit Lahiri and Ms Ashmita Lahiri for talking to us and sharing their invaluable inputs.

16

Two Daggers

On a scorching afternoon in Kolkata, we stood in BBD Bagh (old Dalhousie Square) in front of the General Post Office[1] with Hong Kong House just down the road. Central Kolkata breathes history. Take the old secretariat building, for example. On 8 December 1930, Benoy Krishna Basu, Badal Gupta and Dinesh Gupta entered the Writers' Building, dressed in European attire and carrying loaded Webley revolvers. They shot and killed Colonel N.S. Simpson, the inspector general of prisons, known for his brutality against political prisoners.

Our destination, however, was the Town Hall library. It was a sombre trip, since we were still reeling from the passing of P.T. Nair,[2] often called the 'barefoot chronicler of Calcutta'. Nair, who barely spoke a word of Bengali, was a collector and dedicated his life to documenting Calcutta—its history, its streets and its people. In 1999, the Kolkata Municipal Corporation purchased all his books on Kolkata from Nair, which are now housed in the Town Hall library.

The Town Hall, built in the early nineteenth century, once hosted soirées for the British elite. Standing on its steps today, one cannot help but imagine the historic events its imposing Doric columns have silently witnessed. Among those events was a moment of violence—a calculated act of vengeance and rebellion. On 20 September 1871, the steps of the Town Hall became the stage for a shocking murder, an act that reverberated through the corridors of British authority, leaving a small but indelible mark on its history.

Injustice leads to assassination

The tale of this murder starts with the arrest of the elderly Khan brothers—Ameer and Hashmadad, well-known among Calcutta's business community. On 10 July 1869, the authorities arrested them on suspicion of being Wahabis, who had been active leaders in 1857. It was a common ploy by the British to discredit any acts of rebellion, particularly by the Muslims, perpetuating their divide-and-rule strategy.

They were taken to Patna, Bihar, where they were detained without any formal charges for months. They applied for the writ of habeas corpus, challenging the unlawful detention, and that caught the eye of the British press. In what became known as the great Wahabi case, the British government tried to completely decimate the brothers and their standing and to add to the notion that all Indian Muslims were inherently disloyal to the Queen of England. The controversial trial triggered an extended public debate in India and Britain about the greater harm done by government despotism than by alleged religious fanatics. The murder on the steps of the Town Hall was a direct consequence of this unjust arrest.

Presiding over the case in the Calcutta High Court was John Paxton Norman. Norman was the acting Chief Justice at the time. The High Court those days held its sessions at the Town Hall since the new building was still under construction. The brothers were ably defended by Thomas Chisholm Anstey, a distinguished barrister. A lower court acquitted Hashmadad but Norman held Ameer guilty of waging war against the Queen and deported him to the Andamans.

The brothers' trial caused a sensation not only in the British press but also among the locals who saw this as another case of colonial oppression. Some were willing to exact revenge and among them was Mohammad Abdullah. When the news of Khan's deportation reached Punjab, Abdullah was furious. He made his way to Calcutta and silently waited for the right opportunity. He reconnoitred the

Town Hall and its surrounding area, living as a humble caretaker in a central Calcutta mosque.

On 20 September 1871, just as Chief Justice Norman was ascending the stairs of the Town Hall, Abdullah stabbed him. Crying out in pain, Norman staggered and attempted to escape. Abdullah, gripping the blood-covered dagger, lunged again but missed his mark. Before he could strike a third time, a clerk who had witnessed the scuffle managed to wrestle Abdullah to the ground and disarm him. Writhing in agony, Norman called for a palki, his final words barely audible: 'I shall not live.' Abdullah made no attempt to flee, knowing escape was futile. Later that night, as the clock struck midnight, Norman succumbed to his injuries.

A historical view of Town Hall from Samuel Bourne's *Views of Calcutta and Barrackpore* (circa 1860s), witness to the assassination plot against John Paxton Norman. (Photographer: Samuel Bourne. Public Domain via Wikimedia Commons.)

For the entirety of his fast-paced trial, Abdullah never uttered a word about his comrades, always insisting that he was a lone wolf acting on his own accord. On 28 September 1871, Abdullah was sentenced to death by hanging. While the authorities suspected a larger scheme was at play, they could never prove anything.

Photograph of Abdullah, the assassin of Judge John Paxton Norman, Calcutta, 1871. (Photo courtesy: James Morley. Public domain via Wikimedia Commons.)

Their hunch was right; more was indeed on the horizon. Three thousand kilometres away from Calcutta, another daring plan was being hatched, but this time the catch was even bigger.

The Ross Island Penal Colony was established by the British on the Andaman Islands in 1858. Initially, its purpose was to serve as a prison large enough to hold people who were arrested for their part in the First War of Independence of 1857.

However, why are we going from Calcutta to the Andamans? Let's hear from Lord Argyll who, on 12 February 1872, got up to deliver a message on the floor of the British Parliament.

'My Lords, it grieves me to say that I have a most painful communication to make to your Lordships' House.'

The telegraphic message was from a member of the Indian Council, Mr Ellis, who stated in his message: 'I have to announce with the deepest regret that the Viceroy was assassinated by a convict at Port Blair on the 8th inst., at 7 in the evening.'

Richard Southwell Bourke, the sixth earl of Mayo, was appointed the viceroy of India in January 1869. It was under Lord Mayo that

India's first census took place in 1871. In January 1872, Lord Mayo visited Burma, and while returning he made a detour to the penal colony of the Andamans. During the initial days of the penal colony on Ross Island, most prisoners had ties either with the war in 1857 or with the growing Wahabi movement, but there were some who were there because they had committed some extreme act of violence. One of them was Sher Ali Afridi.

Assassination on an island

Afridi had served in colonial police and armies, including the Presidency armies during the war of 1857, and was quite popular among the British officers. He came from the Afridi tribe in Khyber-Pakhtunkhwa. Afridi was convicted for murdering his cousin to defend the honour of his sister, though he pleaded innocence. The actual reason is lost to history, although some say that internal family feuds were rampant at the time. He was sentenced to life imprisonment and sent to the Andamans. He was well-behaved and so was allowed to work as a barber.

Afridi thought the punishment too severe and sought revenge against the superintendent of the jail and the viceroy. On 8 February, the viceroy, Lord Mayo, and his entourage made routine inspections of the island, concluding the visit by witnessing the sunset atop Mount Harriet (now called Mount Manipur). As they were making their way back to the docks, it had become dark and they heard a noise. The private secretary to the viceroy stopped to look back, and his eyes widened in horror as he saw a man stabbing Lord Mayo. It was Afridi. Chaos ensued, and the security personnel who were leading the group rushed to apprehend the assailant. Afridi was able to stab the viceroy twice—once in the neck. Mayo's coat was torn in places, and a gush of blood was steadily flowing from his wounds. A couple of minutes later he became unconscious, the last words he spoke were 'Hold my head'. When the doctors examined him later, he was already dead.

During his trial, when Afridi was asked about his motives he simply answered, 'I killed him by the order of God.' The official report stated:

> He gloried greatly in the deed, saying that he had heard of Abdullah having killed Justice Norman—that that was a great deed, but that his was much greater than anything ever done before, as he had killed the greatest Sahib in India ... He hoped his name would be glorified in his country for the deed which he had done, and that a monument would be raised to his memory by his fellow-countrymen.

His life sentence was revoked and he was given the death penalty. Afridi was brought to the gallows on 11 March 1872 to be hanged. With a smile of quiet satisfaction, he spoke to his Muslim brethren:

'Brothers, I have killed your enemy. You are witness that I am a devout Muslim.' After that he recited a kalma, and then was hanged.

As with the Norman murder, it was never conclusively established whether there was an underlying conspiracy orchestrated by the Wahabis to assassinate high-ranking officials. Neither Afridi nor Abdullah ever disclosed the involvement of any co-conspirators, leaving the suspected link unproven. The Wahabi trials and the twin murders of Norman and Lord Mayo deeply unsettled the British authorities. If they believed that suppressing the 1857 War of Independence would deter rebellious Indians from resisting colonial rule, they were gravely mistaken.

As we wandered through the museum inside the Town Hall, absorbing the city's past, its written history immortalized by authors like Nair, we were reminded of the countless stories that remain unwritten. A blood-covered dagger, a stray bullet, fleeting whispers of rebellion—martyrs whose sacrifices we know very little of, their names and deeds fading into the shadows of time.

17

The Heist That Shook the Empire

It was Shashthi—the first day of the Durga Puja in 2023. Some of us at the Paperclip decided to watch the Bengali film *Bagha Jatin*—produced by and starring Bengali superstar Dev. The film was a loose biopic of the life of Jatindranath Mukherjee aka Bagha Jatin—one of the most important figures of the nationalist movement in the years leading up to the First World War.

While we broadly knew the major events and milestones that the movie was going to depict, one incident left us in a state of awe. We had read about it, of course, but maybe watching it unfold on the big screen added to the experience. In its daring and audacity, it was mind-blowing and somewhat reminiscent of the Ocean's series of heist movies. We decided to read up more on this incident and when the idea of this book came about, it was one of the first chapters that we put down on our list.

Now for the story.

The first decade of the twentieth century was a tumultuous one for the Bengal province—inspired by the writings and speeches of visionaries like Swami Vivekananda, Rashtraguru Surendranath Banerjee, Bankim Chandra Chattopadhyay and Rabindranath Tagore, Bengalis were discovering a taste for nationalism that did not sit well with the British rulers of India. Viceroy Lord Curzon's nefarious plans for partitioning the Bengal province in 1905, although cloaked in the guise of administrative efficiency, was a vile ploy to destabilize the emerging wave of nationalism by employing the 'divide and rule' policy.

Curzon's move backfired spectacularly, with his partition plans acting like a spark on a mass of gunpowder that was the Bengal state. From this fire was born the armed revolution movement that, in the years to come, would become a real thorn in the side of the English, and eventually witness the shifting of the capital from Calcutta to Delhi. The first wave of the movement, spearheaded by the Ghose brothers Aurobindo and Barin, culminated in the Alipore bombing trials of 1908–09. Aurobindo was acquitted but decided to embrace a spiritual path and retired to Pondicherry. Barin Ghose and most of the other leaders were sentenced to imprisonment in the Andamans. For the time being, the armed revolution movement was stymied. But only on the surface.

The first Christmas Day Plot

Unbeknownst to the British administration, one of the key figures of the movement, who had evaded suspicion till then, was plotting a bigger attack on the colonial government. His name was Jatindranath Mukherjee, better known as 'Bagha Jatin'. He was soon to emerge as a bête noire of the administration. Jatin's first move, the Christmas Day Plot of 1909, aimed at destroying the top echelons of British government in Calcutta, the capital. Mukherjee had convinced the soldiers of 10th Jat Regiment, in charge of security, to blow up the Christmas Ball hosted by the governor of Bengal and attended by everyone from the viceroy to top military officers. It had been foiled by a last-minute act of treachery. Undeterred, Jatin, aided by a new crop of faces, including Amarendra Chatterjee and Narendranath Bhattacharya (later M.N. Roy, Chapter 37), kept at their plans of triggering a great revolution against the British.

While Jatin and his allies were working on reorganizing the revolutionary movement in Bengal, over in north India, another young man was working with similar goals. His name was Rash Behari Bose. Like Jatin, he also held a government job to evade suspicion. Through Rash Behari, Jatin's group established contacts with Indian revolutionary modules in the USA, Canada and Europe—primary among them being the Ghadar Party. This was when global geopolitics favoured the Indian revolutionaries. Tensions were on the rise in Europe, and it was becoming clear that a great war was soon going to engulf the continent. It was also apparent that the British and Austro-German empires would end up in rival camps in such a scenario.

Thus, was born the great Hindu–German conspiracy: a dream of Indian revolutionaries to overthrow the British administration of India with political and armed assistance from Germany. (It should be clarified that 'Hindu' was used back then for any Indian, regardless of religion, and came from 'Hind'.) It is said that during a state visit by the German crown prince to Calcutta in 1912, Jatin and Naren Bhattacharya met him secretly to secure a promise of assistance.[1] To pay for the weapons, Jatin's group planned a number of robberies, targeting mainly wealthy landholders.

To carry out these robberies as well as arm themselves for strikes against the British, the revolutionaries needed the latest arms. From this was born the plans for an audacious daylight robbery, right in the heart of Calcutta.

'The greatest daylight robbery'

Located on Vansittart Row in the heart of Dalhousie Square, the power centre of British Calcutta, was Rodda & Co.—a leading business in the latest arms and ammunitions and a prime supplier to the British garrisons at Fort William and to the Calcutta Police. The revolutionaries, led by Jatin, decided to target Rodda. Over several days, a meticulous plan was drawn up. Jatin entrusted the primary responsibility to Bipin Behari (B.B.) Ganguli—a close associate of Barin Ghose and Rash Behari Bose. One of Bipin Behari's friends, Kalidas Mukherjee, was employed at Rodda. Bipin prevailed on Kalidas to get a young revolutionary named Shrish Chandra Mitra employed at Rodda as customs sircar (agent). Meticulous at his work,

Shrish soon earned the trust of his English superiors. No one had an inkling of his true intentions.

It was through Shrish that news came to the revolutionaries that a large consignment of German-made Mauser C96 guns was set to arrive at Rodda very soon for onward distribution to the British forces.[2] The revolutionaries realized this was the opportunity they were waiting for. The main think tank of the heist was B.B. Ganguli's Atmonnati Samiti headquartered at 39, Malanga Lane, with members Srish Pal (aka Naren), Anukul Mukherjee, Haridas Dutta and Khagen Pal forming the nucleus of the squad assembled to carry out the daring heist.

Dalhousie Square, the heart of British Calcutta, pictured in 1910 by Samuel Bourne. This is where the drama started unfolding on the rainy morning of 26 August 1914. (Photographer: Samuel Bourne. Public domain via Wikimedia Commons.)

It was 26 August 1914. Monsoon rains lashed the city. Mr Prike, Shrish Mitra's boss, sent him to Customs House with the necessary papers to get the consignment of Mauser guns released and transferred to Rodda's godowns in six bullock carts. As the carts lined up near the customs office, no one took particular notice of another cart joining the procession. This cart was driven by a young revolutionary, Haridas Dutta, who was disguised as a simple Hindustani bullock-cart driver. Shrish performed his official duty admirably, getting the 200-odd boxes of guns and cartridges released.

Of these, 190 were loaded in the first six carts. The remaining ten boxes, containing fifty Mausers and 46,000 cartridges, were placed in the last cart being driven by Dutta.

Shrish flagged off the carts back towards Rodda's offices, seating himself in the leading cart. The first six carts duly arrived at their destination. The final one, however, turned away from the entrance of the godown on Vansittart Row at the last minute and drove away towards Bow Bazar Street. Here, Dutta and two other revolutionaries—Srish Pal and Khagen Das—who had walked alongside the cart, abandoned the cart, changed vehicles and took the boxes to Presidency College student Bhujanga Dhar's house in Jeliapara Lane. From there, the guns and ammunition were packed in small steel trunks and distributed to various pockets of revolutionary resistance.

Shrish, the brave young man, returned to office and reported to Mr Prike that he had executed his task successfully. Sometime later, unnoticed, he slipped out of Rodda's office. As per plan, he went to the railway station, bought a ticket and boarded a train for North Bengal, accompanied by Srish Pal. He went into hiding at Rangpur (presently in Bangladesh) from where he is believed to have set out to cross over into China through Tibet. It is here that Shrish vanished from the pages of history. He was never seen or heard from again. His exact fate remains unknown to this day, although it is believed that he was possibly shot dead by a guard while trying to cross the border.

So well had the heist been planned, that it was three days before it was noticed that Shrish and ten boxes of guns and ammunition were missing and Mr Prike filed a complaint with the police.[3] Although they did recover a significant chunk of the stolen weapons and many of the key perpetrators were arrested, it was still a big slap in the face of the British administration that such a robbery was carried out in broad daylight within walking distance of Writers' Building—the seat of the Bengal administration—and Lal Bazar—the Calcutta Police HQ.

The reverberations of the Rodda arms heist were to be felt in Indian history for years to come.[4] Rash Behari Bose carried one of the Mausers with him all the time and before leaving for Japan, handed it over to his comrade Sachindra Nath Sanyal. At the iconic last stand of Bagha Jatin and his comrades on a paddy field near the Buribalam River in present-day Odisha (Chapter 19), the Indian revolutionaries used Mauser guns from the Rodda haul. And much later, during Master Da Surya Sen's Chittagong Armoury raid also (Chapter 15), the Rodda Mausers were claimed to have been used. Even great revolutionaries like Bhagat Singh and Chandrasekhar Azad are said to have received the Rodda Mausers.

Today, the only surviving memory of this incredible tale is a memorial erected on Ganesh Chandra Avenue, one of central Calcutta's busiest thoroughfares. It features busts of four of the key figures in the plan: Anukul Chandra Mukherjee, Bipin Behari Ganguly, Haridas Dutta and Girindra Nath Banerjee. It stands in silent testimony to the audacious bravery of those young bravehearts—obscured by banners and hoardings, some of which we had to manually remove to get a snap.

As homage to this brave and audacious act, we decided to take a walk, retracing and revisiting some of the major points of this heist. We visited Vansittart Row, the RBI Building where the Customs House stood more than a century ago, the narrow Malanga Lane off Bow Bazar Street (since renamed B.B. Ganguli Sarani) where the conspiracy was hatched and Jeliapara Lane, ending our trip at a memorial to the heroes of this memorable incident on Ganesh Chandra Avenue near Hind cinema hall. At every point, we stopped for a few minutes, trying to transport ourselves to that rainy August day, more than 100 years ago, and doff our (imaginary) hats to these intrepid young men who put their lives on the line for the love of the motherland.

18

A Secret Radio Station in Italy

In 2014, a document from the CIA archives was declassified. It was dryly titled *Study of German Intelligence Activities in the Near East and Related Areas Prior to and During World War II*. The 338-page tome was exhaustive and, at times, a mind-numbing read—a list of spies, informants and agents tangled in the covert operations of the Axis powers. However, through all the official jargon and military language, one entry made us stop. It was so incongruous, so wildly out of place, that it begged further investigation.

'Hassan Khan; aka Ajad Singh,' the entry read. 'A Moslem of advanced age, he was a leader of the Indian nationalist movement. He was active in Rome during World War II as a speaker on the Himalaya clandestine radio station and cooperated with Mohammed Iqbal Shedai.'

Clandestine radio stations, Indian revolutionaries in Rome and a secret broadcast aimed at undermining British colonial rule? It was the stuff of spy novels. The document is now in the public archive. But what exactly was this mysterious 'Himalaya' radio station, and why did it merit a mention in a CIA report decades after the war?

To answer that, we have to start with a man whose life reads like a thriller: Mohammed Iqbal Shedai.

the GIS and received GIS support in his fight against the British.
Aid was also provided by the Italian Government, as the Axis
powers planned to stage an uprising in the tribal territory at a
later date and use the Fakir's forces in the attack on India
(operational plan "FEUERFRESSER")[62].

Hassan KHAN, aka Ajid SINGH

A Moslem of advanced age, he was a leader of the Indian
nationalist movement. He was active in Rome during World
War II as a speaker on the "Himalaya" clandestine radio
station and cooperated with Mohammed Iqbal SHEDAI[63].

Hassan KHAN

A Kakar tribal leader in Beluchistan, who was cooperating
with the FAKIR of IPI and the GIS. He is believed to have been
identical with a GIS agent who worked for the GIS from 1941-1943
and whose cryptonym was "ARBEITER"[64].

SECRET

A snippet referencing the Himalaya Clandestine Radio Station, cited in the declassified CIA document *Study of German Intelligence Activities in the Near East and Related Areas Prior to and During World War II.* (Declassified report, CIA Reading Room, Record No. CIA-RDP81-01043R003500080004-7. Available at: https://www.cia.gov/readingroom/docs/CIA-RDP81-01043R003500080004-7.pdf.)

A rebel nomad finds refuge

Born in 1888 in a small village in Sialkot, British India, Shedai seemed to always be on the move, a few steps ahead of the authorities, and with somewhat radical views. By the time World War II was inevitable, Shedai had already made a name for himself as a die-hard anti-British activist. He had joined the Ghadar Party in 1918, a revolutionary outfit determined to rid India of its colonial rulers, and his speeches lambasted the 'imperialist exploiters' Britain and the Indian National Congress alike. To him, both were complicit in keeping the Indian masses shackled in poverty and ignorance.

For Shedai, revolution wasn't just a political goal; it was a mission, a calling. He wanted to ignite the spark of rebellion not just in India but across the globe, and his base of operations became an unexpected one—Italy.

After a whirlwind journey through Afghanistan, Turkey, Russia, France and Switzerland—always staying one step ahead of relentless British agents—Shedai finally found sanctuary in Italy. It was there that fate introduced him to Arnaldo Mussolini, a name that should raise eyebrows for a good reason: Arnaldo was none other than the brother of Benito Amilcare Andrea Mussolini—'Il Duce' ('the Leader') of Italian fascism. What followed was an unexpected and unconventional partnership between Shedai and the Italian dictator. It was an alliance that seemed improbable, but for Shedai, it was bound by a shared disdain for British imperialism. While Mussolini offered him a cushy position to carry on his anti-British activities, Shedai turned him down, preferring to focus on what he really wanted: a platform to speak directly to the Indian masses.

Radio Himalaya broadcasts begin

And so, in February of 1941, Shedai's wish was granted. With Mussolini's blessing, he launched Radio Himalaya, a clandestine broadcast that transmitted directly from Rome, pretending to be based in India. The station was aimed at Indians across the world, particularly those working in British-controlled territories. The Italian government had no idea what kind of sensation they had helped create.

Shedai opened each broadcast with the bold words, 'This transmission comes to you from the Republican Party of Free India.' It was revolutionary rhetoric with a capital R, delivered in Hindustani and aimed squarely at undermining British rule.

For half an hour each day, Shedai would read news updates, offering a pointed critique of the Indian National Congress for cooperating with British authorities, while urging his listeners to rise against their colonial overlords. And at the end of each broadcast, Shedai would make a stirring call to arms in his charismatic voice, demanding freedom for India's working classes.

He wasn't alone in his crusade. He found a great partner in Sardar Ajit Singh, the uncle of the legendary Bhagat Singh and a towering figure from Punjab. It was said that the young Bhagat Singh drew much of his inspiration from his uncle's fearless spirit. A gifted writer and orator, Ajit Singh's revolutionary activities had long placed him on the British Empire's most-wanted list (Chapter 39). Like Shedai, he also lived the life of an exile, dodging warrants and weaving through a maze of nations—Iran, Russia, Turkey, Germany, Brazil, France and Switzerland—before finally landing in Italy.

By the time Ajit Singh reached Italy, he had carved out an unlikely alliance with Benito Mussolini. Under the Italian dictator's watchful support, Ajit Singh was already broadcasting fiery speeches over radio transmissions, addressing Indian and Persian audiences. His goal was clear: to ignite the spark of rebellion in Indian soldiers stationed in India and Africa. This was when he crossed paths with Mohammed Iqbal Shedai. Shedai shared his determination with Ajit Singh and saw Rome as the perfect base for their covert operations. Together, they took their battle for freedom to the airwaves. The CIA report's 'Hassan Khan; aka Ajad Singh' might well be Ajit Singh.

Soon enough, Ajit Singh's broadcasts, delivered in Hindustani, struck a powerful chord with his listeners. This was the language of the vast majority of Indian soldiers, and his words, soaked in conviction and sacrifice, were electrifying. He often opened his speeches with a poignant couplet from Bahadur Shah Zafar, the last Mughal emperor who had defied the British during the Great Indian Rebellion of 1857:

Gaazion mein boo rahegi jab talak imaan ki,
Takht-e-London tak chalegi teg Hindustan ki.

(As long as the spirit of faith burns in the hearts of the valiant,
The sword of Hindustan will rage all the way to the throne in London.)

He would close with verses, composed by Jagdamba Prasad Mishra 'Hitaishi' in 1916, stirring lines of hope and defiance, painting a vision of a liberated homeland:

Maza ayega jab apna raj dekhenge,
Ke apni hi zameen hogi, apna ashiana hoga.

(Oh, the joy we will feel when we see our rule,
Our own land, our own home.)

Shaheedon ki chitaon par lagenge har baras mele,
Watan par marne walon ka yahi nishan hoga.

(On the pyres of our martyrs, there will be fairs each year,
This will be the lasting mark of those who died for their
motherland.)

The British, predictably, were in a panic. They couldn't figure out where the broadcasts were coming from. London suspected the transmissions were being sent from somewhere in the Middle East or perhaps even from deep within India itself. That they were emanating from Rome of all places was unfathomable. All the same, the British government wasted no time in branding the clandestine broadcasts as Axis propaganda. To them, it wasn't just a rogue radio station. They dubbed Himalaya Radio a tool of fascist manipulation, designed to sow dissent among Indian soldiers and civilians alike. In 1941, the Indian Information Series dismissed the station with biting sarcasm, calling it the straight-up 'Himalayan Blunders Show'. The British propaganda service was brutal and candid. They accused the broadcasts of being exploitative and filled with deliberate misinformation. They even called them anti-religious, undermining the station's credibility among its largely devout audience. In the eyes of the colonial authorities, the radio was a puppet of fascist ambitions dressed in the guise of freedom.

A rift appears, and an attempt that failed

But while Shedai was broadcasting his propaganda, there was one man he didn't appreciate much. It was Subhas Chandra Bose.

The two men were both Indian nationalists who shared a profound hatred for British rule, but that was where the similarities ended.

Shedai, with his deeply pan-Islamic worldview, began to drift towards supporting the idea of a separate Pakistan, a notion that was anathema to Bose's vision of a united India. They were de facto rivals.

Additionally, in 1941, with Italian support, Shedai established the Azad Hind Government as a government-in-exile for independent India. He was president and Ajit Singh was minister of information and broadcasting.

Their ideological rift only deepened as Shedai used Radio Himalaya to push a pro-Pakistan agenda, railing against Gandhi, Nehru and the Congress. He accused the Indian National Congress of being pro-British. The tension between the two nationalists would come to a head. Bose, who had his own plans for liberating India, couldn't stand the thought of Shedai using a platform as powerful as Radio Himalaya to sow further division among the Indian revolutionaries.

But Shedai didn't stop there. By 1942, he had gone beyond broadcasting and together with the Italian government, formed a military unit, the Battaglione Azad Hindoustan (Free India Battalion), under the Raggruppamento Centri Militari (Military Centres Group— foreign units in service in the Italian army during World War II). Recruiting Indian prisoners of war held in Italian camps, Shedai tried to forge a fighting force to help take on the British. But the effort fizzled out after a mutiny, and the unit was quietly disbanded. The dream of an Indian military uprising in Europe had evaporated as quickly as it had been conceived.

By July 1943, the tides of war had turned dramatically. Mussolini, who was the primary benefactor of their operations, was overthrown and arrested. The world order was changing, as was the political compass of Rome and Italy. His successor, Marshal Badoglio, had little interest in supporting the radio transmissions that Ajit Singh and Shedai had worked so tirelessly on for months. With Fascist Italy's defeat in World War II imminent, the future of Himalaya Radio began to unravel.

Ajit Singh was arrested by Allied forces. The collapse of Mussolini's regime in 1945 left fascist Italy in ruins. Shedai was forced into hiding, his clandestine broadcasts ceased operations, abruptly halting his revolutionary activities. For months, he lived like a fugitive in Rome, lying low as Allied forces swept through the country. After years of living in exile, in 1946 Shedai was finally allowed to return to the Indian subcontinent, with the help of Maulana Abul Kalam Azad. After Partition, he went to Pakistan. When Shedai returned to Pakistan after decades of exile, his homeland had changed drastically. The British were gone, but the scars of Partition ran deep.

After a few years, he left in the late 1950s, because the Pakistani government was unsympathetic to his progressive views. Shedai returned to Italy and found a quieter role at the University of Turin. From 1957 to 1964, he taught Urdu in the university before he went back to Pakistan for good.

Shedai was a strong advocate of the two-nation theory and believed that Hindus and Muslims could not live together. This was possibly one of the reasons why Congress always kept its distance from him. His approach was questionable, but it is undeniable that he devoted his life to fight against imperialism. After his death, Shedai gradually faded from discussions. Lost somewhere deep in the archives of history, Radio Himalaya was also forgotten.

19

Bagha Jatin and the Christmas That Never Came

The train chugged along steadily, the slowing rhythm of its wheels hinting that a station was drawing near. As the day began to fade into dusk, the lights in the compartment seemed to glow with a greater radiance. Our co-passengers, a curious bunch, were busy sipping tea and nibbling on snacks. We gazed out of the window, watching as the landscape unfolded in a dreamy purple haze. In the blink of an eye, a station marker set in concrete and yellow blurred past us—it was Rupsa Junction.

Situated right on the Odisha–Bengal border, near Balasore, Rupsa is a small nondescript town that might seem unremarkable at first glance. But rewind a little over 100 years, and this seemingly unremarkable station transforms into a vivid tableau surrounded by a rugged rural landscape: the lush, unbroken expanse of the Mayurbhanj forest with its untamed tentacles and dense canopy clouding the horizon. Amidst this bounty of greenery and the rustic charm of the countryside, a fierce gun battle erupts, shattering its serenity. The air crackles with the sharp report of firearms, the earthy scent of soil and foliage mingles with the acrid tang of gunpowder.

A brave last stand

The year was 1915. A *Times of India* report published on 18 September details a serious incident. Officers G.C. Denham and Charles Tegart[1] pursued an intelligence tip about some wanted revolutionaries. Denham and Tegart were part of a special investigation cell of the Calcutta Police, set up to counter rising revolutionary activities. The fugitives had gone into hiding in the Mayurbhanj forest near Balasore. Running out of supplies and fearing capture, they made a last-ditch effort to escape, with Denham and Tegart hot on their heels with a large force.

Having interrogated several villagers, the officers gathered that the revolutionaries were likely to make their way to Rupsa station to catch a train. The district magistrate, another officer and a large posse of armed police arrived at the site, a paddy field nearby, to intercept them on the way to the station. However, the escaping rebels had a surprise for the chasing force who suddenly found themselves caught in an ambush. The revolutionaries, exhausted but still ready to fight to the end, had taken cover in a patch of thorn bushes and made a shallow trench, from where they fired at the surrounding force. A fierce gun battle followed. With a few Mauser pistols at their disposal against a large, heavily armed force, the revolutionaries never stood a chance. But they still attacked, and then gave back as good as they got.

The battle raged for an hour, eventually culminating in the capture of Manoranjan Sengupta and Nirendra Dasgupta, and the death of Chittapriya Ray Chaudhuri, wanted for the murder of Sub-Inspector Suresh Mukherjee. Jyotish Pal and the leader of the group, Jatindranath Mukherjee, aka 'Bagha Jatin', were found severely injured. Jatin, who had sustained a ghastly bullet wound to his stomach, succumbed the next day at the Balasore state hospital. Now, Jatin was a prized target, sought for orchestrating numerous anti-imperial activities. The most recent charge against him was the murder of Nirod Haldar on Pathuriaghata Street[2] in north Calcutta. How this most wanted rebel leader ended up in a ditch in Orissa's forests, along with his compatriots, putting up an audacious last stand, is a tale of defiance and betrayal that spans three continents.

The Christmas Day Plot of 1915

Let's start with the betrayal. A German officer in disguise had landed in Singapore in August 1915 and, based on a tip, was immediately arrested by the authorities. Among his belongings was a map of the Bengal Presidency, with marked points near the coastline, along with other compromising documents. Codenamed Agent X, his identity was expunged. It was a Parsi officer on loan from Bombay Police, Hector Kothavala, who interrogated the German spy. Kothavala was one of Dudley Ridout's men. Ridout was then the general commanding officer for British troops in Singapore.

Under interrogation, the German agent admitted that he had committed an unspecified, terrible act that normally received a death sentence. He was offered an alternative: a secret mission in the East, to organize a plot. He revealed its details: Indian revolutionaries, funded and armed by Germany, planned a simultaneous uprising in Bengal, British Burma and Siam (Thailand). This would be supported by German naval attacks on Madras and the Andaman Islands. The planned date for this insurrection was 25 December 1915.

As the war raged on in Europe, information became a powerful commodity in the grander scheme of things. Agent X, who was later revealed to be Vincent Kraft after imperial documents were declassified, was not the only one who acted as a double agent. According to British intelligence reports, information on the Christmas Day Plot was also given to W.E. Becket, the consul-general of the Dutch East Indies, by an agent codenamed Oren. Oren, according to author Nigel West, was a Baltic double agent who even passed on information about Kraft just before his eventual capture in Singapore.

How did Oren and Kraft come to know about the Christmas Day Plot? And what exactly were the revolutionaries trying to do? The genesis of the story takes place a decade before. In 1905, Bengal was simmering with unrest. The partition had extinguished any lingering traces of pacifism; it was time for action. The Ghose brothers,

Aurobindo and Barin, stood at the forefront of this radical movement. Their organization, Anushilan Samiti (Chapter 15), rapidly gained traction across Bengal, attracting a following of like-minded individuals determined to see a country free from British rule. Among them were Rash Behari Bose and Jatindranath Mukherjee.

When Hemchandra Kanungo, a name you must be familiar with by now (Chapter 15), returned from Paris with a trunk hiding an explosive manual for bomb-making, there was no going back. As the eighteen-year-old Khudiram Bose hurled a bomb at what he believed to be Magistrate Kingsford's carriage, cementing his immortality, he would set in motion a chain of events both dramatic and disruptive. Aurobindo and Barin were arrested in the aftermath of Khudiram's daring act in what became famous as the Alipore Bomb Case. Jatin, who was one of the masterminds, was able to successfully evade the police, his mind now fixed on keeping the fires of revolution burning. His next plan was to incite the 10th Jat Regiment stationed at Fort William to revolt, seize the fort, and immobilize the British from within. An offshoot of this plan was to use the Kanungo bomb to target a ballroom on Christmas Day 1909, in the presence of the viceroy. However, the plan never saw the light of day as one of the soldiers betrayed them and revealed the plan to his superiors. Jatin immediately went underground, but his shadow continued to loom large over the resistance movement. Yet his identity remained obscure to the British police.

Five years later, the 30 August 1914 edition of *The Statesman* carried a sensational news of a heist, which it called 'The greatest daylight robbery'. Members of the Jugantar group, now headed by Jatin, successfully robbed fifty Mauser pistols and 46,000 rounds of ammunition from Rodda & Co. as they were heading for the godown (Chapter 17). Even as winds of war blew through the political corridors of the high and mighty in Europe, the robbery at Rodda & Co. left the British shaken. They could sense something big was on the anvil. The Bengal revolutionaries had established contact with the Ghadar Party in the United States. The latter, with the help of the

Berlin Committee along with the German military attaché, Franz von Papen,[3] had devised an ingenious plan.

Gun runners, ships and betrayal

The plan, hatched by the Ghadar Party and the Berlin Committee, was to procure arms and ammunition from Germany, and then send them by sea to India. The plan was put in motion, the shipment was sent aboard the schooner *Annie Larsen*. The *Annie Larsen* was to meet the SS *Maverick*, which would handle the final leg of the journey. However, due to various delays and challenging weather conditions, the *Annie Larsen* was unable to deliver the goods to the *Maverick*. The cargo of the *Annie Larsen* was confiscated by US Customs, which ultimately led to the Ghadar Party trials.

In the meantime, through German agents in Siam (Thailand), the Berlin Committee had sent word that some firearms would be dropped off near the coasts of Balasore, Sundarbans and Chittagong. Jatin was tasked with setting up operations near Balasore to retrieve the arms.

The plan was set for 25 December—it was to be a major uprising, not only in Bengal but also in the Andamans and Burma, the likes of which hadn't been seen since 1857. However, it was not meant to be. Kraft and Oren revealed the plans, and as word of the uprising leaked, the police finally caught wind of Jatin's movements. Documents found on the rebels after the Rupsa battle in Balasore revealed their role in the plot and its details.

It is believed that Tegart took off his hat upon seeing Jatin's cold body at the hospital after the battle, as a mark of respect. He had later written: 'If he were born in a free country he would be the first general of a nation. I have met the bravest Indian and I have high regard for him.'

The Christmas Day Plot remains one of the biggest 'what if' scenarios in the history of our freedom struggle.

Meanwhile, as our train passed the station, slowly picking up speed, a striking conversation caught our ears.

'Did you know Bagha Jatin was killed in Balasore, somewhere around here?'

'You're getting that from the recent Bengali film, right?'

The first speaker grinned a bit.

'They say he killed a bagh [tiger] with his bare hands. Now, that's a story I've known long before the film.'

The words lingered in the air for a moment, as if the past had softly brushed against us, only to be broken by the shout of the tea vendor: 'Chai garam, chai garam!'

20

Three against an Empire

As we entered the Barhath Haveli[1] in Shahpura, Rajasthan, its faded glory unfolded through crumbling arches and weather-worn balconies. The air hung heavy with neglect. The haveli no longer dazzled with grandeur but stood like a haunting echo of Rajputana heritage.

Within the storied walls of this century-old haveli unfolds a saga of valour, courage and sacrifice—the legacy of a family whose dedication to Swaraj knew no bounds. As we stand before the portraits of the scions of the Barhath family, a question lingers in our minds: Who were the Barhaths of Shahpura?

A bomb at the Durbar

Let us rewind the clock to 23 December 1912, when a large crowd had gathered on the streets of Delhi. The mood among the Indian section of the crowd was indifferent, while the European sections were far more excited. As the viceroy's decked-up ceremonial elephant passed near the clock tower at Chandni Chowk, close to the Red Fort, there was a loud bang! The explosion ripped through the air, jolting the crowd into shock and chaos.

> **Telling the time of rebellion: Clock Tower at Chandni Chowk**
>
> Built in 1870, the clock tower or the Ghantaghar at Chandni Chowk, was considered the centre of Old Delhi. Sadly, it no longer exists, though you might find it in old pictures of Delhi as well as in B.R. Chopra's 1954 film, *Chandni Chowk*.

Although the howdah itself was smashed to smithereens, Lord and Lady Hardinge, the viceroy and vicereine got out relatively unscathed. The umbrella bearer for the viceroy was the unfortunate soul to die, while the elephant brushed it off as if nothing had happened.

Though the assassination attempt failed, its ripple effects were felt throughout His Majesty's Indian Empire. Unlike a silent, calculated strike, this was a public spectacle of violence and that too targeted at the most high-profile British official of the land—designed solely to unleash chaos and mayhem. The Associated Press ran a bulletin the next day: 'Viceroy of India Is Injured by Bomb. Attendant Killed'.

A reward of Rs 10,000 (a fortune back then) was announced for anyone who would disclose the whereabouts of the assassin or assassins. So, who were the daredevils who attempted such an audacious act?

After months of investigation into what became known as the infamous Delhi–Lahore conspiracy case, the police traced the whole plan to a group of men: Lala Hanumant Sahai, Basanta Kumar Biswas, Bhai Balmukund, Amir Chand and Awadh Behari. Sahai was sent to the penal colony in the Andamans, while the other four were sentenced to be hanged. But they were not the only ones involved. While Basanta and Balmukund were convicted for throwing the bomb, the sessions judge admitted that the evidence against them was largely circumstantial.

Today, it is believed by most that it was Thakur Jorawar Singh Barhath of Shahpura, disguised in a burqa, who had stealthily moved into a vantage position and hurled the bomb, aiming to kill the viceroy.

The Barhath legacy of defiance

But the story of Shahpura and the defiant lineage of the Barhaths has an even earlier genesis. Before the bombed Durbar of 1912, there was another Durbar in 1903. The viceroy at the time, Lord Curzon, had invited kings and queens from all the princely states to join the celebrations, among whom was Maharana Fateh Singh of Mewar. But as Fateh Singh was journeying to the Durbar, a letter arrived in his hands—written by Kesari Singh Barhath.

The letter contained a poem by Kesari, titled '*Chetawani ra Chungatiya*', containing couplets such as these:

गिरद गजां घमसांणष नहचै धर माई नहीं |
(ऊ) मावै किम महाराणा, गज दोसै रा गिरद मे ||

The circle of elephants and the fierce battle are unyielding,
Oh Mother, I cannot endure it.
(But) How can the Maharana retreat?
Even if surrounded by elephants in the battlefield.

In this poem, Kesari Singh implored the maharana to reflect on the glorious tradition of staunch independence set by his ancestors, all great Rajput warriors. He contrasted the maharana's legacy of valour and honour with the insult the British had imposed upon him, placing him in a mere 200-yard room (that is, he would be seated in an enclosure 200 yards from the royal visitors)—a mockery of the great Rajput dignity.

The maharana read this and turned back; he didn't attend the Durbar. This was perhaps the first spark of rebellion against the British from the Barhath family. Kesari Singh's plea ignited a fire of resistance, urging the maharana to reclaim his honour and set the stage for future defiance in the fight for Swaraj.

The Barhath family belonged to the Sauda Barhath clan of the Charan community and traced their origins to Gujarat. Kesari Singh grew up on the ideals of Maharishi Dayanand Saraswati, whose words, such as, 'You should become Charan not by your caste but by your deeds,' left a lasting impression on him, quietly influencing his thoughts and actions as he matured. After successfully dissuading the maharana from attending the Durbar, Kesari Singh became more directly embroiled in the freedom struggle.

He formed secret societies in Kota and recruited youngsters who were ready to die for their country. By keeping close connections with counterparts from Bengal, he sought to raise funds and get arms and ammunition for an uprising against the British. Around 1912, Kesari Singh came in close contact with Rash Behari Bose and Amir Chand. Bose and Chand were planning something big. Taking cues from the failed attempts of rebellion in Bengal, they wanted to showcase a public act of defiance—and what could have been more fitting than blowing up the Delhi Durbar.

While multiple members were involved in the planning and logistics, it was Kesari Singh's younger brother, Jorawar Singh Barhath, who ultimately carried out the plan. Pandit Arjun Lal Sethi, who was also involved in the planning, later told a friend that it was Rash Behari who told him that four revolutionaries were involved in throwing a bomb at Hardinge: himself, Basant Kumar Biswas, Bhai Balmukund and Jorawar Singh Barhath. It was Jorawar Singh who actually threw the bomb.

After the failed attempt, Jorawar went into hiding in the ravines of central India. Jorawar was reportedly involved in numerous dacoities in the Chambal region—an area long notorious for its bandits—using these raids as a means to secure funds and ensure survival. He was principal accused in the 1913 Nimej murder case, also known as the Arrah conspiracy. Jorawar and a couple of his associates were accused of killing Mahant Bhagwandas—a Jain holy-man suspected of being close to the British. Jorawar was never caught and spent the next three decades hiding in the guise of a sadhu with the name Amardas Bairag.

While Jorawar went underground, his elder brother Kesari Singh was captured for the murder of Mahant Pyarelal in Kota. He was tried and sentenced to life imprisonment in Hazaribagh Jail, while the jagir at Shahpura and the newly built haveli, completed in 1913, were confiscated. But while one Barhath was absconding and the other was in jail, the youngest scion of the Barhath family was still plotting to bring the British down.

Kunwar Pratap Singh Barhath was trained in nationalist ideals from a young age by his father Kesari Singh. After the failed attempt in Delhi, Jorawar Singh and Pratap Singh (who had accompanied his uncle) fled the scene and made their way back to Rajasthan. While Jorawar went into hiding, Pratap Singh went to Benares in secret to meet Rash Behari Bose, who was now trying to instigate another rebellion together with the Jugantar group from Bengal and the Ghadar Party from Punjab. Bose entrusted Pratap to turn dissident Indian platoons of the British army to their cause. It was decided that on 21 February 1915, an armed rebellion would begin from Benares.

Another plot, bad luck and betrayal

Pratap had become a close confidante of Bose. Writing about him in an article many years later, Bose said, 'He was a lion by nature. His father, uncle, grandfather all sacrificed themselves for the country.'

Coming back to our story, part of the new plan was to assassinate a member of the government, Sir Reginald Craddock, which would have been the signal for dissident garrisons to take up arms against the British. Pratap was entrusted to kill him but when the day eventually came, Craddock never showed up. The assassination plan collapsed. A little earlier, word had reached the Ghadar Party that the British had somehow come to know about the plans, and so the dates were changed, but this information never reached Benares on time. As per the original plan, on 21 February 1915, Sachindra Nath Sanyal and his associates reached the parade ground in Benares and were arrested (Chapter 23). Sanyal got a life sentence, while Bose fled to Japan. Pratap, in the meanwhile, escaped to Hyderabad in Sindh with the police hot on his heels. In Sindh, Pratap disguised himself as a medical compounder, but he was repeatedly asked to come back and take the leadership role since both his father and uncle were now out of the picture. He decided to heed the call of the motherland.

No story feels complete without a betrayal. For Pratap, it was the station master at Ashanada railway station who turned him in while he was on his way back to Jodhpur. The very man who was supposed to facilitate his meeting with other rebel leaders had instead sealed his fate. Pratap was tried for his complicity in the Benares Conspiracy case and on 14 February 1916, he was sentenced to rigorous imprisonment in Bareilly Central Jail. While in jail, Pratap was given various assurances, inducements and offers of clemency to lure him into revealing the names of the co-conspirators. But not once did Pratap utter a word about his colleagues, namely Bose and Sanyal. Pratap succumbed to relentless torture in prison on 7 May 1918, becoming the family's first martyr. He was only twenty-five.

A year later, Kesari Singh was released as part of the clemency shown to celebrate the ending of World War I. The loss of his son didn't deter him from restarting his fight with the colonial government. He continued to write inflammatory material for local newspapers, advocating for self-rule, till his last breath. Meanwhile, efforts to nullify Jorawar Singh's warrant did not work and he spent the rest of his life in hiding, eventually dying in 1939 from a bout of pneumonia.

The government museum in Shahpura was established by the Archaeology and Museums Department of Rajasthan in the Barhath haveli. Like any other similar museum devoted to an aristocratic family, it displays everyday objects used by the family, such as books, pens, clothes, turbans and also guns. Mute and inert, these objects fail to convey the immense scale of the family's involvement in the struggle for freedom, their sacrifices and their martyrdom.

21

Rebels of Rampa

In the southern parts of India, mainly in the states of Kerala, Andhra Pradesh and Tamil Nadu, toddy—locally known as kallu—is a natural alcoholic beverage made from the fermented sap of palm trees. Toddy tappers take a lot of risk, from the dangers of slipping and falling down to being stung by wasps, in order to get this white liquid from coconut trees, which after fermentation is rushed to the toddy 'shaaps' as shops are locally called.

These unassuming shops tucked away in unobtrusive corners are not hard to find if you know where to look, and in the rush hour or usually during lunchtime, it's difficult to find an empty spot. The air buzzes with lively, unfiltered chatter, mingling with the deep, familiar aroma of age-old spices and slow-cooked meals. For generations, these shops have represented a distinct way of life. They have served as gathering spots where stories are exchanged and friendships are forged, and, in the process, they have kept the local culture thriving.[1]

But toddy shops have played significant roles beyond mere socializing. They once served as clandestine meeting places for revolutionaries, while the drink itself once paved the way for a rebellion.

The story of this rebellion takes us to Rampa, a region in the Eastern Ghats, in the East Godavari district of Andhra Pradesh, not far from the port city of Visakhapatnam. It is home to the Konda Reddis, a Telugu-speaking tribal community that has long inhabited the densely forested hills surrounding the area. The lands, for the most part of the nineteenth century, were under the control of a self-styled zamindar who was nothing but a puppet of the East India Company. Toddy tapping was an integral part of the tribe's culture; so, when the Madras government decided to introduce a new law, an excise regulation making toddy tapping illegal and imposing a severe tax, matters came to a boil.

Tribal rebellions

The rebellion started in March 1879 and engulfed the local police stations. Several constables and officers were killed. Led by a group of men—Kakur Reddy, Bhim Reddy, Amal Reddy and Tammanna Dora—it spread like wildfire to the neighbouring regions of East Godavari and before the authorities could step in, flames of the revolt had spread from Chodavaram Taluk, to Visakhapatnam and all the way to Bhadrachalam.

This was, however, not the first time that Rampa had rebelled. The first rebellion happened around 1839, when a man also called Tammanna Dora, in a daring act, ambushed a police party. Twelve policemen were killed and twenty others were injured. Dora became a cult hero, but he mysteriously disappeared a few years later. It was generally believed that Dora had been killed, although no proof or evidence of the same was found. Nor was his corpse ever discovered.

A second rebellion in the region took place in 1857–58, followed by a third in 1861–62, both largely driven by resistance against oppressive British policies.

In 1879, Dora reappeared under mysterious circumstances— some believed it was the same man returning, while others argued that it was his nephew carrying forward the legacy of defiance. Whatever the reality may have been, under Dora, the rebels looted police stations and executed two policemen to set an example. As the fight waged on multiple fronts, Dora led a band of rebels to join the fight in Malkangiri—some 170 kilometres away, and soon he was declared the liberator and subsequently the king of Malkangiri.

Realizing that the revolt was spiralling out of control, the government responded by deploying six regiments of Madras Infantry, two companies of sappers and miners, a squadron of cavalry, and a regiment from Hyderabad to quell the unrest. In July 1880, Dora was tracked down and killed. He was decapitated and his head brought back as a prize—an act of brutality that cemented his place as a hero even further. The rest of the rebellion wasn't quelled until November 1880, and many rebels were sent to the Andamans.

The fourth Rampa rebellion of 1879 would have a considerable impact on the area and its administration. The Madras government was forced to make new laws that were amicable to the tribal community of the region.

Fighting wars, fighting malaria

An intriguing detail emerges from the rebellion—while British soldiers fell in battle, many more were claimed by an invisible enemy: malaria. Swarms of mosquitoes attacked the troops relentlessly, leaving men fever-stricken or dead. Just after the 1879–80 rebellion, Ronald Ross, a surgeon in the Indian Medical Service, arrived in India and served in the Madras Presidency for several years.

During his stay, Ross came across numerous cases of soldiers infected with malaria fever, which piqued his interest. In 1880, Alphonse Laveran, a French military doctor in Constantine, Algeria, had made the groundbreaking discovery of the malaria parasite (*Plasmodium falciparum*) in the blood of infected patients. Ross began to work on finding out more. In 1897 he discovered that the Anopheles mosquito was the primary vector responsible for transmitting malaria. He solidified his findings in a small lab in Calcutta the following year, working with an Indian scientist, Kishori Mohan Bandyopadhyay.

Ross was awarded the Nobel Prize for his work on malaria in 1902 and Bandopadhyay was not included in the Nobel award but received the King Edward VII's Gold Medal at the Delhi Durbar in 1903. Laveran was awarded the Nobel in 1907.

After the rebellion of 1879–80, although the tribes had been quelled, the land and the forest were still a standing problem for the British authorities as controlling them had been made more difficult by the prevalence of malaria fever. So, in 1882, the government introduced the Madras Forest Act, which closed off large areas of the forest within the Rampa administrative region, thus trying to establish greater administrative control. The new Act not only restricted the movement of the tribes but prevented them from doing anything inside the forest without prior permission. Even their traditional way of agriculture, the 'podu', was restricted. This discontent among the tribes paved the way for the rise of another rebel hero.

Between 22 and 24 August 1922, under the dense canopy of the forests of the Eastern Ghats, a band of 500 rebels led by Alluri Sitarama Raju struck like a storm. Moving with precision, they raided the police stations of Chintapalli, Krishnadevipeta and Rajavomangi, seizing an arsenal of twenty-six muskets, 2,500 rounds of ammunition, six .303 Lee-Enfield rifles and a revolver. When the authorities arrived the next day they found a written note in the station's diary by Raju, detailing the date and time of the raid, and the weapons seized during it—a new rebellion had begun.

Revolution in movies

If the name Alluri Sitarama Raju sounds familiar, you may have heard it from Bollywood star Deepika Padukone at the 95th Academy Awards. While introducing the live performance of the song 'Naatu naatu' from the film RRR,[2] she highlighted

> the song's cultural significance and its energetic beats, which had set people dancing across the world. She also referenced Alluri Sitarama Raju, the revolutionary leader who served as the inspiration for the character portrayed by Telugu superstar Ram Charan.

Sadhu turned rebel leader

Born sometime around July 1897—though this date remains a matter of debate—Alluri Sitarama Raju came from a modest middle-class family in Mogallu in the West Godavari district near Visakhapatnam. From an early age, he was deeply influenced by the rising tide of patriotism sweeping across the country, a fervour that would later shape his path as a revolutionary.

At eighteen, Raju renounced worldly life, embracing the path of a sanyasi and wandering through the hills of the Eastern Ghats. Though he had dropped out of school, his acquired knowledge of astrology and medicine earned him reverence among the tribal communities, who saw him as a healer and guide. Yet, beneath his ascetic life burned a raging purpose—to overthrow British imperial rule and reclaim the land for its people. During his pilgrimage across the country, Raju is believed to have crossed paths with revolutionaries from Bengal, from whom he allegedly learnt the art of bomb-making.

Raju found some common ground with Gandhi's Non-Cooperation Movement but believed more in armed revolution. He cleverly drew people towards his own cause, channelling their growing discontent into an armed uprising against British rule. Raju's first band of followers was drawn from the Peddavalasa and Makaram muttas (muttas under the British Rule were considered as divisions) of the Gudem hills. Among them, his most trusted lieutenants were the brothers Gam Gantayya Dora and Gam Mallayya Dora, unwavering in their loyalty—men who would follow him to the ends of the earth. Soon enough, everyone wronged by the British was joining Raju's rebellion.

Thus came about the coordinated attack by 500 rebels in August 1922, which began the Rampa Rebellion of 1922.

In September 1922, Raju struck again. With the same ferocity and precision, his forces carried out three more daring raids. At Dammanapalli Ghat, the conflict turned ugly—two British police officers were killed, sending shockwaves through the colonial administration. By the year's end, Raju was no longer just a rebel—he had become a myth, a messiah-like figure in the eyes of the people, a warrior who had risen to rid the land of its wicked foreign oppressors.

The rebellion continued for two more years. Raju managed to evade several attempts to capture him. The British even tried to lure people to give information by announcing a princely reward of Rs 10,000 for the head of Rama Raju, and Rs 1,000 each for his lieutenants the Gam brothers, but the tribal community never gave them up.

Eventually though, luck ran out. Raju was captured near the forests of Chintapalle, was tied to a tree and executed by firing. It is estimated that the British government of the time had spent almost Rs 40 lakh to quell the rebellion.

He changed his name to hers

In his youth, Raju is said to have been deeply in love with a girl named Sita, whose untimely demise left him heartbroken. In her memory, he is believed to have prefixed her name to his own, and thus, he came to be known as Sitarama Raju.

By the time of his death, Raju had earned the stature of a demigod who defied the might of an empire. To the British, he was a relentless terror, a ghost in the hills who refused to be caught. The sheer scale of the military force deployed to crush his rebellion speaks volumes about the threat he posed to colonial rule.

Rampa's various rebellions illustrate the vast magnitude of our freedom struggle—fought gallantly—regardless of whether they were won or lost—on multiple fronts by countless unsung heroes like Tammanna Dora and Alluri Sitarama Raju, whose defiance still echoes across the length and breadth of this nation.

22

A Chilling Revenge and a Fearless Witness

On 18 April 1930, a group of brave freedom fighters, led by the enigmatic Surya Sen aka Master Da, met in Chittagong, which is now in eastern Bangladesh. Among them were Ganesh Ghosh, Lokenath Bal, Nirmal Sen, Ambika Chakrabarty, Naresh Roy, Sasanka Datta, Ardhendu Dastidar, Harigopal Bal, Tarakeswar Dastidar, Ananta Singh, Jiban Ghoshal, Anand Gupta, and the valiant Pritilata Waddedar (Chapter 28) and Kalpana Dutt. And there was a boy, barely in his teens, Subodh Roy, whose heart was as big as his dreams.

The Chittagong liberation raid

Master Da had the plan all set. The group quickly sprang into action. In no time, they cut off telegraphic and railway communications to the rest of India, and took control of two government armouries and various government establishments. However, they were unable to get light machine guns as they had planned, and there was no ammunition for the .303 rifles, so those were useless. In a bold and historic move, they declared independence under the Provisional Revolutionary Government, operating under the Indian Republican Army. To mark the victory, Master Da raised the Indian national flag. It was a moment of sheer pride.

The British forces, fully trained and equipped, were taken aback by the audacity of these revolutionaries. Surya Sen and about sixty of his fellow revolutionaries had liberated Chittagong that day, but they knew they couldn't hold their ground against the oncoming British army reinforcements. They made a strategic retreat, marching towards the Jalalabad Hills in search of a safe haven.

Surya Sen, revered as 'Master Da', the revolutionary mind behind the 1930 Chittagong Armoury Raid. (Photo author unknown. Public Domain via Wikimedia Commons.)

The great Jalalabad siege

What unfolded next was a tale of bravery and defiance only rarely seen in history. The siege that followed was of remarkable magnitude, and a testimony of the courage and determination of these freedom fighters. Hidden in the forests of the Jalalabad Hills, a great gun battle ensued between the armed revolutionaries and the British army. Despite being massively outnumbered and outclassed in terms of weaponry, these indomitable fighters, fighting with obsolete muzzle-loading musket rifles, stood their ground against the British, who were armed to the teeth with machine guns and .303 magazine rifles.

The revolutionaries, who had taken refuge in the hills, had braced themselves for the worst but hardly knew they were about to make history. Since the First War of Independence in 1857, there had been no event as glorious as this. A handful of men, many of them young boys and teenagers, armed with limited resources, were battling a much larger and well-armed British army in an open battle.

As they resisted valiantly despite all the odds, they frustrated their powerful opponents. The police and military kept returning to Jalalabad with larger forces and arms, only to be thwarted by the iron will of the brave Indians. Yet there was no denying that the Indians could match neither the numbers nor the weapons of the oppressors. So, eventually they fell, one fearless revolutionary at a time. With most of his force dead, Master Da ordered a retreat, opting to fight another day. The remaining fighters scattered into the forested hills of Jalalabad.

Meanwhile, desperate to capture Master Da, the British government announced a large monetary award for anyone who could give them information to arrest Master Da. The news sent shockwaves through the community, and the stakes were higher than ever.

People lived in fear, not knowing who among them might betray their leader for the reward. The revolutionaries, too, were cautious, knowing that every move they made was being watched. Yet, they remained undeterred in their loyalty to Master Da.

The drama unfolded like a thrilling tale of espionage and intrigue, with the British government leaving no stone unturned in their pursuit of Master Da. But the revolutionaries were equally determined to protect their leader and continue their fight for freedom. The reward only served to strengthen their resolve, and the legend of Master Da grew even more significant.

Master Da, constantly pursued by the police, had no choice but to go into hiding. He found refuge in the house of Sabitri Devi, a widow living near Patiya. On 13 June 1932, a police and military force led by Captain Cameron surrounded the house. The tension was palpable as the revolutionaries inside prepared for the worst. As Cameron ascended the staircase, a shot rang out, and he was killed instantly. In the chaos that followed, Surya Sen, along with Pritilata Waddedar and Kalpana Dutt, managed to escape to safety.

> ### A lesson in unity
>
> The poor Muslim peasants of Chittagong also played a crucial role. As Asghar Ali Engineer noted in *They Too Fought for India's Freedom*, they gave Surya Sen and his comrades shelter to help them evade the police, as Hindu homes were often raided. The British also tried to incite communal riots by spreading stories of Hindu oppression. But their plan failed. When Hindu revolutionaries were hunted, Muslim peasants kept their doors open—a lesson in unity for the nation's future.

But the drama was far from over. In the tumultuous days of India's struggle for independence, betrayal could come from the most unexpected sources. Netra Sen, a relative of Surya Sen, had also chosen to walk the path of revolution under his guidance. But, driven by either greed for monetary rewards or consumed by jealousy, or perhaps a toxic mix of both, Netra made a fateful decision.

Treachery

On 16 February 1933, he made a deal with the devil and informed the British authorities that Master Da was at his house. As Master Da sat down to have lunch with his relative, unaware of the impending danger, the police stormed in and captured him.

After Master Da's arrest, Netra Sen was murdered by an unknown assailant. The air was rife with rumours and whispers of the encounter, the tale morphing with each telling, leaving the world wondering who was responsible for the traitor's death. Films and documentaries have been made on India's freedom struggle, but there's hardly any mention of this assailant.

Yet, there was a lone eyewitness to Netra Sen's murder, who became the real hero: the slain man's wife. This is her story, a tale of courage and truth in the face of danger. A story that sheds light on the dark corners of history, where heroes often go unrecognized. We unravel the drama and chilling tale of Netra's murder and the bravery of the lone eyewitness.

Revenge

In 1915, a boy named Kiranmoy Sen was born into a world of turmoil and revolution. From a young age, Kiran became one of the working members of Surya Sen's revolutionary party, even when he was a young student. As a boy, he would risk his life to carry secret messages of the party from one place to another, and help absconding members move from one shelter to another. Thanks to a video released by Kiran Sen's family, we heard Kiran's own account of the entire incident.

When Master Da was captured in 1933, Kiran was just an eighth-grade student. But his heart was filled with a sense of duty and a desire for justice. With his friend Rabindra 'Khokon' Nandi, Kiran decided they would not let the betrayer Netra Sen live any longer. As the British prepared to hang Master Da, Kiran and Khokon plotted to make Netra pay for his betrayal.

They formed a group and undertook two missions at the same time. The first was to attack the European cricket club and the second to kill Netra. Himanshu, Nityagopal and two others would go to the European cricket club; Kiran and Khokon would go for the execution. The plan was to shoot Netra, but the boys couldn't collect the pistol from the person who was supposed to give it to them. Then they decided they would use a billhook (ramdah). Kiranmoy Sen in an interview later revealed that they used a billhook for multiple reasons—there wouldn't be any noise, no one would be alarmed and bullets wouldn't be wasted on the traitor.

Kiran and Khokon joined a game of football at a local ground, and kept a lookout for Netra. They saw Netra was coming home from the town market, carrying hilsa fish and vegetables. Kiran recognized him from a distance and made an excuse that he had hurt his foot and could not play anymore. Khokon followed suit. The two boys went to their friend Deben Dutta's house. Though Deben was not involved in party matters, he admired Kiran's spirit. He lent them a huge billhook and Kiran took another one from his own house.

The two boys headed for Netra Sen's house. Kiran knew Netra's house well enough to find his way to the kitchen area. They positioned themselves in the south of the kitchen, from where they could see Netra being served his food, and his wife leaving for the kitchen to get more food. The boys decided that as soon as his wife left and Netra lowered his head to take his first mouthful, thus exposing his neck, they would kill him. There was a hurricane lamp in front of Netra while he was eating. Kiran mentally calculated that it would take him two to three steps to reach him. Just when Netra bent forward to eat, Kiran struck his neck with the billhook. His wife came back from the kitchen just then, in time to witness the murder. The boys fled the scene immediately.

In the meantime, a rumour spread in the village that the two boys had killed Netra's entire family. When Netra's dead body was being taken away, Kiran was assured that he had succeeded in his mission.

Loyalty and courage

The police stormed into the house; they demanded that Netra's wife reveal the identity of her husband's killer.

'You have to tell us!' they shouted.

But the widow stood her ground, her eyes flashing with defiance.

'No!' she declared, 'You can kill me. I will not tell you. I do know who the person is.' Despite their threats and intimidation tactics, she refused to betray her husband's killer. 'If you want to arrest me, arrest me,' she said. 'If you want to kill me, kill me. I am ready.'

Her courage was born out of love and loyalty to her country. Her conscience wouldn't let her betray someone who had avenged the betrayal of their beloved leader, Master Da. She resolutely faced the police and their demands, willing to sacrifice her own life to protect the truth.

After her husband's death, Netra's wife made the courageous decision to seek out Surya Sen. When she approached him, he greeted her with kindness and wisdom in his eyes. Just before he was hanged, Surya Sen blessed her and said something that would forever change her life.

'I am not the hero,' he said. 'You are the hero. I am not the real leader. You are the real leader. The sacrifices that you have made for Mother India have made you the true leader of Chittagong's revolution for our liberation.'

With those words, Surya Sen comforted her and bestowed on this brave woman the mantle of moral leadership—an acknowledgement of her immense strength in choosing patriotism over family ties. It is awe inspiring to imagine what courage must have been needed to show such defiance: a simple housewife from the interiors of Bengal, refusing to identify those who killed her husband. She must have known that it would lead to her being ostracized—not just by her husband's family but also, in all likelihood, by her own. And yet she stood firm and unmoved with her conviction. In some ways, it feels fitting that Netra Sen's widow remains unnamed in the pages of history. It further adds to her mystique as a symbol of strength and sacrifice.

Her name is perhaps deliberately hidden to shield her family from public scrutiny, or because society often alienated women who broke stereotypes and social conventions. Women like Netra's wife, Yamuna (Chapter 33) and Nanibala Devi (Chapter 46) bore not only the immediate pain of sacrifice but also the lifelong weight of alienation.

Tragedy and inspiration

On the dawn of 12 January 1934, Surya Sen was led to the gallows. He was in a pitiable condition—his teeth and knuckles broken and the nails of his hands and feet pulled out (Chapter 24).

Master Da had written a final letter to his followers from his cell in Chittagong Jail. With the shadow of the noose hanging over him and death knocking at his door, Surya Sen had reflected on the legacy he would leave behind. 'What shall I leave behind for you?' he wrote. 'Only one thing—a golden dream, the dream of a Free India.'

He implored his comrades to carry on the fight, even if it meant sacrificing their own lives. 'If you die before the goal is reached, then give the charge of your further pursuit to your followers, as I do today,' he wrote. 'Onward my comrades, onward—never fall back.'

Surya Sen's words were filled with hope and determination, even in the face of his own impending demise. He believed that the days of bondage were coming to an end, and that the dawn of freedom was close at hand. 'Be up and doing,' he urged his followers. 'Never be disappointed. Success is sure. God bless you.'

23

Banarasi Baghis

The play, or rather the Lila,[1] begins with the birth of the demon king Ravana. For the next thirty-one days, our guide explained, Ramnagar in Kashi (also called Varanasi, Banaras or Benares) transforms into a grand stage—with different parts designated as Ayodhya, Lanka, Janakpuri and other places that feature in the Ram Lila. The audience watches in hushed silence as years pass in moments, while Ravana prays. His penance is so intense that even the heavens tremble. Pleased with his devotion, Lord Brahma appears in front of him.

'Grant me immortality, O Creator! Let no god, demon or celestial being ever lay me to waste!' Ravana says.

Brahma, bound by the laws of the universe, shakes his head. 'All who are born must one day perish, Ravana. Ask for another boon.'

Ravana pauses, his mind calculating his next words.

'Then grant me this—let me not be slain by any god, demon, celestial being or beast. Let only a man, a mere human, be capable of my death!' And with those words, the demon king seals his fate, blinded by his own arrogance. The irony spills over, for in dismissing humans as weak and insignificant, he unknowingly paves the way for his ultimate downfall.

But is all evil triumphed over? We sought the answer while we were in Kashi; our next stop was one of the city's most ancient parts: Bangali (Bengali) Tola.

144

A little Bengal in Benares

Kashi or Varanasi, which some still prefer to call Benares, is a confluence of paradoxes. American writer Mark Twain once described Benares as 'older than history, older than tradition, older even than legend, and looks twice as old as all of them put together'. Within its complex tapestry of narrow lanes, Benares never fails to offer something to those in search of answers and solace.

It's hard to pinpoint where Bangali Tola actually starts as there is no clear marker. Locals say it stretches from Dashashwamedh Ghat to Raja Harishchandra Ghat. While walking along the road, if you pay close attention, you will see signboards written in Bengali and many vendors screaming in Bengali too. Bengaliness is infused into Benares in more ways than we can comprehend, but it has toned down in the last few decades as many Bengalis have left Benares for greener pastures. Imran, a documentary filmmaker who has a keen eye for finer details, tells us that it's sad to see the Bengali houses being sold or converted into lodges and dharamshalas.

The 'Calcutta Lodge' is still there, he says. 'You know, the one from *Joi Baba Felunath*,' he adds. Though it's known as Dashashwamedh Boarding House, it is one of few remaining boarding houses which is still fully Bengali in identity and operation.

While the Bengali identity itself is being questioned today, let's not forget that a major part of the Bengali identity of Benares is infused with blood and revolution—and that ultimately leads us to Pandey Haveli Road, where the Bengali Tola Inter College now stands.

Initially established as a school for teaching Bengali and English near Ramapura by Keshab Chandra Sen, it moved to its current location on Pandey Haveli Road under the stewardship of Girish C. Chatterjee in 1865. During the next three to four decades, the Bengali Tola School, which had by then become a high school and had gained popularity, received various grants and increased its student capacity tenfold. But by the beginning of the twentieth century, it had also become a hotbed of anti-imperialist thinking.

When we went to visit, the gates were closed since classes were still in progress, leaving us disappointed. But then our guide showed us a photograph—an image of a plaque which now stands inside the college premises. It bore the names of the teachers and students who had been part of the freedom struggle.

A school that made revolutionaries

In 1906, the Prince and Princess of Wales (the future King George V and Queen Mary) were on a tour of India, and on their list of visits was Benares. A year after Curzon's decision to bifurcate the Bengal Presidency, the youth of Bengali Tola High School decided to take matters into their own hands. Secret societies were formed. Inspired by the actions of Anushilan Samiti, students in Bengali Tola handed out pamphlets containing inflammatory writings, openly debated British policies, and even advocated for strong and violent measures. This brought them into direct conflict with Rai Bahadur Jitendra Nath Mukherjee, who was the deputy superintendent of the Benares branch of CID.

A teacher who was a hero

Sensing unrest during the prince's visit, Mukherjee launched a series of sedition cases against the students of Bengali Tola, leading to several arrests. Among them, Vinayak Rao agreed to turn approver. In response, a group of students decided to execute Rao. Enraged by the turn of events, Mukherjee had Sushil Lahiri, a science teacher, imprisoned, hoping to pressure him into revealing the assassin's identity. However, Sushil remained steadfast. When presented in court, he is believed to have declared, 'I know who killed Vinayak Rao, but I will not tell.' Ultimately, he was hanged, sparking widespread outrage and further strengthening Bengali Tola's defiance. Sushil Kumar Lahiri's name is first on the memorial tablet.

Brothers in arms

Sachindra Nath Sanyal's name appears second on the plaque and his brothers Rabindra Nath and Jitendra Nath are somewhere lower down, though by no means less important—they played their roles a little later, in 1915, in the Benares Conspiracy case (Chapter 20). The Sanyals, according to Sanjeev Sanyal, the former principal economic advisor to the finance minister and present generation of the family, settled in Benares sometime in the mid-eighteenth century. Back then it was not known as Bangali Tola—that moniker only appeared in the 1940s, when a huge influx of Bengalis into Benares began.

A viceroy's inglorious escape

Incidentally, the defiance of Benares against British rule was not new. In 1781, Governor-General Warren Hastings found himself in a financial crisis. A few years earlier, the Treaty of Faizabad had bound Raja Chait Singh of Kashi to pay a hefty tribute to the East India Company. However, driven by greed, Hastings demanded additional compensation. When Chait Singh refused to comply, Hastings marched to Kashi with a small battalion, only to be met with fierce resistance. Chait Singh's forces retaliated, killing Hastings's men and capturing him. Though some advised executing him, the raja hesitated—a fateful mistake. Hastings ultimately escaped, allegedly disguised as a woman, giving rise to the famous saying:

घोड़े पे हौदा, हाथी पे जीन,
ऐसे भागा वॉरेन हेस्टिंग्स।

The couplet humorously describes Hastings's escape, suggesting he fled in such haste that he mismatched traditional riding equipment—placing a howdah (a seat used on elephants) on a horse and a saddle on an elephant.

Let us now turn to a daring dacoity. On 9 August 1925, the 8-Down Saharanpur Lucknow passenger train was stopped at Kakori, near Lucknow. Members of the Hindustan Republican Association (HRA), notably Ashfaqullah Khan, Sachindra Bakshi, Rajendra Lahiri and Ram Prasad Bismil, overpowered the guard and looted cash meant for the treasury. Within a month of the attack, the vengeful colonial authorities arrested more than a dozen HRA members. Among them was Sachindra Nath Sanyal. Sanyal's involvement in revolutionary activities was nothing new; he was a notorious thorn in the empire's flesh.

Early in his revolutionary career, Sachindra Nath joined forces with Rash Behari Bose and the Ghadar Party to incite an armed rebellion, to start at Benares. He had also founded the Benares branch of the Anushilan Samiti (Chapter 15). Information of the impending revolt was, however, leaked to the authorities and Sanyal was captured in February 1915 in the Benares Conspiracy case (Chapter 20). He was sent to the penal colony in the Andamans.

Sanyal loses patience with Gandhi

With Bose fleeing to Japan and Jatindranath Mukherjee dead, Sanyal was the senior-most revolutionary leader in the country. But times were changing, and the freedom movement was charting a new course, away from armed revolution. In 1920–21, Gandhi launched his Non-Cooperation Movement and appealed to the revolutionary leaders to cease their activities for a year. Sanyal, who had been released by now, was doubtful but went along. When the movement dissipated, Sanyal wrote to Gandhi:

'Now the experiment is over and therefore the revolutionaries are free from their promise, or, as a matter of fact, they promised to remain silent only for a year and no more.'

It was Sanyal, along with Ram Prasad Bismil, who formed the Hindustan Republican Association. Sanyal wrote its manifesto, titled 'The Revolutionary'. It advocated the overthrow of British colonial rule and the establishment of what it called a Federal Republic of the United States of India. The HRA's efforts came to the forefront during the Kakori dacoity.

In the aftermath, Sanyal and the other leaders of HRA were arrested. While Ashfaqullah Khan and Ramprasad Bismil were hanged, Sanyal was sentenced to another term of life imprisonment in the Port Blair Cellular Jail, and his ancestral home in Benares was confiscated. A nineteen-year-old Chandrashekar Azad, who was also part of the Kakori dacoity, was the only one who managed to evade the police. Azad later reorganized the Hindustan Republican Association (HRA) as the Hindustan Socialist Republican Association (HSRA) and infused it with new blood, notable among them Bhagat Singh and Shivaram Hari Rajguru.

Sanyal shared a tense and often confrontational relationship with Gandhi as exemplified by a series of letters between the two. In one of them, Sanyal writes:

'The non-violence that India preaches is not non-violence for the sake of non-violence, but non-violence for the good of humanity, and when this good for humanity will demand violence and bloodshed, India will not hesitate to shed blood just in the same way as a surgical operation necessitates the shedding of blood.'

Sanyal died of tuberculosis on 7 February 1942 in Gorakhpur while serving his fourth prison term.

Though Sachindra Nath stands out, the younger brothers were not to be left behind. Both Rabindra Nath and Jitendra Nath were arrested in the Benares Conspiracy case of 1916 but were sentenced to shorter jail terms. The youngest one, Bhupendra Nath Sanyal, whose name isn't mentioned in the plaque, later went to jail as well for his involvement in the Kakori dacoity.

The list at Bengali Tola College goes on.

Surendra Nath Mukherjee, a student who, in 1913, is said to have smuggled a revolver to Mughal Serai station in an attempt to kill the viceroy, Lord Hardinge. Hardinge, seemingly favoured by fate, escaped yet another assassination attempt. After his release, Mukherjee played an important role in the Benares Conspiracy case and was sentenced to prison multiple times.

Suresh Chandra Bhattacharya was a part of HRA as well as of the Kakori dacoity, for which he was sentenced to prison, but he escaped the gallows and got away with a ten-year sentence.

Many of the students were banished from Benares, like Romesh Chandra Jowardar, and some were put under house arrest. The list could have gone on and on but space on the plaque was restricted. Looks can often be deceiving, and nowhere is this truer than in Bangali Tola. Tucked away in a corner of this ancient city—where death is a permanent presence, and the struggle between good and evil is eternal—it stands as a testament to our hard-fought freedom.

Speaking of good vs evil, our visit was perfectly timed with the burning of Ravana's effigies as part of the conclusion of Ramnagar's fabled Ram Lila. It felt like a quiet yet powerful reminder of the enduring struggle between dharma and adharma. The empire that once loomed over us has long since faded, but history whispers its lessons to those willing to listen.

Acknowledgement: Imran Ahmed, a storyteller, traveller and entrepreneur, has embarked on countless journeys fuelled by his passion. We appreciate his valuable insights on the Bengali community in Varanasi. You can find his work at https://akaimu.com/author/aka-imu/.

24

A Hanging, a Funeral and the Worst of the British Raj

Act One

Date: 21 November 1908
Time: Approximately 7 a.m.
Place: Alipore Jail, Calcutta

A young revolutionary is hanged to death. His offence: he murdered, inside the prison, a man who had turned traitor to the cause, testifying against his former comrades in exchange for clemency. In early-twentieth century Calcutta and Bengal, this wasn't really an uncommon act. Bengal, especially the colonial capital Calcutta, was the hotbed of the armed nationalist movement. But what happened after the hanging was certainly unusual.

The young man whose life had been cut short tragically at just twenty-six was Satyendranath Basu. He was a member of Jugantar[1] and had been arrested in the aftermath of the Muzaffarpur bombing case.[2] As soon as he was declared medically dead, preparations were in full swing to cremate him. Right there, inside the jail walls. Not his family, not his comrades who were incarcerated at Alipore, no one was allowed to be present. Quickly and efficiently, Satyendranath's remains were consigned to the flames.

Act Two

Date: 23 March 1931
Time: Close to midnight
Place: Banks of the Sutlej River, about two hours from Lahore

Two holy men, a Sikh and a Hindu, stand by the Sutlej. Three pyres lie prepared. Several men are milling around, in prison guards' uniforms. Gunny sacks are hauled down from a truck parked nearby. Their grisly contents are soon revealed: chopped human remains. The mortal remains, of what had been three of the finest young men in India, are laid out on the pyres. The priests are urged to quickly perform the last rites. And soon, the three pyres are burning. The fidgety guards cast worried glances around. They don't even wait for the pyres to burn out but drag the half-burnt remains and throw them into the Sutlej, before driving away. Soon a large crowd gathers, some of them dive into the river and retrieve some of the charred remains and re-light the pyres, giving the deceased a final dignified farewell.

The three men who met with such an undignified end were none other than: Bhagat Singh, Sukhdev Thapar and Shivaram Rajguru.

Act Three

Date: 12 January 1934
Place: Chittagong Jail, Chittagong, East Bengal (present-day Bangladesh)

A forty-year-old man has been mercilessly beaten, hands and feet fractured, his knuckles and toes broken, teeth and nails pulled out. He has been reduced to a bloody pulp. Now his near-lifeless form is dragged to the hanging ground where all is ready for a quick execution.

The man who had been put to such a brutal death was Master Da Surya Sen the man behind the Chittagong Armoury raid, about which you have already read earlier in the book (Chapter 22). But further ignominy awaited Master Da. He was to be denied even the dignity of a funeral by his British captors. Master Da's mortal remains were put in a large iron box which was quietly taken to the sea and dropped into the wild waters of the Bay of Bengal, consigning him to a watery grave.

These three instances bear testimony to the unimaginable cruelty that the British administration in India could resort to. However, their reactions in the above three cases were not in isolation. They all trace their origins to one of the earliest hangings of an Indian revolutionary and its aftermath.

The botched assassination attempt on Magistrate Kingsford on 30 April 1908 in Muzaffarpur was an eye-opener for the British Raj. It revealed to them the threat that the Bengali nationalists posed and the firepower they had amassed. They struck back swiftly and hard.

A band of heroes and one traitor

It was the calm before the storm on 1 May 1908. Overnight, in the early hours of 2 May, the British forces were launched, like a predator unleashed from chains, and conducted simultaneous raids across more than twenty locations in Calcutta. Aurobindo Ghose, the prime brain behind the revolutionary movement, was arrested from a house on Grey Street.

A simultaneous raid at 32, Muraripukur Road was the most productive. This was the principal bomb-making unit of the revolutionaries (Chapter 15). Apart from a huge cache of arms and ammunition, they recovered material for making bombs, detonators and fuses, as well as some ready bombs. The principal leaders, Barindra Kumar 'Barin' Ghose (Aurobindo's younger brother and the 'commanding general' of the movement) and Ullaskar Dutta, were arrested and twelve other revolutionaries were picked up from here. As many as twenty-four others were arrested from hideouts spread all over Calcutta.

Among them was twenty-year-old Kanailal Dutta, his comrade Satyendranath Basu (whom you have already 'met' in Act One) and another man, Narendra Nath Gossain. Gossain came from landowning stock, and unlike his tougher colleagues, he was unable to withstand the harsh treatment in jail. This fact didn't escape the attention of his captors. Detective Inspector Shamsul Alam, one of the main figures involved in the raids and arrests, began to meet Gossain regularly. Soon it came to light that the latter had turned approver and would be the King's witness[3] against his own comrades.

The British government wanted to secure a death penalty for Aurobindo Ghose. However, despite their best efforts, they were unable to secure any incriminating evidence against him. That's when they turned to the traitor Gossain. Gossain stated that it was Aurobindo Ghose and not his brother Barin who was the real leader of the movement and everything that happened, including the Muzaffarpur assassination attempt, was on Aurobindo's orders. The case against Aurobindo Ghose would rest almost solely on Gossain's testimony. The British correctly deduced that he was now a prime target for his erstwhile comrades, and Gossain was moved to the European block of the jail to protect him before he gave his testimony in court.

They silence the traitor

A few days later, Satyendranath and Kanailal got admitted to the jail hospital. There, the two sent out feelers to Gossain about how the inhumane treatment in jail was becoming too much to bear. They indirectly expressed a desire to 'cut a favourable deal' with the authorities.

On 31 August 1908, Gossain came to the jail hospital to meet Kanailal and Satyendranath, escorted by a European convict overseer. The three of them stepped out onto a veranda to hold a discussion. Unknowingly, Gossain had just signed his own death warrant. Some pistols had earlier been smuggled into the jail, as tools for a potential escape plan. Kanai and Satyen were now armed with two of them.

As they walked outside, the duo pulled out their guns. Gossain, realizing what was afoot, now broke out into a run, with Kanai and Satyen in hot pursuit. The overseer tried to stop them, but was shot through his wrist. A hot chase now followed. Nine shots were fired, and the last of them, from Kanailal's gun, proved to be the fatal one. The traitor crashed into a drain, his life slowly ebbing away. Kanailal and Satyendranath were apprehended and overpowered by a European prisoner named Linton, aided by a few other jail guards.

Satyendranath Basu (second from left) and Kanailal Dutt (second from right), under arrest after the shooting of Narendra Nath Gossain. (Photo author unknown. Public Domain via Wikimedia Commons.)

Later, while being interrogated, Satyendranath refused to give a statement. Kanailal however, readily admitted to shooting Gossain, with these iconic words: 'I wish to state that I did kill him. I do not wish to give any statement why I killed him. Wait, I do wish to give a reason. It was because he was a traitor to his country.'

A trial was immediately ordered, which lasted just two days. In light of his statement, Kanailal was found guilty and sentenced to death by hanging. Satyendranath was later tried at the High Court and given a similar sentence.

Meanwhile, with the elimination of Gossain, the case against Aurobindo Ghose had collapsed. Aided by Chittaranjan Das's gritty and meticulous defending, the court had no option but to acquit Aurobindo. If there was something that the Bengali society hated more than the oppressive colonial master, it was a traitor among their own ranks. By murdering Gossain, Kanailal and Satyendranath had become near celebrities and the talk of the town. Kanailal, especially, because of his bold statement, was touted as an example for all patriotic Bengali youth.

Meanwhile, Kanailal's hanging had been scheduled for 10 November 1908. His calm demeanour and conduct leading up to the dreaded day left his captors in awe. So much so that one of the British jail officers incredulously asked Barin Ghose, 'How many more like him do you have?'

Martyrdom and public frenzy

Act Zero

Date: 10 November 1908
Place: Alipore Jail, Calcutta

Kanailal Dutta bravely embraced death by hanging. Afterwards, his mortal remains were handed over to his family. Already, hundreds had gathered outside the jail to get a last look at the brave young martyr. As the procession set off for the Keoratolla cremation ground, its ranks started swelling by the minute. Hundreds became thousands and thousands turned into a lakh. Cries of 'Jai Kanai!' (Hail Kanai!) filled the air. The massive crowd jostled to touch the bed on which Kanai's remains were being carried.

The gallows at the Alipore Central Jail. We are extremely grateful to the Information & Cultural Affairs Department, Govt. of West Bengal, for sharing this image with us.

An azadi saint's relics

In an uncanny incident, after the funeral, there was a mad rush to get hold of some of the ashes left over from the cremation. Some unscrupulous men soon set up an impromptu trade of 'Kanailal's ashes'. It is said that people paid as much as Rs 5 for half a *chhotak* (one *chhotak* = approx. fifty-nine grams) of Kanai's ashes! A less-than-amused British police officer had dryly remarked that what was sold that day in the name of 'Kanailal's ashes' must have been fifty times his actual ashes.

The frenzy around Kanai's death and last rites, far from dampening the Bengali spirit, worked as a stimulant for Bengali youth to embrace the cause of armed revolution. It also alarmed the British rulers. By this time, Satyendranath's hanging had been set for 21 November. The authorities were apprehensive of a repeat act. They immediately ordered that under no circumstances was Satyendranath's corpse to leave the jail premises.

Thus began a tradition and an unspoken rule that spread as far and wide as Lahore to the west and Chittagong to the east and continued till the last day of the British Raj: the remains of Indian armed nationalists who had been executed were never handed over to their families and instead disposed of in the most heinous manner.

We say a silent prayer of deep respect for all those souls who embraced death for the cause of the motherland and created such terror that even after their death, they continued to haunt the minds of the British.

May their memories be forever sacred.

25

When a Harvard Scholar Planted a Bomb

On 19 April 1944, the *Indian Express* published a brief yet striking report titled 'Keezhariyur Bomb Case Judgement'. The article described the case as the most sensational in Malabar's history and proceeded to list the accused—twenty-seven individuals in total. At the top of this list appeared the name of Dr K.B. Menon. What stood out, however, was the additional detail next to his name: 'PhD from California'.

It was a surprising contrast. A highly educated scholar from one of the world's top universities was now the main suspect in a bombing case in Kerala. How did his life take such a drastic turn?

Rewinding two decades, to 30 November 1923, another small insignificant news item was published in the *Berkeley Daily Gazette*. This report, titled 'Hindusthan Club to Give Social Tonight', referred to a student organization at the University of California, Berkeley. Among the names mentioned in the article was none other than K.B. Menon, who was the president of Hindusthan Club.

It is startling to realize that both reports refer to the same individual. How did a scholar, once a member of an intellectual student collective in UC Berkeley, find himself implicated in an insurrectionary conspiracy in colonial India?

K.B. Menon's life is more than just the story of a personal journey. It is also about education, political beliefs and the fight against colonial rule. His journey deserves a closer look. So, who was K.B. Menon? At first glance, he seemed like an ordinary man. There was nothing unusual about his appearance. But those who looked closer would recognize in Dr K.B. Menon a brilliant mind, a man of conviction and a steadfast freedom fighter.

Aristocratic academic turns nationalist

Konnanath Balakrishna Menon, born on 18 June 1897 into the aristocratic Konnanath family of Taliparamba in North Malabar, was not destined for an ordinary life. He studied philosophy at the Madras Christian College before becoming a teacher at the Nizam College in Hyderabad. His brilliance earned him a scholarship to the University of California, Berkeley, where he pursued postgraduate studies and a PhD in economics. After he achieved this, he moved to the University of Colorado for further studies in economics and sociology. His academic journey led him to a prestigious position at Harvard University, where he briefly joined as a faculty member.

Meanwhile, another prominent nationalist, Jayaprakash Narayan, arrived in the USA for higher studies. Amarnath Seth, in his biography of Jayaprakash Narayan, recounts Narayan's arrival in California in October 1922, his stay at a segregated hotel and experience of racial discrimination. Within days, he met UC Berkeley students from the Nalanda Club and soon shared a room with K.B. Menon, a connection that profoundly shaped Menon's political path. This relationship proved transformative for Menon, altering the course of his political and intellectual pursuits.

According to the article by Jayaprakash Narayan et al., 'Congress Socialist Party (CSP) at a Glance and Short Profiles of Its Leaders', Menon ultimately resigned from his professional career, returned to India and resolved to immerse himself in the freedom struggle. The Harvard lecturer had returned—not to lecture in classrooms, but to mobilize the masses in the Quit India Movement.

Back in India, Menon plunged headfirst into the freedom movement. Soon after, he became the general secretary of the Civil

Liberties Union, chaired by Nehru, in 1936 and the joint secretary of the All India State Peoples Conference in 1937.

However, Menon's most defining moment came during the Quit India Movement in 1942. By this time, the British administration had pre-emptively arrested most senior Congress leaders in Malabar, leaving a power vacuum. Into this breach stepped a group of young, determined nationalist workers who formed a socialist group under the leadership of Dr Menon. This group included N.A. Krishnan Nair, V.A. Kesavan Nair, C.P. Sankaran Nair, Mathai Manjooran and many other fiery revolutionaries who refused to back down. It is quite interesting to observe how, shifting from Gandhian principles of non-violence, Menon led the socialist group to adopt the path of a violent resistance in Malabar.

A bomb plot in Malabar

They orchestrated what came to be known as the Keezhariyur Bomb Case, a daring and ambitious plot to disrupt British rule. It was a bold, yet ultimately unsuccessful, attempt to disrupt British infrastructure during the struggle for independence. At the heart of the operation was K.B. Menon, who was the mastermind behind this operation.

Incidentally, we also met Sujit Saraf. He is a man of many talents, with an effortless charm that makes him instantly likable. Sujit earned an engineering degree from IIT Delhi and went on to complete a PhD at UC Berkeley. He worked as a space scientist in California, a brilliant techie by all measures. But that's only one side of him.

Beyond science and technology, Sujit has a deep passion for storytelling and theatre. He runs Naatak, a theatre company in the San Francisco Bay Area dedicated to producing intelligent and engaging plays, often centred around South Asian narratives. Founded in 1995 by students from UC Berkeley and Stanford, Naatak has staged over 100 productions over the past twenty-nine years, making it the largest Indian theatre company in the United States.

In 1996, Sujit came across an article that intrigued him, and two years later, Naatak brought it to life on stage. The result was 'Vande Mataram: A Play about Greed, Gunpowder, and Gandhism', performed in San Jose in 1998. What made it even more fascinating was its subject—Dr K.B. Menon and the Keezhariyur Bomb Case and that the play was being staged in the San Francisco Bay Area where Dr Menon first set foot in the United States in the early twentieth century, bringing his story full circle.

So, what exactly happened in Keezhariyur?

The plan itself was daring in its simplicity. Originally scheduled for 9 November 1942, the date was later pushed back to 17 November, as the bombs were not fully prepared in time. The target locations were carefully chosen—key government offices, bridges and railway stations, critical to the British colonial structure. The bombs were manufactured in Keezhariyur, a serene village located by the Akalapuzha backwaters. The village would soon find itself at the centre of a high-stakes operation that would change its history.

Distrust and confusion bring failure

However, as the plan progressed, paranoia and suspicion began to take hold. It seemed that the police might have infiltrated their ranks, leading the conspirators to shift their operations to Parappanangadi. The gunpowder and the bombs were transported discreetly in buckets. Adding to the tension was the timing—it was Thulam Masam, a period of heavy rains in the region, which heightened the risk of exposure and complications.

But the mission was doomed from the start. Several bombs were stolen along the way and used to settle personal grudges. This transformed the mission from an act of defiance to something chaotic and absurd. The seriousness of the plan was lost due to these betrayals. The situation became tragic and confusing. To make matters worse, some members of the group leaked the plans to

British authorities. By the time the saboteurs were ready, the police were already waiting. Some members, exhausted and anxious, fell asleep at their shelter and missed their chance. Others hesitated at the last moment and failed to carry out the attack.

What began as a carefully planned mission soon unravelled. The authorities outmanoeuvred them, and within hours, most were arrested. The operation that had promised so much ended in failure, with the original intent of disrupting British control ultimately falling apart under the weight of internal betrayals, poor timing and the inexorable force of fate.

Sujit had a slightly different take on the story. He staged the play twice—once in 1998 and again in 2013. While the narrative was based on the real events of Keezhariyur, he relocated the setting to Patna, where the rebels in his version attempted to blow up the Patna–Hajipur bridge.

Drawing inspiration from real-life figures, Sujit crafted a story that was both a lament for Indian nationalism and an exploration of the absurdity of being a rebel in the 1940s—how grand revolutionary plans often collapsed in the most ridiculous ways. In an effort to make the play as realistic as possible, they even built a makeshift bomb using aftershave lotion, a metal tube, and some wiring.

Sujit chuckled, 'I still don't know how the authorities in San Jose allowed that.'

Regardless of the creative liberties, he managed to keep the memory of Dr K.B. Menon and the Keezhariyur conspiracy alive—right in San Jose, not far from Menon's alma mater.

The ensuing trial of the conspiracy was sensational, closely followed by the people of Malabar. Dr Menon was convicted and sentenced to ten years in prison. He was released after five years, following India's independence, and went on to lead the Socialist Party in the region, continuing his political activism and efforts towards nation-building.

A dramatic scene from *Vande Mataram* by Naatak—the final bomb blast sequence staged in California, USA, commemorating the Keezhariyur Bomb Case, courtesy of Sujit Saraf, founder and artistic director of Naatak. (Photography: Swagoto B.)

Dr K.B. Menon was more than just a politician. It is rare to find someone with an elite education from UC Berkeley and a faculty position at Harvard—two of the most prestigious institutions in the world—who would then choose to leave everything and dive into one of the most daring events of the Indian freedom movement. While it's difficult to fully judge the ethics of that era, figures like Menon stand apart for their honest commitment to a cause greater than themselves.

26

The Robin Hood of Kathiawar

A few years ago, on a cold winter evening, we stopped at a roadside dhaba in Himachal Pradesh. The air was chilly, and the food was hot. In one corner, a small television played an episode of *Taarak Mehta Ka Ooltah Chashmah*. We were not fans of the show, but with a plate of steaming rajma chawal and crispy parathas in front of us, we watched it anyway.

The show is one of India's longest-running television comedies. It is known for its simple humour and everyday stories. It follows the lives of the residents of Gokuldham Society, a fictional middle-class neighbourhood in Mumbai. Gokuldham is a microcosm of India, where families from different states and backgrounds live together as a close-knit community.

The episode revolved around kids playing cricket, and at one point, the affable yet ever-flustered Gujarati man Jethalal, played by Dilip Joshi, made an exasperated remark to his wife, Dayaben. He was particularly frustrated with his son, Tappu, whose mischief had reached new heights. As the episode neared its end, someone jokingly asked his wife, 'Dayaben, which book have you read after Tappu was born?'

With her usual exaggerated enthusiasm, Dayaben, played by Disha Vakani, replied, 'It was a book about Kadu Makrani!'

Jethalal promptly scoffed. 'Why would you read a book about a bandit? No wonder Tappu is so mischievous.'

The episode moved on, but at our table, an elderly gentleman named Dinanath, a regular at the dhaba, chuckled and shook his head. 'Kadu Makrani was not a bandit,' he said in Hindi. 'That's just what the British wanted us to believe. If you ask the old folks of Kathiawar, they'll tell you—he was a revolutionary.'

Intrigued, we listened as Dinanath leaned forward and spoke with the quiet authority of someone who knew his history well. 'You can call him a bandit if you like, but that's not his only identity. He was a rebel, a man who fought the British in his own way. He was our own Robin Hood.'

To prove his point, he pulled out his old Android phone—handling it with some difficulty—and played a few YouTube videos. Folk singers in Gujarat still sing of Kadu Makrani's daring exploits in the ballad '*Dungre kadu tara dayra*' (The tales of Kadu are heard and celebrated on every hill).

So, who was Kadu Makrani? His real name was Qadir Bukhsh Rind Baloch. He was born in Makran, Balochistan, but it was in Kathiawar, Gujarat, that he made his mark.

Kathiawar's outlaw chief

The nineteenth century was a turbulent time. The British were expanding their hold over India, squeezing communities with taxes and restrictions. Life became difficult for the working classes of Makran, forcing many—including Kadu Makrani and his tribe—to migrate to Kathiawar, living more or less as outlaws.

To understand Kadu Makrani, one must first understand the land he made his home. Kathiawar had a long and rich history. It was a large peninsula in western India. Many princely states, such as Junagadh, Bhavnagar, Porbandar and Rajkot, were part of it. The land had seen quite a few battles. Rajputs, Marathas and later the British, had all fought for control. Amidst these conflicts, shifting loyalties and resistance to British rule, the legend of Kadu Makrani was born.

When Kadu and his people arrived, they were noticed by the royals. The nawabs of Kathiawar saw their bravery and fighting skills.

They asked Kadu and his men to fight against other outlaws who caused trouble in the region. In return, they gave them land and protection. This was when Kadu Makrani's power and influence began to grow.

Most likely, the book mentioned by Dayaben in the TV show was *Sorathi Baharvatiya* (Saurashtrian Outlaws), a collection of stories written by Jhaverchand Meghani in Gujarati. We have discussed Jhaverchand Meghani in detail earlier in the book (Chapter 9). The book tells the tales of several baharvatiyas—outlaws or people who lived outside the law, often rebelling against rulers and the British.

The term baharvatiya has deep roots in the history of Saurashtra. It refers to people who defied authority, rejecting the rules of the land. Some were ruthless dacoits, while others were seen as folk heroes—stealing from the rich, protecting the poor and fighting against unjust rulers.

Many of the events in *Sorathi Baharvatiya* are so dramatic that they seem unbelievable. Yet, they are deeply ingrained in local folklore, passed down for generations. Kadu Makrani was one such figure, and his real-life story reflects the baharvatiya way of life—brutal, rebellious and fearless.

Dr Manjula K. Patel, in her book *In Search of Paradise: A Saga of Courage, Resilience and Resistance*, highlights how internal power struggles among the Kathiawar royals led to anarchy, allowing outlaws like Kadu Makrani to thrive. His reputation grew so strong that his name alone could instil fear. It is said that Kathiawari mothers used his name to frighten their children into good behaviour.

But the British saw this growing power as a threat. They wanted to disarm Kadu Makrani's tribe, using the pretext of a census and social work programmes to enter their homes. Kadu refused. The British gave him an ultimatum: surrender his weapons or prepare for battle. But as the legend goes: a Baloch warrior does not surrender.

What followed was fierce resistance. Kadu Makrani and his men, though vastly outnumbered, used guerrilla tactics to fight back. They ambushed British forces, attacked supply lines, and struck fear into colonial officers. Furious, the British placed a huge bounty on his head for anyone who could capture or kill him.

The surgeon who did 300 nose jobs

Here's another fascinating story worth noting. It's about Tribhovandas Motichand Shah, a young plastic surgeon and the chief medical officer of Junagadh State. In 1889, his paper, 'Rhinoplasty: A Short Description of 100 Cases', was published by the Junagadh Sarkari Press. After studying in Bombay, he gained clinical experience in Gujarat and caught the attention of the nawab of Junagadh. Impressed by his surgical flair, the nawab appointed him as chief medical officer at Junagadh State Hospital. There, Tribhovandas pioneered reconstructive surgery, performing over 300 nose reconstructions during his short career—a record unmatched by any surgeon back then.

But how did he get the chance to perform so many reconstructive surgeries? It was because it was Kadu Makrani's territory. Kadu was notorious for punishing his enemies by cutting off their noses. As noted by Paolo Santoni-Rugiu in his book, *A History of Plastic Surgery*, the presence of Kadu Makrani in Junagadh created a constant need for Tribhovandas's expertise in nasal reconstruction. Nasal amputations as punishment were not so uncommon in Indian culture; even Surpanakha in the Ramayana bears a similar story. Kadu's brutal tactics were well known, and it's said that the royals and British in Junagadh were terrified of him. In fact, the proverb *'Kadu kape nak, Tribhovandas sande'* in Gujarat translates to 'Kadu cuts off noses, and Tribhovandas repairs'—a testament to Tribhovandas's unmatched legacy and Kadu Makrani's fearsome reputation.

For years, Kadu Makrani remained undefeated, a ghost in the British records—always appearing where they least expected him, always vanishing before they could strike back. But every legend has an end. Tired of being hunted, Kadu planned his escape to Balochistan in the late 1870s. He made his way to Karachi and sought help from a local camel trader to cross the desert.

But greed is a dangerous thing. The camel handler recognized Kadu Makrani and saw an opportunity. He lured Kadu to a supposed meeting place behind Baghdadi Police Station. But instead of meeting an ally, Kadu found himself ambushed.

Even then, he did not go down easily. As the legend goes, armed with just a dagger, he killed the handler and a policeman who had come to capture him. Yet, as he tried to escape through the narrow streets of the old city quarter of Lyari, a labourer—unaware of who he was—dropped a heavy stone on his head to stop him. Kadu was captured, unconscious. After a brief trial, he was sentenced to death. In 1878, he was executed in Karachi Central Jail.

The final resting place of Kadu Makrani in Karachi.
(Photo courtesy: Mirbaloch. Public Domain via Wikimedia Commons.)

The stone said to have been dropped on Makrani by a labourer—marking his death—has been preserved beside his grave. His tombstone bears the inscription: 'Martyr — Resident of Kathiawar'. (Photo courtesy: Mirbaloch. Public Domain via Wikimedia Commons.)

Feared and beloved antihero

There are hardly any detailed documents about Kadu Makrani's life, but his legend lives on in rural folklore. He is probably one of the few revolutionaries on whom movies have been made in both India and Pakistan. Several legends and anecdotes about Kadu Makrani were brought to life through these films. In 1960, *Kadu Makrani*, a Gujarati historical fantasy film, was directed by Manhar Raskapur in India. The titular role was played by Arvind Pandya, a veteran Gujarati star and a freedom fighter himself who participated in the Quit India Movement. Another Gujarati remake was released in 1973 by Manu Desai, where Upendra Trivedi played Kadu Makrani. One of the film's famous dialogues was also part of Kathiawari folklore:

'એક ગામ ભાગે તો સાધુ...ત્રણ ગામ ભાગે તો કાદુ'

(If one village flees, it's because of a sadhu. If three villages flee, it's because of Kadu.)

The quote highlighted his fearsome reputation, as he was believed to raid three villages each day.

The promotional poster for *Kadu Makrani* (1960), Manhar Raskapur's Gujarati classic inspired by the legendary outlaw who defied British rule in Kathiawar. (Photo courtesy: Sadhna Chitra. Public Domain via Wikimedia Commons.)

From the author's private collection: a rare 1973 vinyl record of the Gujarati film *Kadu Makrani.*

One of the most memorable scenes in the film showed a British officer running away in fear from Kadu's gang, leaving his wife and child behind. When Kadu's men surrounded them, Kadu stepped in and ordered his men to lower their weapons. He declared that his army would never harm women or children. He told his men to make sure the woman and child reached safety. This act of gallantry, often repeated in stories, showed Kadu's unique moral code. The film even made its way into an episode of *Taarak Mehta Ka Ooltah Chashmah.* It was mentioned that *Kadu Makrani* was Jethalal's favourite childhood film. After watching it, young Jethalal would pretend to be a bandit, re-enacting his favourite scenes for weeks at home.

The man, the myth

In 1966, Pakistani filmmaker Habib ur Rehman paid tribute to Kadu Makrani in his Urdu film *Jaag Utha Insan*, directed by Sheikh Hasan. Mohammed Ali played the lead role. One timeless scene from the film shows Kadu raiding a Hindu village, where a young woman named Parvati, his sworn sister, desperately needs money for her wedding. In a bold move, Kadu offers himself to be captured and turned over to the British, to allow Parvati's family to claim the 25,000-rupee bounty, and use it to fund her marriage. The story, though probably apocryphal, remains one of the many legends that define Kadu Makrani.

History is often shaped by those in power, and over time, Kadu Makrani's name has largely faded from official records. He is rarely recognized as a freedom fighter—at least not in the conventional sense. But India's struggle for independence took many forms, some beyond what textbooks acknowledge. Today, he is reduced to a mere footnote or, worse, remembered only as a criminal, bandit or outlaw. Perhaps he was one, but it is difficult to erase the generational memory of a man who, despite being on the wrong side of the law, also protected villagers from British forces. While history may have overlooked him, folk tales continue to celebrate his defiance, and in the dry and harsh land of Kathiawar, his name is still spoken with respect.

007
VOTE FOR GHOSE
CHICAGO RADIO
She Who
Dared

27

The Rebel Begum of Lucknow

In the last decade or so, it has pretty much been the norm for the Hindi film industry to make movies based on historical figures and for a part of the ecosystem to immediately follow up with claims of how real history has been obfuscated.

The release of the Vicky Kaushal-starrer *Chhaava*, chronicling the life of Maratha warrior king Chhatrapati Sambhaji, ignited a heated debate on the contents of India's history textbooks. Renowned public figures weighed in on the matter but the jury is still out on this matter.

Meanwhile, as storytellers, we would like to tell a story of a girl—a story that we somewhat fortuitously discovered while having a delicious lunch at Manzilat's, a restaurant owned and operated by a direct descendant of the Awadh royal family—who overcame her humble background and cruel twists of fate to emerge as a queen and an icon. She became a thorn in the flesh of the British Raj and refused to kowtow before the mighty Queen Victoria. It is quite possible that you are hearing her story for the first time.

Steely resolve—from slave girl to queen

Today, Faizabad, located on the south bank of the Saryu River, 130 kilometres east of Lucknow, may be a poor cousin to its twin city, Ayodhya. But go back 300 years and Faizabad was the first capital of the kingdom of Awadh (Oudh). It was in Faizabad in 1820 that the heroine of our story, Muhammadi Khanum, was born. But life was rather unfair to little Khanum. She lost both her parents at a very young age and was brought up by her uncle. A life of struggle went from bad to worse when she was sold off by her aunt to two women, former courtesans of the royal court of Lucknow, who trained young girls in the same trade. It was hardly the fate that a young girl would desire, but the vagaries of life had steeled Khanum by the time she stepped into her teens. All she needed was a lucky break.

Inside Manzilat's, Kolkata's celebrated Royal Awadhi dining destination, the walls tell stories—adorned with images and newspaper cuttings of Begum Hazrat Mahal.

And that came when she caught the eye of the young crown prince of Oudh—Wajid Ali Shah. Khanum was initially recruited as a khawasin[1] (lady's maid) into the Awadh royal harem. Despite coming from a humble background, Khanum was blessed with a powerful personality. Soon, she was promoted from khawasin to pari (fairy; one of the many beautiful and talented girls housed in the parikhana—house of fairies—and given special training by experts in dance and music). Shortly afterwards, she was accepted as a concubine to Wajid Ali Shah and became one of his begums (wife/consort) with the new name of Hazrat. In 1845, Hazrat bore Wajid Ali a son—named Birjis Qadr—and thus became a mahal (favourite wife). When Wajid Ali

Shah became the nawab of Oudh in 1847, life had come full circle for Hazrat Mahal.

Corporate greed in the 1850s

But there were dark clouds on the horizon of Awadh. By the time Wajid Ali Shah ascended the throne in 1847, the East India Company was bleeding white the coffers of this prosperous state, with the royal treasury funding the maintenance of the Bengal Army besides being forced to advance loans to the Company regularly. Eventually, citing breakdown of law and order in the state and the precarious position of the royal coffers—ironically caused by the Company itself— Awadh was annexed formally into Company-controlled territory on 11 February 1856. Nawab Wajid Ali was exiled to Calcutta, where he spent the rest of his life. Begum Hazrat Mahal, however, did not accompany her husband and chose to remain in Lucknow with her minor son Birjis Qadr.

The annexation and exile of the nawab had not gone down well with the populace of Awadh. As a matter of fact, Sir William Sleeman,[2] the British resident at Lucknow from 1849 to 1856, despite being a staunch critic of the nawab, had repeatedly recommended against the annexation. On 20 March 1857, Sir Henry Lawrence arrived in Lucknow as the chief commissioner of Awadh and quickly realized he had inherited a proverbial crown of thorns. Apart from the resentful royal family, the move had infuriated the talukdars (land owners), many of whom had been enjoying properties bestowed by the kings, but which they were now dispossessed of due to the absence of Company-approved title deeds. And with the nawab's court shifting to Calcutta, small traders, artisans, craftsmen and many others were suddenly left without their biggest patron.[3] Awadh, particularly Lucknow, was the proverbial powder keg as the summer of 1857 dawned. And ironically, it was a gun, or more specifically a bullet, that provided the spark to light the keg.

The Bengal (Presidency) Army,[4] whose maintenance bill the Awadh State had been footing for many years, unlike its counterparts in the Bombay and Madras Presidencies, was mainly composed of upper-caste Hindus from the northern Gangetic plains, primarily Awadh and Bihar. These men were strongly opposed to crossing the high seas as it was prohibited in their religion. Till 1856, they were exempted from this ordeal but the passage of the General Service Enlistment Act, 1856, now made even the Bengal Army battalions open to overseas campaigns. This caused widespread resentment.

The final trigger came with the introduction of the Enfield Pattern 1853 musket rifles. The rifles used pre-greased paper cartridges which the sepoys had to bite open to release the powder. A rumour spread like wildfire among the army ranks that the grease used for the cartridges used tallow derived from beef—forbidden for high-caste Hindus, and lard derived from pork—forbidden for Muslims. Efforts by the British officers to dispel such rumours only added fuel to fire. Coming on the heels of the General Service Enlistment Act mandating overseas postings and the rapidly rising presence of Evangelical Christian missionaries in India, the rumour now sparked a conflict that threatened the survival of the East India Company rule in India.

Fire and fury across the land

It started with the rebellion in March of sepoy Mangal Pandey of the 34th Bengal Native Infantry (34th BNI) at Barrackpore (Chapter 40), who opened fire at his British superior officers. Pandey was court-martialled and executed by hanging on 8 April 1857. His Indian commander was also similarly executed for refusing to arrest Pandey and the 34th BNI was disbanded. But the news spread to the other cantonments across north India.

On 10 May, men of the 3rd Bengal Light Cavalry in Meerut rose in violent revolt after eighty-five of their comrades had been court-martialled for refusing to use the new greased cartridges, and sentenced to prison. A great number of British officers and civilians were slaughtered. A large section of the revolting sepoys left Meerut for Delhi. The First War of Independence had formally begun.

In Lucknow, the situation was tense for reasons narrated already. In early April, the house of the surgeon of the 48th Native Infantry was set ablaze. The surgeon and his family had a lucky escape. Shortly after, the men of the 7th Oudh Irregulars refused to bite the Enfield cartridges and threatened to murder their officers. Sir Henry Lawrence quelled the rebellion with his European troops, and the men had returned to work, but it was obvious that the truce was fragile and temporary.

Begum Hazrat Mahal had observed these developments with keen interest. She knew that there was already a lot of discontent on the ground against the Company Raj.[5] Moreover, with the majority of the Bengal Army sepoys being from Awadh's villages, popular support lay with the sepoys. She figured her best hope of reclaiming power was to throw in her lot with the rebelling soldiers.

Shortly after 9 p.m. on 30 April, when Sir Henry was having dinner at his residence, the native sepoys rose in revolt.[6] By the end of the night, his residence was the only British house in the cantonment not ransacked or burnt. Subsequently, following a decisive defeat in the battle of Chinhat on 30 June 1857, the remnants of European presence in Lucknow, as well as survivors from the outstations, were holed up in the Residency. The great siege of Lucknow had begun.

The siege of Lucknow—and a clever queen

With the Company administration collapsing, there was a vacuum that resulted in looting and riots. This was the moment Begum Hazrat was waiting for. Seizing the opportunity, she had her minor son Birjis Qadr installed as the new ruler with herself as the regent: Qadr's formal anointment took place on 5 July. In the meanwhile, the rebelling soldiers from Meerut had marched into Delhi and proclaimed allegiance to the ageing Mughal monarch Bahadur Shah II 'Zafar'. Begum Hazrat was quick to realize that having the blessings of the Mughal throne would offer the highest form of legitimacy to her son's ascension—both against outside forces and intrigues in the royal harem. Thus, Qadr's elevation was made subject to the payment of a tribute to the Mughal Badshah.

In the coming days, Begum Hazrat proved her mettle as an administrator. Days after Qadr's anointment, an executive council of state was formed to look after affairs of the state. Although outwardly democratic, she ensured the key positions were all manned by people close to her. Also, in a remarkable display of judgment, she ensured equal representation of both Hindus and Muslims in the council to avoid alienation of any group.[7] Every important decision—whether civil or military—was personally reviewed and vetted by her.

By the end of September, both Kanpur and Delhi had been wrested back by the Company. In the last week of September, a campaign was launched on the besieged Residency but was beaten back. One of the great successes of Begum Hazrat was to keep the various disparate elements—the rebelling sepoys, the general population and the land-owning talukdars—united in a common cause. To keep the anti-British sentiment on the boil, Begum Hazrat ordered periodic proclamations in the name of Birjis Qadr across Awadh, Rohilkhand, Moradabad, Azamgarh and so on—reminding the people to remain united and defend their land against the colonial oppressors. These were pasted across the kingdom in all the thanas (police outposts). She was a Muslim ruler with predominantly Hindu subjects but the fact that the population of Oudh remained loyal towards their queen bears evidence of Hazrat Mahal's tact and wisdom.

In November, the British were able to secure their first success, as Campbell's forces rescued the survivors from the Residency. From November 1857 to March 1858, the fortunes of the two warring parties started changing, with the British now in ascendancy. By the middle of March, the Company forces, led by General James Outram, had claimed control over much of Lucknow. Still, the rebel forces held firm and the Company had to appeal to Jung Bahadur Rana of Nepal for assistance, who now entered the fray with his Gurkha force. During this period, Begum Hazrat regularly appeared on the battlefield, exhorting the soldiers to hold firm. By then however, the writing was on the wall. Far away in Calcutta, her husband—the deposed nawab—observed everything and penned these immortal lines to express his anguish and helplessness:

Usse angrezi fauj ghere hai,
Khanjar-e-gham jigar pa phere hai.

(She is surrounded by the English army
Running the knife of sorrow on my heart.)

(We are incredibly thankful to Irfan Ali Mirza—great-grandson
of Birjis Qadr—for sharing the above couplet with us.)

Kamran Mirza, Irfan Mirza, and Manzilat Fatima (left to right—direct descendants
of Begum Hazrat Mahal) photographed at Manzilat's, a restaurant in Kolkata, where
they graciously shared rare anecdotes and memories preserved in the family's
archive with the Paperclip.

Defiant survivor

Eventually, with the tide turning completely, Begum Hazrat Mahal, accompanied by her son Birjis Qadr, fled Lucknow. But not before one final act of defiance. In November 1858, the control of India passed from the Company to the British Crown, as Queen Victoria was declared the monarch of India. The royal proclamation offered amnesty to all rebels except those who were guilty of murdering British nationals and assured non-interference of the Crown in religious matters. Begum Hazrat responded to this with a proclamation of her own that conveyed perfectly the warrior spirit in her:

To eat pigs and drink wine, to bite greased cartridges and to mix pig's fat with sweetmeats, to destroy Hindu and Mussalman temples and mosques on the pretence of making roads, to build churches, to send clergymen into the streets to preach the Christian religion, to institute English schools, and pay people a monthly stipend for learning the English sciences, while the places of worship of Hindus and Mussalmans are to this day entirely neglected; with all this, how can people believe that religion will not be interfered with?[8]

Till the last days of 1858, Begum Hazrat Mahal kept up her fight from the Baundi fort in present-day Bahraich district before finally crossing over to Nepal with her son.[9] The Rana, a British ally, however, initially refused her asylum and even threatened to have her evicted by force. He had a change of heart, though, and allowed Begum Hazrat Mahal to settle in Nepal where her final years were spent. His decision was most likely influenced by the treasure the pragmatic Begum took along with her, besides a vast train of other exiles. Even in Nepal, Begum Hazrat carried on with her duties, spending generously on the well-being of her compatriots in exile, and also hosted Nana Saheb and other rebel leaders. She breathed her last in Kathmandu in April 1879 where she was buried on the grounds of the local imambara that she had built herself. And to this day, she lies there in eternal sleep.

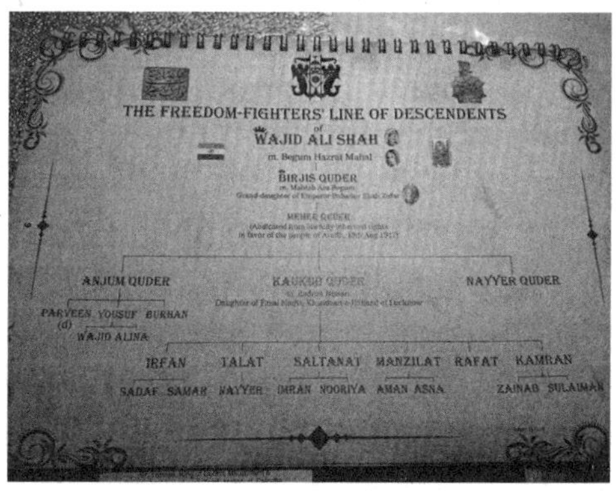

The illustrious family tree of Nawab Wajid Ali Shah and Begum Hazrat Mahal, preserved in the personal archive of Irfan Mirza, Manzilat Fatima, and Kamran Mirza.

28

The Curious Case of an Eighty-Year-Old Mistake

In January 2025, while we were working on this book, Bollywood star Kartik Aaryan was in the news for receiving his engineering degree from his alma mater over a decade after graduating.

This news got us thinking of a similar delayed awarding of degrees at Calcutta University. In that case, however, it wasn't a gap of a decade. The recipients could not receive the degrees personally as the degrees were being awarded nearly eighty years after they were originally due and the recipients had long since left this world. And it wasn't a case of oversight that held up their degrees. Their degrees were withheld as they had dared to take up arms against the draconian colonial rule that had subjugated our country for nearly 200 years. This is their story. And when you are done reading it, surely you will agree with Aamir Khan's iconic dialogue in the film *Dangal*: '*Humari chhoriyaan humare chhoron se kam ke?*' (Are our girls any less than our boys?)

Bengal of the 1920s. The frenzy of armed revolution that had engulfed the state in the years leading up to World War I had become somewhat stymied as the state entered the third decade of the twentieth century. From 1919 to 1922, with the rising popularity of Gandhiji's Satyagraha model, armed resistance took a backseat. Some of the factions of the latter actually decided to suspend activities on request from Deshbandhu Chittaranjan Das. But on 12 February

1922, in response to the Chauri Chaura incident,[1] Gandhiji called off the Non-Cooperation Movement. This led to a revived rise of the revolution in Bengal[2] with a new crop of young leaders coming to the fore, most prominent being Subhas Chandra Bose.

Born to be a rebel

The first of the protagonists of this story had a personal connection with the man who would be hailed as 'Netaji' in time to come. They say the apple does not fall far from the tree. In the case of Bina Das, it was certainly true to the hilt. Her father, Benimadab Das, a leading figure of the Brahma Samaj movement, had been a teacher and mentor to a young Subhas Chandra at Cuttack's Ravenshaw Collegiate School. Her mother, Sarala Devi, was one of the prominent faces of the progressive women's movement in Bengali society. It was in this environment that Bina was born in Krishnanagar on 24 August 1911. Bina met Subhas Chandra when they were both quite young—it was the start of an enduring bond that would have a strong influence on Bina's life.

Closer home, her older sister, Kalyani, also inspired her immensely. A feisty young woman, Kalyani had been among the founding members of the Chhatri Sangha,[3] an outfit exclusively formed in 1928 for training Indian girls in armed warfare, espionage, driving, cycling and so on. In 1930, while leading a protest against the lieutenant-governor of Bengal, Kalyani was arrested and subjected to brutal torture at the hands of the British police. The incident left young Bina deeply traumatized.

Her rebellious streak had already come to the fore before this. The viceroy's wife was scheduled to visit Bina's school, Calcutta's St. John's Diocesan School. All the students were told to bring a bouquet and present it to the lady. This instruction created a lot of turmoil in young Bina's mind. Eventually, she ripped apart the bouquet, left the event and was found by her friends, crying, huddled at the back of the classroom.

She also caused a lot of consternation when in the English paper in her matriculation exam in 1926, she mentioned Sarat Chandra Chattopadhyay's *Pather Dabi* (Demand of the Road) as her favourite novel. The book had been banned by the government for its seditious and 'anti-national' themes, but Bina had already read it by then. She was penalized for her answer but had little regret.

The humiliation meted out to elder sister Kalyani and other female revolutionaries in prison steeled Bina's resolve. She joined Chhatri Sangha and trained to become a revolutionary—her only aim was exacting revenge on the cruel administration. After her matriculation, she had joined Bethune College in Calcutta, but her regular involvement with Chhatri Sangha meant she eventually dropped out, before coming back to her alma mater, Diocesan, to pursue her graduation.

Bina's tryst with destiny arrived in early 1932. She had completed her graduation from Diocesan with flying colours. The convocation ceremony of the graduating batch of Calcutta University was scheduled for 6 February 1932. The chief guest on the occasion was Bengal's governor, Sir Stanley Jackson.[4] The Jugantar revolutionary group decided to assassinate Jackson. The person chosen to carry out the task was none other than Bina Das. Another firebrand female revolutionary, Kamala Dasgupta, arranged for the revolver. In the intervening period, Bina religiously practised firing with this revolver to perfect her aim.

The D-day arrived. The Senate Hall was decorated lavishly for the convocation ceremony. Jackson had just started delivering his welcoming speech when, suddenly, the interior of the hall reverberated with the sound of gunshots. Unfortunately for Bina, she had been spotted by Vice-Chancellor Hasan Shahid Suhrawardy in the act of taking out the revolver and aiming it at Jackson. Suhrawardy lunged at Bina and tried to disarm her. Bina resisted and while struggling with Suhrawardy, fired five rounds. Jackson was, however, alerted by this time and escaped unhurt, one of the bullets hitting a professor albeit non-fatally.

The power of her pen

Bina was overpowered and arrested. While in custody, Bina wrote a stirring nine-page confession statement. One paragraph of that in particular became such a talking point that the administration ordered it to be censored. We got goosebumps while reading it:

'My object was to die, and if to die, to die nobly fighting against this despotic system of Government, which has kept my country in perpetual subjection to its infinite shame and endless suffering—and fighting in a way which cannot but tell ... I have been thinking—is life worth living in an India so subjected to wrong, and continually groaning under the tyranny of a foreign Government, or is it not better to make one's supreme protest against it by offering one's life away? Would not the immolation of a daughter of India and of a son of England awaken India to the sin of its acquiescence to its continued state of subjection and England to the iniquities of its proceedings?'[5]

A special court convicted Bina Das for attempted murder under section 307 of the Indian Penal Code and sentenced her to nine years of rigorous imprisonment. The university chose not to award her degree.

In 1939, Gandhiji secured the release of all political prisoners across India. As part of that, Bina Das was also released. She became a full-time member of the Indian National Congress and immersed herself in the Quit India Movement. While organizing a protest rally at Kolkata's Hazra Park, she was again arrested and spent the next three years in prison. On Gandhiji's instruction, she was one of the first to arrive in riot-torn Noakhali in 1946.

In subsequent years, Bina Das became a vocal activist for workers' rights; her stints in the Bengal Provincial Assembly (1946–47) and West Bengal Assembly (1947–51) were marked by fiery speeches on the issue. She also earned fame as a writer, regularly contributing to the monthly magazine *Mohini*, run by Kamala Dasgupta, and also penning her autobiography.

In 1948, she married freedom fighter Jatish Chandra Bhaumik. Post Independence, the couple declined the freedom fighters' pension from the Indian government. Increasingly disillusioned with the prevailing political situation, Bina and Jatish Bhaumik quit politics and receded from the public eye. Bina Das's story faded from public memory.[6]

And so it stayed till the start of the second decade of the present century. And perhaps unsurprisingly, the movement to reclaim Bina's story originated in a place that was a major hotspot of the armed revolution in Bengal back in the early 1930s: Chittagong. In late 2011, the Chittagong Parishad, an entity that had its roots in the revolution movement, got in touch with Calcutta University and reminded it about the degrees that were never awarded. One of them was for Bina Das, the other for a girl who etched her name in the highest echelons of sacrifice for the motherland: Chittagong's own Pritilata Waddedar.

A firebrand for freedom

Like Bina, Pritilata Waddedar was also born in 1911, on 5 March at a village called Dhalghat in the Chittagong district of then East Bengal. Unlike Bina, however, there was no immediate nationalistic influence at home. Her father was a government clerk and her mother a simple housewife. For Pritilata, the first inspiration came from a teacher at her school who used to regale the girls with tales of the valour of Rani Lakshmibai of Jhansi, one of the foremost figures of the First War of Independence in 1857.[7]

After completing her matriculation, Pritilata enrolled at Dacca's Eden College where she stood first in the college in the intermediate exam. It was while studying at Eden that she came under the influence of the legendary Leela Nag,[8] joining her organization Deepali Sangha, and imbibing a deep sense of love and duty for the motherland. It was at this point that Pritilata's life crossed with Bina's, as the former moved to Calcutta and enrolled at the Bethune College where Bina had also taken admission. It is not known for sure if the two had met during Bina's brief tenure at Bethune. But if they had, each would have found a kindred spirit in the other.

During her stay in Calcutta, Pritilata proved her mettle. Ramkrishna Biswas was a member of Master Da Surya Sen's group, who had been tasked with the assassination of Inspector General Craig of Chittagong. Unfortunately, the attempt failed and Biswas was arrested and incarcerated in Alipore Jail in Calcutta. His family was of very humble means and could not afford to visit him in Calcutta. On getting to know of this, Pritilata volunteered her services. She regularly visited Biswas in jail and spent time talking with him till his execution in August 1931. To deceive the police, Pritilata pretended to be Biswas's cousin.[9] These meetings left an indelible impact on Pritilata.

Pritilata passed her graduation exams in philosophy with distinction and was due to receive her degree at the same convocation where Bina fired upon Governor Jackson. However, her involvement with anti-government protests hadn't been missed by the authorities and the university refused to award her degree. Pritilata went back to Chittagong and started work as a schoolteacher. Her selfless actions of visiting Biswas in jail had found her an admirer in the man who was an icon and role model for almost all Bengali youth then—Master Da Surya Sen. Soon, Pritilata was asked to meet Master Da and his trusted lieutenant, Nirmal Sen,[10] and was invited to join their unit. When one of the other revolutionaries objected to involving women in the field, Master Da ruled out the objection and ordered that no discrimination should be made against Pritilata, or any other woman, for that matter.

And it didn't take long for Pritilata to prove her worth. The police had somehow traced Master Da to the hideout and, surrounding the house, opened fire with machine guns. The rebels responded in kind with their handguns. Pritilata, who till then had never used a firearm, was soon seen firing a revolver at the police force!

This incident made Pritilata a trusted lieutenant of Master Da and he entrusted her with several important assignments during the legendary attacks on the British establishments in Chittagong. During the last stand at Jalalabad Hills, about which you have read earlier in this book (Chapter 22), Pritilata handled vital logistical responsibilities. Her shining moment would come soon.

While in hiding after the battle, Master Da planned an attack on the Chittagong Pahartali European Club in retaliation for the lives lost at Jalalabad. Master Da had initially considered Kalpana Dutt, Pritilata's schoolmate, to lead the mission. But Dutt was arrested days before the operation while on a reconnaissance of the target, so Master Da decided to pass on the leadership role to Pritilata. It spoke volumes both about Master Da's trust in Pritilata's abilities and about his modern and progressive outlook on life.

In the next few weeks, Pritilata immersed herself in arms training for the attack planned for 24 September 1932. That evening, Pritilata, dressed as a Punjabi man, set out for the European Club with her eight male associates dressed in usual Bengali attire. The attack commenced around 9 p.m. First setting fire to the club building, the revolutionaries stormed inside, firing their revolvers. One English woman was killed and eleven others were injured. One British police officer, who had been enjoying an evening at the club, fired at Pritilata, injuring her. Soon, as reinforcements arrived, the revolutionaries were outnumbered. Pritilata, despite her injury, engaged the police force, and covered her comrades' escape.[11] At last, realizing capture was imminent, she consumed a vial of potassium cyanide and embraced death over arrest. She is believed to be the first female martyr of the revolution.

Justice and degrees at last

In 1947, with Independence came Partition. Chittagong became a part of East Pakistan. The stories of the revolutionaries of former East Bengal slowly became faded memories in India. That's the way it stayed till the Chittagong Parishad raised the matter with Calcutta University in 2011. On learning of the matter, then West Bengal governor, M.K. Narayanan, who was also the chancellor of the university, ordered the verification of records, which showed that the two girls had indeed graduated in 1932 and had been denied their degrees by the British administration.

Finally, on 15 March 2012, an eighty-year-old mistake was rectified as the long-delayed degrees of Bina Das and Pritilata Waddedar were formally awarded by Calcutta University. Obviously, neither was present to receive them. But we would like to believe that somewhere up there, the two firebrands were watching, with contented smiles on their faces.

29

A Courtesan-Turned Spy

There have been many battles of supremacy that have entertained us over the decades. Be it Pelé vs Maradona or Jordan vs LeBron in sports or ilish (hilsa) vs chingri (prawn) or Kolkata biryani vs Lucknowi biryani in food. Though we'd prefer staying mostly neutral, when it comes to biryani, the Awadhi style is our clear favourite.

It's said that Wajid Ali Shah, the last king of Awadh, introduced biryani[1] to the people of Calcutta while he was living in the city from 1856 to 1887. The great thing about legends is, once you start digging deeper about them, you may end up finding stories that are even more interesting.

This is the story of a woman who lived when Wajid Ali Shah was still on the throne of Lucknow. A woman who justified her name and shook the core of the Raj during the First War of Independence. Yet, she remains in the shadows of history.

A world of beauty and culture

During the Nawabi era in Lucknow, the city became an epitome of excellence in classical music and performing arts. And who would entertain the king and his esteemed guests? The courtesans. The nawab's personal passion fuelled this golden age, and courtesans throughout the city enjoyed considerable wealth and influence. Among them was the captivating Azizun Nisa. Her stunning beauty and extraordinary talent in classical singing and dance drew considerable attention.

We have all seen the characters of Umrao Jaan and Chandramukhi in movies and are mesmerized by their beauty and tragic romanticism. But there never has been a biopic or movie based on the character of Azizun Nisa. Why might that be, do you think? Maybe because her story wasn't just about her beauty and tragic love. Maybe because her story was unlike the stereotypical image of courtesans that has been painted in our minds. The word 'Aziz' or 'Azeez', derived from the Arabic word 'azza', meaning 'to be mighty', resonates with power and respect. It's also one of the ninety-nine names of Allah, appearing in the Quran.[2] Azizun Nisa, also known as Azizun Bai, determined to prove her success was self-made, rejected her privileged position and comfortable life in Lucknow and relocated to Kanpur. She would have to rebuild her reputation and establish herself in a new city, starting her own kotha from scratch.[3]

As mentioned in Tripurari Sharma's book *San Sattavan Ka Kissa: Azizun Nisa*, Azizun quickly became a sensation in Kanpur. Lurkee Mahal,[4] the residence of Umrao Begum, which had now become Azizun's kotha, attracted a diverse clientele, from wealthy zamindars to high-ranking British officials. Her stunning beauty, talent in the performing arts and clever wit made her the centre of attention within its exquisite walls. A different kind of drama, one that would transform Azizun Nisa from a renowned courtesan into a brave warrior, was boiling beneath the surface of grandeur and entertainment.

Love forged in a fire storm

The mid-nineteenth century brought the first dawn of change in India. Whispers of rebellion, fuelled by the controversial Enfield rifle cartridges and the recent hanging of Mangal Pandey (Chapter 27), swirled through the crowded bazaars and opulent kothas. The cartridges were rumoured to have been greased using the fat of pigs and cows—hurting the religious sentiments of both Hindus and Muslims.[5] The Kanpur cantonment, when the first sample of these bullets arrived, immediately became a cauldron of unrest. The year was 1857, a year that would etch itself in blood and fire in the annals of Indian history. The British Raj, seemingly invincible, was about to face a challenge unlike any it had encountered before.

Shamsuddin Khan, a sowar (rider) in the Scottish Highlanders Regiment 42nd Cavalry,[6] was a man caught between two worlds. Because of his allegiance to the British Crown, he could live well and enjoy the same pleasures as the English, which Azizun Nisa's kotha provided; at the same time, he was increasingly unhappy with conditions under the British. He first saw her there, amidst the enchanting music and spectacular dances. They bonded straight away, and their mutual admiration quickly developed into a passionate love affair. Khan was drawn to Azizun's zeal and intelligence, while she was captivated by his genuine affection.

However, their romance blossomed in the face of rising political instability. Tantia Tope and Nana Saheb, two powerful individuals, were secretly organizing a resistance movement and mobilizing support for what would become known as the First War of Independence. Khan was drawn more and more into their covert meetings as he sought to reconcile his feelings for Azizun, his duty to his British regiment, and his growing concern over the British presence.

Spy queen and fighter

One evening, a group of British officers arrived at Lurkee Mahal. One of them was very drunk and full of arrogance. He proudly talked about killing an Indian sowar at the regiment, almost as if it were something to brag about.[7] Azizun quietly listened to his cruel words. She was revolted by what he said, and his evident hatred for her people. Her anger grew inside her. It made her determined to protect her beloved Shamsuddin Khan and her motherland.

Azizun first wanted to protect Khan, the love of her life. If his loyalty towards his fellow countrymen was exposed, he would be branded a traitor and would probably end up dead. But soon, she found a bigger purpose. Her kotha, once a place only for music and dance, also became a secret meeting spot where revolutionaries gathered at night to plan against the British. It also became a means of intelligence-gathering: Azizun still entertained British patrons; she listened carefully to their conversations and passed important information to the rebels.

Driven by this newfound purpose, Azizun, with Khan by her side, devised a plan. They followed the officer to his favourite club, and waited outside patiently till he came out. Using her charm and allure, Azizun enticed the officer into a dark, deserted alley. There, waiting in the shadows, was Khan. With a swift, decisive movement, he plunged a dagger into the officer's heart.[8] In that moment, as the officer gasped for his last breath, Azizun Nisa's transformation was complete. She was no longer just a courtesan; she was a revolutionary.

The murder was a turning point. Azizun knew she couldn't stay on the sidelines anymore. She put down her ghungroos and picked up swords and guns. She started learning about warfare. Azizun wasn't there to just watch—it didn't take long for her to earn respect and rise through the ranks of the rebels. Soon, she formed a brigade of women, the Mastani Toli. The brigade was trained in espionage and combat, becoming a strong force over time.

On the night of 1 June 1857,[9] Nana Sahib convened a secret meeting with the top leaders of the rebellion. Among them, standing shoulder to shoulder with the men, was Azizun Nisa. Six days later the Siege of Kanpur had begun.

Azizun was no longer confined to her kotha. She had become a vital cog of the resistance. She skilfully managed espionage operations. Her group collected intelligence and sent it to the rebel leaders. The women in her brigade cared for the wounded and maintained the supply line for the fighters.

Then, tragedy struck. On 23 June, the lifeless body of Shamsuddin Khan was brought to Azizun's doorstep.[10] The sight of her lover, killed in the service of their shared cause, shattered her. As her grief turned to fury, she swore to exact revenge for his death. It is said that, in a fit of righteous rage, she snatched up his weapons and raced into the battlefield.

What happened next is shrouded in legend. One account claims that she was captured by the British, and brought before General Henry Havelock. The general, captivated by her beauty, offered her mercy in exchange for information about Nana Sahib's trusted commander, Azimullah Khan. Azizun, refusing to betray her comrades, was ultimately executed.[11]

Another version of the story, talked about among the people of Kanpur, paints a different picture. They say that Azizun Nisa escaped, disappearing into the chaos of the rebellion. Some claimed to have seen her, riding on horseback, disguised as a man, a gun in her hand and a sword at her side,[12] a symbol of resistance.

It is said that Azizun's role in the First War of Independence became the reason why the Raj merged the brothels with the kothas so that it would suddenly become a forbidden place for civil society, a place the British officials could raid at will, making sure another Azizun was not in the making.[13]

30

Nehru's Queen

On 24 August 2015,[1] at New Delhi's Vigyan Bhavan, Prime Minister Narendra Modi inaugurated the birth centenary celebration of Gaidinliu Pamei and announced the construction of a statue to commemorate her life and contributions. The Prime Minister, in his speech, referred to her as 'Rani Maa' (Queen Mother). However, historical records do not indicate the existence of a queen named Gaidinliu Pamei in Manipur (Gaidinliu Pamei's birthplace). This raises several questions: Why then refer to her as one? Was she a queen from elsewhere? Where was her kingdom? And the most important question of all, why had she remained so unknown?

The key to finding these answers lies in understanding the origins of Gaidinliu's story. Som Kamei's book *Rani Gaidinliu: Legendary Freedom Fighter from the North East* provides a detailed insight of Gaidinliu's life. Her story is inextricably linked to the rise of Haipou Jadonang,[2] the 'messiah' of the Zeliangrong Nagas in Assam, Manipur and Nagaland.

In the ethnic landscape of Northeast India, the Zeliangrongs are a unique ethno-cultural tribe, spread over the area where Nagaland, Manipur and Assam meet. The name 'Zeliangrong' is a combination of the four tribes that share ethnic and linguistic roots—Zemei, Liangmai, and Rongmei and Puimei (Ze+Liang+Rong).[3] Historically, the Zeliangrong territory encompassed a vast mountainous region of some 10,000 square kilometres of richly varied terrain, difficult to access. The Zeliangrong people, treated as insignificant by the ruling

British Raj, started to find their voice through their mystical leader Haipou Jadonang.

A leader and an identity

From a young age, Jadonang was deeply religious. He often visited Bhuvan Cave and Zeilad Lake, which the Nagas saw as holy places. This made him popular among the Zeliangrong people. They believed he had mystical powers given by the gods. In the mountains, where medical care was rare, Jadonang's knowledge of herbal medicine helped many. As word spread about his healing powers, more people came to him for help.

But the mystical 'guru' soon became a rebel against British rule. The British imposed heavy taxes on the Zeliangrong people but did not protect them during the 'Kuki Rebellion' (1917–19). In these hard times, the Zeliangrong people turned to traditional beliefs for comfort. As Christianity began to spread across Naga territory, Jadonang viewed it as a form of foreign imperialism, firmly opposed both and began to advocate for 'Makam Gwangdi'—an independent Naga kingdom.

Jadonang initiated 'Heraka', a socio-religious movement grounded in ancestral Naga traditions known as 'Paupaise'.[4] The movement focused on purity, spiritual renewal and the revival of worship of 'Tingkao Ragwang', their supreme God. Traditionally, Naga faith did not have dedicated temples. However, Jadonang encouraged the building of Heraka temples, called 'Kao Kai'.[5] Gradually, the Heraka movement went beyond just spirituality.

Jadonang strategically employed spirituality to unite the Zeliangrong people against British imperialism. He encouraged them to overcome historical grievances, such as intervillage feuds and communal tensions, and stand united against the colonial oppressors.

Haipou Jadonang openly defied British rule. He dressed like British officials and rode a pony through Zeliangrong lands. S.J. Duncan, the British subdivisional officer, saw this as an insult to

British authority. When Jadonang refused to remove his hat and get off his pony as ordered, he was jailed for a week.[6]

His imprisonment made him even more popular. When he was released, people welcomed him as a hero. With this support, he formed an army called 'Riphen' with 500 men and women to fight British rule. They trained in military tactics, weapon use and survival skills.

A very special girl

Among them was a thirteen-year-old girl who soon became second-in-command. This remarkable individual, tasked with training the Riphen in singing, dancing, secret messaging, enemy troop counting and coded communication,[7] was none other than Gaidinliu Pamei, Jadonang's closest disciple.

You might question how a teenager could become the deputy commander of a rebel army, particularly in a time when Indian society defined gender roles rigidly, and women were often perceived as inferior. While the image of a child leading an army might evoke fictional narratives like Harry Potter, this was a real struggle against the formidable British Raj, a far more potent adversary than any fantastical monster. And there she was, a mere child, instructing adults in combat strategy.

A goddess is born

If legend is to be believed, Gaidinliu's early rise to leadership suggested a destiny foretold, rather than mere coincidence. Zeliangrong society was deeply rooted in folklore, a vital part of their cultural heritage. They strongly believed in myths about their gods, finding solace and hope in these narratives during challenging times. One such legend around Gaidinliu is that, witnessing the suffering of the Zeliangrong people, the god Bisnu (not the Hindu god Vishnu) decided to send his

daughter, the goddess Cherachamdinliu, to alleviate their pain and liberate them from oppression. According to the prophecy, she was destined to be born on 26 January 1915.[8]
It was a Tuesday, the date 26 January 1915. Kaluatlienliu, a woman of Longkao village, experienced a strange dream. Two tall figures stood beside her bed. She woke up in fear, and they disappeared into thin air. Outside, the weather changed suddenly. Thunder and lightning scared the villagers. Many left their work in the fields and went home. But Kaluatlienliu was not afraid. She went into the nearby jungle to collect firewood. When she came back, she went into labour. That day, Gaidinliu was born.

Gaidinliu was believed to have extraordinary abilities. It was said she could communicate with the divine, converse with animals and make accurate predictions.[9]

While Jadonang was aware of Gaidinliu's purported mystical abilities, these alone were insufficient to gain the trust and leadership of the Zeliangrong people. Zeliangrong society had a unique system called the morung[10]—separate dormitories for unmarried boys and girls, where they were educated in the customs, history and social norms of their community, and trained in practical skills such as warfare and craftsmanship. This rigorous system tested the youth through a demanding and challenging environment. Gaidinliu excelled in the morung, earning the deep respect of her elders, and solidifying her position as a respected leader within the Riphen.

By the end of 1930, the Riphen had gained significant influence across Naga territory, alarming British officials. To quell the growing resistance, they arrested Jadonang on 19 February 1931, and imprisoned him in Silchar jail.[11]

J.C. Higgins, the British political agent of Manipur, escalated the situation further. He led a detachment of Assam Rifles to Puiluan,

Jadonang's birthplace, and desecrated the Heraka temples. This act of aggression further inflamed tensions across Naga territory.

Higgins's actions took a cruel turn when he paraded Jadonang, shackled and chained, atop Tamenglong Hill. It was a deliberate attempt to undermine his perceived divine powers and demonstrate British dominance. On 29 August 1931, Jadonang was unjustly hanged on fabricated charges of conspiring to murder four Christian traders from Manipur.

People's leader at seventeen

Jadonang's untimely demise thrust Gaidinliu into the forefront of the resistance. In response to the growing Heraka movement, the British Indian government intensified its oppression, imposing heavier taxes on the villagers. All firearms were confiscated to suppress the rebellion, but as the saying goes, 'Leave one wolf alive and the sheep are never safe.'[12] Gaidinliu boldly declared to her people: 'We are a free people. The white men should not rule over us. We will not pay house tax to the government. We will not obey their unjust laws like forced labour and compulsory porter subscription.'[13]

The British Indian government immediately recognized the escalating threat posed by the socio-religious movement that had morphed into a full-blown political rebellion. In response, they imposed draconian measures: anyone suspected of sympathizing with Gaidinliu faced immediate arrest. Villagers who sheltered her faced crippling fines and impossible tax burdens. To incentivize informants, the government offered substantial rewards for information leading to her capture.

Despite facing severe repercussions, the Naga people stood firmly behind Gaidinliu, recognizing her as their only hope for freedom. A relentless manhunt ensued for the seventeen-year-old rebel across the rugged Naga terrain, but the region was practically a maze. The villages were surrounded by fields, caves, ravines and deep forests. Every house had secret passageways and hiding spots. The villagers gave shelter to Gaidinliu and her followers. They also developed an ingenious system of communication. They used beacons and smoke signals to warn each other about approaching British patrols.

While the government was chasing her shadow, on 18 March 1932,[14] Gaidinliu's army, led by one of her commanders, Heungchang Zemi, launched a surprise attack on the Assam Rifles outpost at Hangrum village in broad daylight. Despite a more powerful enemy, the Riphen's unwavering determination caught the British forces off guard. Both sides suffered losses, but the Riphen strategically withdrew to avoid a massacre.

The British Indian government was struggling to capture a young girl in an area that now spans Manipur, Nagaland and Assam, and her army's continued resistance only frustrated them more. In desperation, they put the area in blackout for days, cutting off all public communications, access and supplies, and burned entire villages. They tortured senior citizens for information. But nothing seemed to work.

In the early winter of 1932, Gaidinliu established a base in Pulomi village, approximately thirty kilometres from Kohima. Pulomi's strategic location and abundant resources made it an ideal headquarters for the Heraka movement. Her loyal followers embarked on an ambitious project. They planned to build a wooden fortress that could house a battalion of 4,000 soldiers. The message was clear: Gaidinliu was not afraid to confront the British Indian Army head-on. However, fate intervened. On 17 October 1932,[15] an Assam Rifles contingent, led by Captain MacDonald, launched a surprise attack on Pulomi village, and Gaidinliu was captured. A watchman was suspected to have revealed her whereabouts, leading to her capture. Her followers killed the watchman to avenge her capture.

The British government exploited this incident, falsely accusing Gaidinliu of abetting murder. This fabricated charge resulted in a life sentence for Gaidinliu, while many of her comrades in the Riphen faced imprisonment or worse.[16]

A queen by worth not birth

When the president of the Indian National Congress, Pandit Jawaharlal Nehru, was touring undivided Assam in 1937, he first heard about the heroism of Gaidinliu. An excerpt from one of his notes said:

> I heard a story which India ought to know and cherish. It was a story of a young woman of their tribe belonging to the Kabui clan in the Naga Hills ... Gaidinliu was her name ... She dreamt of freedom for her people and the ending of all restrictions they suffered from, she raised the banner of independence and called her people to rally around it ... And I thought of Gaidinliu, the Rani, sitting in her prison cell. What thoughts were hers, what regrets, what dreams?[17]

Determined to secure her release, Nehru appealed to Lady Nancy Astor, an influential Conservative member of the British Parliament. However, his repeated pleas were dismissed by the British Indian government. Later that year, Nehru went on to Shillong (the capital of what was then Assam) and finally met Gaidinliu in person in Shillong Jail. She remained imprisoned until India achieved independence. Upon assuming the office of interim Prime Minister, Nehru finally secured her release from Tura Jail.

Upon her release, she continued to work for the upliftment of the Zeliangrong people. However, her movement was strongly opposed by the Naga National Council (NNC) rebels. They were advocating for secessionism while Gaidinliu's vision was focused on creating a separate Zeliangrong territory within the Union of India. The strong backlash forced her to go underground for six long years (1960–66). Finally, after much persuasion, the then deputy commissioner of Kohima, Subodh Chandra Dev, convinced the Rani to come out of hiding and give up the path of violence. She agreed, on condition that the government must arrange a meeting with the then Prime Minister of India, Indira Gandhi, in Delhi.

The chief minister of Nagaland ensured Gaidinliu met Mrs Gandhi in February 1966. By then she had chosen the non-violent, democratic and peaceful route to work for the welfare of her people and convinced her fellow rebels to embrace spirituality for peaceful, collective welfare. The Rani of the hills dedicated her whole life to seeking freedom for the Zeliangrong people, sometimes leaning on mysticism but mostly relying on her grit, determination and strength as a warrior.

31

Kamala, in Her Own Right

In 1893, a twenty-four-year-old Indian lawyer was travelling in South Africa. We all know him. He was Mohandas Karamchand Gandhi. He had a valid ticket for a train ride but was still asked to leave a compartment reserved for white passengers. Racial segregation was brutal and very real there. When he refused, he was thrown out.

That wasn't just another incident. It was a rare and defining moment in history. On that day, Gandhi didn't just witness prejudice—he felt its full weight. And for the first time, it was personal.

Most people know this story. It often marks the beginning of Gandhi's fight against discrimination. But fewer know that decades later, something uncannily similar happened in Louisiana, USA.

In the spring of 1941, an Indian woman got on a train deep in the American South. She was travelling through Louisiana. But this wasn't the Louisiana you hear about—the one with spicy Cajun food, lively music and the colourful Mardi Gras festival. This was a very different Louisiana. It was a place where black and white people were forced to live separate lives. There were strict laws. One of them, called the Separate Car Act, said black and white passengers couldn't sit in the same train compartment. Interested readers may refer to *Plessy v. Ferguson* to understand how the US Supreme Court decision upheld racial segregation and legitimized Jim Crow laws.

What Kamala didn't know was that she had accidentally entered a section meant only for white passengers. When a ticket collector noticed a 'coloured' woman sitting in a compartment reserved for white passengers, he quickly approached her and, in a condescending tone, ordered her to move.

But what followed was nothing short of remarkable.

The woman remained seated. She looked up calmly and asked a simple question: 'Why?'

He replied, 'That's the rule, and you better obey it.'

But she didn't move. He left, fuming, but soon returned. It seemed he had realized she wasn't African American. In a softer tone, he asked, 'Where are you from?'

At this point, she could have revealed her distinguished status. After all, she was Kamaladevi Chattopadhyay, a prominent figure in India's independence movement, a respected advocate for women's rights. On top of that, she was an honoured guest of President Roosevelt at the White House. But instead, she replied firmly: 'It makes no difference. I am a coloured woman, obviously, and it is unnecessary for you to disturb me, for I have no intention of moving from here.' At that moment, Kamaladevi did something radical. She could have dropped names. She could have claimed the safety of her privilege. But she didn't. She chose to stand, by sitting still, in solidarity with those whose everyday reality was shaped by racial injustice. So, why was this woman seated unflinchingly in a segregated train car in 1941, deep in the American South?

Woman with a voice

The answer is worth thinking about. And to understand it fully, we need to know who Kamaladevi really was. In today's world, the name Kamala brings to mind Kamala Harris, the first woman Vice President of the US, or Kamala Khan, Marvel's first Muslim protagonist. But long before them, Kamaladevi was breaking barriers in a world that expected her to stay in the background.

Kamaladevi Chattopadhyay was the first woman in India to contest a legislative seat. It was she who urged Mahatma Gandhi to actively involve women in leading roles within the freedom movement. But there is more to her story.

Kamaladevi was born on 3 April 1903 in Mangaluru, Karnataka. At the age of seven, she lost her father, a tragedy that forced her and her mother to seek refuge with her maternal uncle. Though born of difficult circumstances, this change proved formative. Her uncle was a committed revolutionary, deeply connected with leading figures of the time, including Gopal Krishna Gokhale, Annie Besant and Ramabai Ranade. Watching them, listening to their conversations, and being in their presence lit a spark in young Kamaladevi. It was in those formative years that patriotism and activism began to take shape in her, and kindled her love for swadeshi ideals.

Her mother and grandmother were fiercely independent and outspoken women, and gave a foundation of respect for her intellect and her voice. She was an outstanding student and also studied traditional theatre. All this developed Kamala's strong, independent personality.

She was married off at just fourteen, as was common in the day. At the age of sixteen, she was widowed after two years of marriage. But later, when love came knocking, she wasn't about to turn it away. She fell in love with Harindranath Chattopadhyay, a poet and playwright, and brother of Sarojini Naidu, whom she met when she went to college after being widowed. People fondly called him Harin. If you're from Bengal, you might know him as Sidhu Jyatha, or Uncle Sidhu, from Satyajit Ray's Feluda films. Their love was about to grow into a lifelong bond.

But there was a problem: Kamaladevi was a widow from a Saraswat Brahmin family, where remarriage wasn't just taboo; it was considered sacrilege. Yet both Kamaladevi and Harin were remarkably modern in their outlook. They decided to brush aside the naysayers and boldly choose love over orthodoxy—they married despite familial outrage.

In 1922, Harindranath and Kamaladevi travelled to Europe, where they met Harindranath's elder brother, the formidable and enigmatic

Virendranath Chattopadhyaya. In the underground political circles people knew Virendranath by his pseudonym, Chatto. A towering figure in the Chattopadhyaya family, Viren came across as a tragic soul—a man deeply committed to India's liberation, yet exiled and unable to return home. His conversations left a profound impact on Kamaladevi.

A tragic hero in exile

Virendranath Chattopadhyaya, widely referred to as Chatto, emerged as a prominent leader in taking India's freedom movement to the global stage. Brother of Sarojini Naidu, he studied in England and became active in revolutionary circles, including the India House movement. During World War I, he co-founded the Indian Independence Committee in Berlin, seeking German support against British rule. Later, in Moscow, he worked with the Communist International to promote anti-colonial solidarity. Tragically, he was executed during Stalin's Great Purge. His legacy remains as a bold voice for Indian independence on the global stage.

By then, India was entering a brutal and decisive phase in its struggle for independence. Kamaladevi was not one to be left behind. When Gandhi gave the clarion call for the Non-Cooperation Movement, she returned to join the cause.

In 1926, Kamaladevi had a chance encounter with Margaret E. Cousins, the Irish suffragette and the first woman magistrate in India. Inspired by Cousins' words and ideals, Kamaladevi decided to participate in the political movement and not remain a bystander. Although she narrowly lost the election to the Madras Provincial Legislative Council by just fifty-five votes, her candidacy marked significant new ground for women in politics.

'Magistrate sir, buy our Freedom salt!'

It was in 1930 that Kamaladevi really rose to the occasion. A revolution was brewing; the idea was simple—make salt yourself. It was a simple act of defiance. As people from all walks of life came to join the Salt Satyagraha, Gandhi remained hesitant to include women in direct political action. To women, this exclusion felt unjust, and rightly so.

Kamaladevi decided to address the matter herself. During the Salt March to Dandi, while Gandhi was halting in a village, she approached him directly and voiced her concerns. In her book *Indian Women's Battle for Freedom*, Kamaladevi recounts how she explained to Gandhi that this was a historic opportunity where Indian women could achieve true liberation only if they were treated as equal participants in the movement. Although Gandhi was initially sceptical, he eventually understood Kamaladevi's concerns, recognizing that this was an issue that affected everyone.

Later, Kamaladevi was handpicked by Gandhi to lead a seven-member team to break the salt laws on the sandy beach of Chowpatty, Marine Drive in Bombay. On 6 April 1930, Kamaladevi and her group of women marched with makeshift chulhas (stoves) in hand, as a large crowd gathered to witness the event.

Though the authorities charged them with lathis (bamboo sticks), the women managed to make salt before the gathering was forcibly dispersed. Packets of this symbolic salt were later sold outside the Bombay High Court and even at the Bombay Stock Exchange. In a daring act, Kamaladevi entered the high court herself and shocked a British magistrate by offering to sell him the 'Freedom' brand of salt. Kamaladevi's strong personality, her defiance of social norms and her influence—especially on women—often unsettled those around her. Even Gandhi had mixed feelings about her.

After 1930, Kamaladevi relentlessly fought for women's rights, enduring imprisonment on several occasions. She also travelled extensively, visiting the USA and China. During her visit to Japan, she became quite a celebrity, reportedly receiving up to 100 letters a day from admirers who had only read about her in the newspapers.

Her visit to the US was deeply political. She was initially denied a visa and was eventually allowed to visit only on a temporary visa. During her stay in Washington, Kamaladevi was invited to the White House for tea with President Roosevelt and his wife, Eleanor Roosevelt. There was a great deal of mutual admiration between Kamaladevi and Eleanor for their shared commitment to standing up for what was right.

Making common cause

But her journey to the US wasn't just about seeking support for India's independence. It was something more. For Kamaladevi, the struggles against racial, colonial and gender injustice were all part of a common fight. During her eighteen months in America, she travelled across the country, often choosing to stay with African-American families in the segregated South. This decision was quite extraordinary and risky for the time. However, it caught the attention of the press on both sides of the Atlantic. Nico Slate, in his paper, '"I Am a Coloured Woman": Kamaladevi Chattopadhyaya in the United States', has beautifully explained the profound impact Kamaladevi had during her time in the USA.

African-American newspapers called her 'India's foremost woman leader' and 'Gandhi's aide', recognizing her effort to build connections with black communities. New York papers announced her farewell talk before she headed South, while the *Bombay Chronicle* described her stay with black families as 'daring', given the racial tensions of the time.

She didn't see herself only as an Indian challenging colonial rule. She saw herself as part of a global fight against racial injustice and she truly believed that India's freedom struggle was deeply connected to the civil rights movement of black Americans. By the end of her visit, her actions had planted seeds of solidarity. Kamaladevi's presence and bold support for the black civil rights struggle left a lasting impact. She helped bridge the struggles of two communities fighting different but parallel battles. In 1942, a US survey showed that 87.8 per cent of black Americans supported India's quest for independence. It was quite a remarkable achievement by any standard.

While on Kamaladevi's story in Southern America, let's take a quick detour back home to Faridabad. Around fifty kilometres south of the national capital, Delhi, Faridabad was built by the Mughals as an outpost to protect the capital and the imperial highway from raiders and enemies. Its origins, however, date back to the time of the Mahabharata. The city and its economy fell into decline in the nineteenth and early twentieth centuries.

Independence—a new chapter begins

Shortly after Independence, the national capital was struggling under the immense pressure of a massive influx of refugees. In 1949, during a visit to a refugee camp near Purana Qila, Kamaladevi was shocked by the appalling conditions she witnessed. There was hardly any hygiene. People were living in makeshift tents. Food and other basic supplies were running out. The whole camp felt like a humanitarian disaster.

Kamaladevi wrote to the President and Prime Minister, alerting them to the dire condition of the refugees and proposing a resettlement plan. Faridabad was chosen as the site for their rehabilitation. Under the leadership of Kamaladevi, along with Sudhir Ghosh and Laxmi Chand Jain, a comprehensive plan was drawn up. Funds were mobilized, and remarkably, the execution was carried out by the refugees themselves. In just two to three years, a small city took shape near Old Faridabad. It had roads, houses, schools and bazaars. Everything was built from scratch. Around 25,000 people, mainly from the North West Frontier Province (NWFP), came together to create this little township. It was a brilliant showcase of human ingenuity and resilience.

After Independence, Kamaladevi shifted her focus to shaping India's cultural and economic identity, promoting arts and crafts, developing cottage industries, and revitalizing traditional handicrafts. She played a pivotal role in establishing the All India Handicrafts

Board and served as its chairperson for many years. Her vision and tireless efforts made her a participant in creating some of India's most important cultural and educational institutions: the National School of Drama, Bharatiya Natya Sangha, Lady Irwin College, Sangeet Natak Akademi, the Central Cottage Industries Emporium and the Crafts Council of India. The list goes on.

Her life was anything but ordinary. She remarried after being widowed—a rare thing at the time. She also became the first woman in India to be granted a legal divorce through the courts. She broke norms quietly at every step. She even acted in Kannada films, at a time when being in cinema was considered disgraceful for someone from her elite background. But she didn't let that stop her. She did what she believed in.

Her entire life, in some ways, can be captured in that defining moment in America. By refusing to leave her seat on a segregated train in Louisiana, Kamaladevi risked upsetting the very white Americans who supported India's independence but turned a blind eye to racism at home. She chose courage over comfort. It was a quiet act of defiance that still challenges all of us who often overlook injustice in our own backyard.

32

Behind the Veil

Cross-dressing has long transcended basic clothing across the vast Indian subcontinent. It is a long-standing, spiritually meaningful habit that occasionally arises in times of acute need. The line between male and female has frequently blurred, from the lively, flowing performances of Maharashtra's Lavani dancers, in which male actors represent women's elegance and sensuality, to the Hijra community's age-old customs, in which gender identification is inherently fluid and multifaceted.

But occasionally, the hard facts of life, as well as the fears and superstitions that held on to communities like monsoon mists, have also influenced the practice of cross-dressing. Ironically, though, this same practice—which was formed out of extreme need—became a powerful weapon and a means of defiance that at times altered the trajectory of India's fight for independence.

'Ram with a nose-ring'

Fear and despair might push people to extreme measures in the rural heartlands, where life-and-death cycles were frequently uncertain. Vinayak and Lakshmi[1] were one such couple. They were caught in a vicious circle of grief in one such Maharashtra village where the earthy smell of cow dung blended with the scent of burning incense. Infant mortality had claimed the lives of their first three sons, each small life flickering out like a frail candle. The burden of their previous losses weighed down on them when Lakshmi became pregnant again.

The village priest, a man whose pronouncements carried the weight of ancient wisdom, declared that the deaths were not random. They were the sign of a cosmic imbalance. The fact that their daughter had survived while their sons had perished was a clear indication that a male child bore a curse. The only way to trick fate, to appease the unseen forces, was to raise their next son as a girl.[2]

And so, Ramchandra was born, and the family embarked on a desperate deception. His nose was pierced, a delicate nose-ring was placed, and he was dressed in girls' clothing. He became Nathuram, 'Ram with a nose-ring', a boy forced to live a lie. The cross-dressing was not a performance, not a ritual, but a shield, a desperate attempt to protect a child from an unseen enemy.

As far as fate goes, Nathuram did live to win the war against destiny and became the infamous assassin Nathuram Godse.

Cross-dressing to cross enemy lines

However, not all necessity leads to an infamous history such as this. While some shaped the nation's future in the most controversial way, some risked their lives to snatch freedom from the enemy by infiltrating its fortress.

Consider the story of Saraswathi Rajamani, born into a world of wealth and privilege in Rangoon (present day Myanmar). In this case, cross-dressing was a tool of defiance and a means to an aim, rather than a desperate act of survival. Rajamani's family was a strong supporter of Indian nationalism, and revolutionaries found refuge in their house. Her childhood was steeped in the language of resistance, her spirit forged in the fires of patriotism.

In 1937, Gandhi paid a visit to her family mansion, where he saw a young Rajamani busy polishing her shooting skills with a rifle. The ten-year-old girl appeared to be already certain that shooting the British down was the only way to oppose them, even though Gandhi tried his best to persuade her with his philosophy of non-violence.

'Violence is not the answer, little girl. We are fighting the British through non-violent ways. You should also do that,' Gandhi urged.

'We shoot and kill looters, don't we? The British are looting India, and I am going to shoot at least one British person when I grow up,' replied the determined child.[3]

Their brief conversation, documented in Harsha Sharma's book *Raw Secret Agents: Thrilling Stories of Intelligence Operations by Indian Spies,* paints Rajamani's fierce character from even the early days of childhood.

During World War II, Subhas Chandra Bose came to Rangoon to raise money and recruit volunteers for the Indian National Army (INA). He urged everyone to unite and fight the British. His words deeply inspired Rajamani, now a teenager. She saw in him a leader who shared her belief in action. She donated all her jewellery and was ready to risk everything for the cause. Bose recognized her dedication and gave her the name 'Saraswathi'.

In 1943, Bose started the Rani Lakshmibai regiment[6] of the INA, where, at the tender age of sixteen, Saraswathi Rajamani became the youngest spy[7] of the Indian freedom struggle. She seemed to have found her purpose in life, as she moved, seen but unnoticed, in broad daylight through the British camps. Her ability to transform herself, to slip into the guise of a young boy, was crucial to her mission. This cross-dressing was not a performance, but a strategic manoeuvre. It was a way to gain access to information that could change the course of the war. It was hard for a young girl in pre-Independence India to dress as a boy. The idea itself was shocking.

Trolled to death for cross-dressing

Let's be honest. Even though cross-dressing has been part of Indian culture, it has always been the target of stigma and bullying. Society does not fully accept it. Not so long ago, in 2023, a sixteen-year-old boy from Ujjain, Madhya Pradesh, reportedly died by suicide. He used to create and share makeup and beauty content on social media. During Diwali, he posted a reel on Instagram, wearing a saree. The reel received so many hate comments that it may have pushed him to take such a drastic step. Cross-dressing is still a major taboo in India.

Her first assignment was to cross-dress as a sweeper boy and enter a British camp, along with a few other comrades of her ilk. She used to wash the clothes of the British soldiers and polish their shoes and sweep the grounds, and while doing so, collect critical information by overhearing their conversation. Thus, in the midst of World War II, she sent valuable information from the British camp to Bose who, in turn, gave the information to the Japanese army.

Army men who were women

Cross-dressing as a wartime tactic is a fascinating subject. It has been used in different eras for various purposes. For example, Maria Quitéria fought in the Brazilian War of Independence while dressed as a man. Frieda Belinfante was a talented musician and Dutch Resistance fighter during World War II. She disguised herself as a man for months to escape the Nazis. Then there was the legendary French spy Chevalière d'Éon, who fought in the Seven Years' War as a man and later infiltrated the Russian royal court dressed as a woman.

Another obscure story is that of Hannah Snell, who travelled to India in the eighteenth century dressed as a man. Her life was tragic. Her husband, a British soldier, abandoned her while she was pregnant. After her baby died in infancy, she joined the British army posing as a male to search for him. She was later sent to India, where she fought in two wars—one in Pondicherry and another in Theevukottai—while disguised as a man. She was injured multiple times and even operated on herself to keep her identity hidden.

Hannah's story has been largely forgotten. But in the wild world of cross-dressing spies and soldiers, another name was added—Saraswathi.

Dangerous rescue: Valour has no gender

Things soon took a dangerous turn. Saraswathi's comrade and fellow spy, Durga, was caught and imprisoned by the British. Saraswathi had to make a tough choice: escape to save herself or risk everything for Durga. She chose to stay. Durga, her sister in arms, was in peril, and Saraswathi would move heaven and earth to free her.

Discarding her usual guise of a young sweeper boy, Saraswathi embraced a new persona: a young dancer.[8] The transformation was complete. Despite her internal turmoil, she walked around the soldiers in the camp with a calm assurance.

Saraswathi acted after noticing a momentary weakness in the prison's security. She drugged the British officer in charge of her comrade's cell and deftly picked the lock. Their retreat was a blur of panic and adrenaline. They were racing through the prison's maze-like passageways when a British officer noticed them. The tense silence was broken by the piercing sound of bullets as shots rang out. Saraswathi felt a sharp pain in her leg that nearly knocked her to her knees. But she refused to give up.

Despite the agonizing wound, they escaped into the nearby forest. The thick trees offered some shelter. To hide from the British forces, they climbed a huge tree and remained atop it for three agonizing days. Their bodies were sore, and they felt weak from hunger and thirst. The heat was intense during the day, and the nights were cold. But they didn't despair. When they had the chance, they went to a nearby village. There, they got on a bus for a dangerous 700-kilometre journey back to Rangoon.[9] The bullet injury left Saraswathi with a permanent limp.

Saraswathi's extraordinary courage and resilience to rescue her comrade in the face of danger was a symbol of the indomitable spirit of the Indian freedom fighters, irrespective of their gender. Surprisingly though, despite her valour at such a young age, her story remains largely untold. A person's attire often declares their gender or religious identity. Sadly, even though years of evolution went into the making of modern society, we often forget that beneath the attire lies a human, capable of unimaginable things.

33

The Fake Wife

If you walk just a few minutes from Shinjuku Station in Tokyo, you will find a Western-style building tucked into a narrow alley. This is Nakamuraya, a small but historic Japanese eatery. Established in 1909, it has grown into a chain of over twenty restaurants and bakeries. Among its many offerings, one dish stands out: a Bengali-style spicy chicken curry called 'Indo Karii'. Served in an elegant sauce boat with rice, this dish has an unusual place in Japanese cuisine.

Its origins trace back to an unexpected source—the Indian revolutionary Rash Behari Bose. In the early 1900s, Bose was on the run from British authorities. He found refuge in Tokyo, thanks to Aizō Sōma, the owner of Nakamuraya. Sōma was not just a businessman but a man of deep convictions, sympathetic to the cause of Indian independence. When Aizō Sōma gave shelter to Rash Behari Bose, Bose taught the Soma family the recipe for this Indian chicken dish, which they began serving in their food joint. The dish gradually became extremely popular.

When we visited Tokyo, we were determined to try this dish. We took the Fukutoshin Line local train from Tokyo's Shibuya Station for a short ride to Shinjuku-sanchōme Station. Upon arrival, we followed the signs towards the Shinjuku District Gate, and within five minutes, we reached the striking Nakamuraya building, which is now a commercial complex. Our destination was Manna Restaurant, located on the second basement floor of this flagship store.

This is the very place where Rash Behari Bose introduced and popularized the '*Jun Indo Karii*' (pure Indian curry)—a dish markedly different from the British-style curry that was more common in Japan at the time. Today, the restaurant is one of Tokyo's most beloved curry houses, catering primarily to a Japanese clientele. And now, we were about to witness that history firsthand.

There was a queue when we arrived, so we added our names to the waiting list. After about a twenty-minute wait, we were called in and shown our seats. The walls were adorned with framed photos capturing moments from the restaurant's rich history. The establishment is run entirely by Japanese staff. We managed to strike up a conversation with the floor manager, mentioning that we were from West Bengal in India—the same region Rash Behari Bose hailed from. He nodded in recognition, acknowledging that Bose was indeed from Bengal, and kindly allowed us to take photographs inside the restaurant.

We ordered the signature chicken curry and a seafood curry to excite our taste buds. Served with Japanese-style sticky white rice, and cucumber and leek pickles, the curry clearly reflected Japanese culinary influences. Yet, thanks to the use of authentic Indian spices, it retained its Indian essence. The result was a refined, unique curry that gracefully bridges the cultural and culinary divide between Japan and India.

A runaway takes refuge and finds love

Over time, Bose became part of Sōma's family, marrying his daughter, Toshiko, in 1918. Kokkō Sōma, his Japanese mother-in-law, became his protector, his family, his shield. Along with her husband, she ran a modest bakery in Tokyo that doubled as a sanctuary for artists, rebels ... and one runaway revolutionary from India. Two weeks after Bose arrived at their home, hiding from the British, Kokkō Sōma lost her infant son. But even in the midst of that grief, she didn't turn him away. She stood by him. A grieving mother still found the strength to protect a stranger hunted by an empire.

We keep thinking—would any of us have made the same choice if we were in her shoes? That's the kind of revolution that humbles us.

Toshiko, on the other hand, was not just his wife but also his translator, confidante and strongest support in exile. Their marriage eventually led to Bose gaining Japanese citizenship in 1923. The couple had two children, but their happiness was short-lived. Toshiko passed away from pneumonia just seven years after their wedding.

In Shinjuku's Manna Restaurant (Nakamuraya chain), Rash Behari Bose's legacy is on display everywhere—on the walls, all over the menu selection, and in the famed Indo-Karii he took from India to Tokyo.

This story is well known. A famous photograph of Bose with Toshiko, possibly taken in a studio, captures a moment of their shared life. But there was another woman in Rash Behari Bose's life, a woman whose story remains largely forgotten. She was his wife for just fifteen days. Not in reality—but in disguise. Her sacrifice was as brave as any act of armed resistance.

Disguises and deceptions

Not many people know that Rash Behari Bose played a crucial role in founding the Indian National Army (INA). From a young age, he was drawn to the revolutionary movement and joined Anushilan Samiti (Chapter 15), an organization preparing for an armed uprising under his leadership.

The story begins in December 1912, just two days before Christmas. Chandni Chowk in Old Delhi was alive with celebrations as the British marked the transfer of India's capital from Calcutta to Delhi. Lord Hardinge, the viceroy, rode through the streets in a grand procession, sitting on a decorated elephant, until an explosion shattered the moment.

A bomb was thrown at Hardinge (Chapter 20). Although he survived, it sent shockwaves through British rule in India. A massive manhunt began, but the mastermind had already vanished.

Bose was a master of deception. That same night, he quietly slipped away to Dehradun, and by the next morning, he was leading a public march condemning the attack. His performance was so convincing that even locals believed he was loyal to the British. For the next two years, he stayed one step ahead of the police, constantly changing his appearance while continuing his revolutionary work.

He was also a master of disguise. Historian Uma Mukherjee tells a story of him hiding in Chandernagore, where he disguised himself so convincingly as a Brahmin that a British spy, sent to arrest him, actually bowed down and touched his feet in reverence. But this story isn't just about Rash Behari Bose. It's about a woman—a woman who has been nearly erased from history.

In 1915, Rash Behari Bose was deeply engaged in planning a major armed revolt against British rule in India, part of the Ghadar Rebellion (Chapter 19). As the mastermind behind this effort, he needed a safe base in Lahore to organize his activities. However, there was one significant problem: the British police had given strict orders—no house could be rented to a bachelor. Since Bose was unmarried, he found himself unable to secure accommodation, which would have jeopardized his operations.

It was then that a young woman named Yamuna stepped forward to help. She was the wife of Ramswaroop Shukul (Ramswaroop Das based on some other accounts), one of Bose's trusted associates. There is very limited historical information about her, but we believe it's important to shed light on her story, especially in an era when women's capabilities and character were often judged harshly and unfairly. Even now, decades after Independence, many women continue to face this kind of scrutiny, and Yamuna's story offers a necessary counterpoint to that narrative.

The lady who became a disguise

The primary source we have about Yamuna comes from Narayan Sanyal's book, *Ami Rashbehari ke Dekhechhi* (I Have Seen Rash Behari). This anthology of witnesses who closely worked with Rash Behari blends historical research with necessary creative liberties to dramatize the storytelling. The book is a work of creative nonfiction, drawing on Sanyal's extensive research and conversations with credible sources. Sanyal makes it clear that the characters in the book are real, and the events are historically accurate.

According to Yamuna's account in the book, she was the daughter of an Indian who had married a French woman. Tragically, her mother passed away during childbirth. When Yamuna grew up, she married Ramswaroop, a telegraph official in Amritsar, who eventually became a close associate of Rash Behari Bose. There are several versions of this story, but here we follow Sanyal's account. However, neither Yamuna nor Ramswaroop's names are real. In Sanyal's book, the identities have been deliberately concealed for anonymity, as the witness did not want to reveal her real name for fear of damaging her family's reputation.

This was the time when the Ghadar Party—a group of revolutionaries mostly from Punjab and largely living in the Americas—was planning their uprising against the British. The revolutionaries were determined to overthrow British rule, inspired by the events of the First War of Independence, the Great Rebellion of 1857. However, there was no clear or unified plan for what would happen once they returned home. Rash Behari Bose emerged as one of the key leaders of the movement (his Lahore conspiracy was part of it, as was the Benares one), and 21 February 1915 was chosen as the day the widespread rebellion would begin (Chapters 20 and 23).

Vishnu Ganesh Pingle, a very close associate of Bose, a key member of the Ghadar Party and one of the main coordinators of the revolution, was working closely with Bose to drive the vast plan alongside the Ghadarites, the Bengal revolutionaries and other revolutionaries spread across different cities in India. In the late hours of a January night, Pingle arrived at Yamuna and Ramswaroop's home in Amritsar. Bose was also present. They had been discussing Bose's need for a safe house in Lahore. Pingle came with frustrating news—no house could be rented to an unmarried man without the British police's approval, a barrier that seemed impossible to bypass.

Up until this point, Yamuna had been a quiet participant in the movement, helping to arrange meetings, offering shelter and preparing meals for the group. But when the situation grew more dire, she realized she was the only one who could solve their problem. She found herself in a position where she had to make a choice. And without hesitation, she made it.

Yamuna offered to pose as Rash Behari Bose's wife. Pingle and Bose were initially taken aback, but her husband, Ramswaroop, reassured them that if she was willing, it was the right course of action. She quickly packed her belongings, gathered household essentials, and prepared herself to take on this new role. This act of deception was crucial in allowing Bose to rent a house and continue his underground activities without attracting suspicion. Tirtha Mandal, in his book *The Women Revolutionaries of Bengal, 1905–1939,* mentions, 'A house was then taken at Lahore where Rash Behari and Yamuna started staying as "husband and wife", and thus Rash Behari got the opportunity to organize his plan.'

From 4 to 19 February 1915, for fifteen days, they shared one room and one bed but lived as husband and wife in name only. At the time, the social implications for a woman in Yamuna's position were enormous. A woman's reputation could easily be ruined by even the slightest hint of impropriety, and yet, she carried out this brave act to serve a cause much bigger than herself.

Revolutionary living on the edge

The idea of living together outside of marriage might seem like a modern choice today, but in the early twentieth century, it was practically unheard of. In some ways, Yamuna's decision to take on this role was as revolutionary as the uprising itself. Even now, in many parts of India, the very concept of cohabitation without marriage is seen as a direct challenge to social norms, and relationships that don't conform to traditional expectations still provoke judgment in most quarters. Yamuna's situation was even more complex—she wasn't just choosing an unconventional living arrangement; she was a married woman, taking on the identity of another man's wife in a time when a woman's honour and reputation were everything.

Unfortunately, the secret didn't remain hidden for long. After fifteen days of Yamuna's living as the fake wife of one of India's greatest freedom fighters, the British police got wind of the plot. A betrayal within the ranks led to the movement's downfall. By the time the revolt was supposed to begin, many of the revolutionaries were either arrested or disarmed, and the British were able to prevent the uprising before it gained momentum. Rash Behari Bose managed to plot his escape as he did several times, but Yamuna was not so fortunate. She was arrested and taken to Lahore jail.

Others who were caught were tried in the First Lahore Conspiracy Trial. Many revolutionaries, including Vishnu Ganesh Pingle, were executed, while others, including Yamuna's husband, received life sentences. Rash Behari Bose's clever disguise as a relative of the famous poet Rabindranath Tagore allowed him to secure a spot on a Tokyo-bound ship from Calcutta. He sailed away from his beloved motherland and spent the rest of his life in Japan, where he passed away peacefully in 1945.

But what happened to Yamuna was beyond imagination.

No good deed goes unpunished

After she was arrested, for three long days, Yamuna was interrogated relentlessly. But despite the pressure, she refused to betray the movement or reveal any names. The authorities, frustrated by her silence, transferred her to the barracks of the Baluch Regiment. What followed was a horrific chapter in the history of India's struggle for freedom.

Yamuna was subjected to brutal and unimaginable torture. As Y.D. Phadke noted in *Women in India's Freedom Struggle*, she was mercilessly gang-raped by soldiers of the Baluch Regiment for harbouring an absconder. After several days of this unthinkable cruelty, she was left unconscious and abandoned by the roadside. She survived, but had paid a horrific price.

We also examined the 582-page report of the Lahore Conspiracy Trial, and unsurprisingly, there is no mention of anyone like Yamuna—she was never formally charged. However, the other details in the report align closely with Narayan Sanyal's account, lending credibility to his research and the broader narrative. Sanyal had documented further aspects of her life, but he himself acknowledged that some characters in those narratives were fictional. Keeping this in mind, we have omitted those elements and retained only the parts from his book that he confirmed as historically accurate.

We may never know her real name, but she could have been anyone around us, which is why her story is so important. It represents the countless unsung women who have gone unrecognized, but whose sacrifices shaped the course of history.

007
CHICAGO RADIO
VOTE FOR GHOSE
The
Travellers

34

A Restaurant by Times Square

It's easy to feel starstruck as dazzling neon billboards and majestic skyscrapers overlook the skyline in Times Square. The colours are vivid. The displays are bold. It is a lot to take in at once. Our base in New York City was in Flushing, Queens. Yes, the same Flushing known for Flushing Meadows, where the US Open is held. We took a nearly one-hour train ride to Times Square. But we didn't go for those giant billboards. We were headed uptown to 49th Street, following Jatinder Guha's notes in his guidebook. Our destination was an Indian restaurant. Back in 1939, a fifteen-minute walk from Grand Central took him to a now-forgotten Indian restaurant.

An article from the Berkeley Daily Gazette in 1934 by James Aswell described a restaurant named Ceylon India Inn as an 'unpretentious walk-up eatery' that served fiery Indian curry to its customers. Among its regulars was Rudolph Valentino, aka the 'Latin Lover', a popular actor of the 1920s, who used to frequent the joint until his untimely death in 1926.[1] A humble walk-up, perhaps Manhattan's first curry haven, a flicker of the East in the Roaring Twenties, the eatery is lost in the bright clamour of present-day New York.

It was an interesting time. Many immigrants came from Europe, especially Italians, Irish, Jews and Eastern Europeans. Ellis Island was a bustling gateway, and immigrant communities shaped neighbourhoods like Little Italy, the Lower East Side and Harlem. Harlem also became the home to people from the Indian community. Many hailed from regions of Bengal that have now become part of

226

modern-day Bangladesh. For a lot of these early immigrants, the Ceylon Inn became a cherished spot, offering not only good food but also providing a welcoming space for mingling and community.

It was in the same Ceylon India Inn that an early version of the Indian national flag was unveiled by Indian nationalists in 1930.

Dancer turns restaurateur

Let's start at the beginning. The story of Ceylon Inn starts with a man named K. Yaman Kira, a native of Kandy in modern-day Sri Lanka. Kira was a performer of one of Sri Lanka's most revered traditions, the Kandyan Dance[2]—also known as Udarata Natum. Rooted in rituals often associated with the supernatural, this dance form is typically performed by male dancers and is celebrated for its vibrant cultural significance. Kira is believed to have toured the Americas during the early twentieth century, coinciding with the first wave of South Asian migration to the region. His journey reflects a cultural bridge between Sri Lanka's artistic heritage and the burgeoning South Asian diaspora arriving on American shores.

Kira supposedly stayed back after his second tour in 1909 and, in 1913, he married a German immigrant, Elizabeth Eckhard. Perhaps it was Elizabeth who gave Kira the idea to give up dancing and touring, and settle down and open a restaurant. According to historian Vivek Bald, the first couple of Indian restaurants to come up were near Eighth Avenue—Ceylon Restaurant on Eighth Avenue and 42nd Street, and the Taj Mahal Hindu Restaurant on 43rd Street between Ninth and Tenth Avenues. Ceylon Inn was perhaps the first and most recognized at the time, opening its doors wide open to Americans and South Asians alike. While Americans were getting their first taste of curry, sailors from Ceylon and India, who were commonly called lascars, found safe harbour in Ceylon Inn under Kira's watchful eye.

Helen Josephy and Mary Margaret McBride, in their 1931 book *New York Is Everybody's Town*, provide a vivid description of the eatery. They write:

The Ceylon India Inn, 148 West 49th Street, has curry as good as curry ever is, murals of Hindu figures, ladies riding on elephants, and Nautch dancers. The owner, with a little pigtail done up in a bun behind, greets guests. On Sunday nights, all kinds of turbanned yogis and devotees of other Oriental cults gather here for dinner.

Serving curry spiced with revolution

The year Kira opened his restaurant in New York City, a revolutionary flame was igniting on the West Coast in sunny California. It was here that the Ghadar Party was established, with the mission of liberating India from colonial rule. Central to their movement was a weekly publication, also called *Ghadar*, which spread their message of resistance and called for courageous individuals to join the fight for freedom. Through fiery rhetoric in print and bold organizing, the Ghadarites sought to inspire a global struggle against British imperialism.

The paper's masthead declared its aim 'to stir up rebellion in India. Pay—death; Price—martyrdom; Pension—liberty; Field of battle—India'.

The reason for the uprising was a series of events. Between 1903 and 1913, approximately 10,000 South Asians emigrated to North America, seeking better economic opportunities. However, this migration wave faced severe backlash as Canada began implementing stringent anti-immigration policies aimed at restricting Asian immigrants.[3]

Meanwhile, back in New York, the Kiras, known for their remarkable tolerance—some might say to a fault—welcomed a diverse mix of patrons to their restaurant, many among whom were young radical Indian students and revolutionaries. These individuals, however, often steered clear of the fiery Sinhalese pepper steak, a house favourite and popular among American customers. After the Hindu–German conspiracy trial in 1917 which led to the convictions of twenty-nine people, including fourteen Indian nationalists, the remaining Ghadarites were scattered. Ceylon Inn by then, in the 1920s to the '40s, had become a hotbed of anti-colonial activities. Secret meetings were held and strategies were discussed, though how many saw the light of day is debatable.

By the mid and late 1930s a few more restaurants had also opened up in the neighbourhood—the Bengal Tiger on 336 West 58th Street and the East India Curry Shop on 117 East 60th Street just to name a couple. The Ceylon Inn, however, hosted the inaugural banquet of the New York branch of the India League of America. By now the eatery had moved into a new address on 148 West 49th Street. The India League of America would play a small but significant role in US–India ties in the years to come, steered by a man named Jagjit (J.J.) Singh. Singh, a native of Rawalpindi (now in Pakistan), had come to the United States in the 1920s and found financial success in a set of import businesses in NYC.

> ### Plots and stratagems over a meal
>
> There are many instances where Indian freedom fighters gathered at eateries to discuss strategy. Kyani & Co., the vintage Irani café in Mumbai's Dhobi Talao, was a hub for freedom fighters and journalists. They often held meetings there. Dadar's Pritam Punjab Hindu Hotel had a similar story. In Kolkata, Paramount, a famous sherbet shop, also served as a meeting place for freedom fighters. The shop's founder, Nihar Ranjan Majumdar, was a freedom fighter himself. Netaji was a regular visitor. The list is long and quite fascinating.

Raja Mahendra Pratap, a prominent freedom fighter, noted the role of the lively eatery in his autobiography *My Life History of Fifty-Five Years*. He wrote: 'The Ceylon India Inn proved to be the best meeting ground. It was an Indian restaurant run by a Ceylonese gentleman who had a German wife. Here, I met several

Indian friends.' He frequented the restaurant several times for dinner and meetings during his stay in the USA.

Well-balanced flavours in political statements

On 15 November 1943, several American intellectuals and Indian nationals from the India League of America gathered at the Ceylon India Inn. They were there for a dinner and meeting to celebrate Jawaharlal Nehru's fifty-fourth birthday. During the gathering, a resolution was passed demanding the release of Nehru, Mahatma Gandhi and other prominent leaders. As mentioned by Jagat S. Bright in his book *Jawaharlal Nehru: A Biographical Study*, the resolution demanded:

> That the British Government in India be asked to immediately release Jawaharlal Nehru, one of the greatest champions of democracy and a crusader against fascism, totalitarianism, and imperialism ... That along with Nehru, other popular leaders including Mahatma Gandhi, should be released so that their services may be utilized in famine-relief work.

As World War II paralysed much of Europe and the Pacific, the India League of America (ILA) contended that Britain's refusal to set a clear timeline for Indian independence not only undermined India and its freedom movement but also weakened the Allied war effort. This indecision, they argued, hindered the ability to rally colonized Asian populations against Japanese aggression, thereby impairing the broader strategy of mobilization in the fight against the Axis powers.

The ILA were well known for their critical views of the British and the US government at the time. Singh, who rose to prominence and became a widely recognized figure in political circles, was instrumental in the passage of the Luce–Celler Act of 1946.[4] The act allowed a limited number of immigrants from India and the Philippines to enter the United States and become naturalized citizens. Though the legislation was introduced by Republican

Clare Boothe Luce and Democrat Emanuel Celler, Gandhi credited Singh for his instrumental role in lobbying for the act's passage. This landmark law not only signalled a breakthrough for Indian immigrants in the United States but also marked the beginning of a new chapter in US–India relations.

Fading glory

By the 1940s, many events and activities connected to the Indian freedom movement had shifted to the Rajah, a popular establishment on 48th Street, just west of Broadway. The Rajah became a cultural and political hub, offering a taste of home with its Calcutta Club Dinner priced at $2.25. The menu featured enticing dishes like Moorgi Curry, Unda Curry and Bengal Loochi, delighting patrons with flavours reminiscent of Calcutta. Ceylon Inn appeared to have endured, though perhaps less so, as a hub of political activity. Its role as a meeting point for revolutionaries and intellectuals seemed to wane over time, shifting focus to its culinary appeal. The Kiras supposedly sold the place to a Bengali restaurateur in the 1950s and retired to Long Island.

148 West 49th Street, New York City—within walking distance of Times Square, once home to the Ceylon India Inn, a gathering spot for prominent revolutionary minds. The inn no longer exists; it was later an Indian restaurant 'Curry India' and now houses a Vietnamese eatery. (Photo courtesy: Tanuka Ghoshal)

It took us only a few minutes to reach 148 West 49th Street from Times Square. The signboard on the first floor now says 'Curry India' (now replaced by a Vietnamese restaurant). The Ceylon India Inn is long gone. So are the people who had once gathered here, sharing spicy curry and dreams of a free nation. The new restaurant is permanently closed and is now looking to rent out the place. However, the signboard still says, 'Oldest Indian Restaurant in USA'.

35

The Lamentable Goose

A lamentable goose might not seem to mean much at first. It's a strange, rather silly phrase, and when we first read it, we thought so too. This came from the book *Bandobast and Khabar: Reminiscences of India* by Colonel Cuthbert Larking. The author was touring Benares around 1886–87 with his companion, Raja Sivaprasad, an Indian scholar, linguist and historian. Larking described Raja Sivaprasad as a great admirer of the British government and a staunch conservative. He also had a tendency to look down upon young, educated Indians, particularly disliking Bengali babus and intellectuals. In a light-hearted moment, the author made a joke, calling an intellectual from Bengal named Lalmohan Ghose the 'lamentable goose'. It was old-fashioned schoolboy humour that amused Raja, as he apparently didn't like the person either. What was interesting, however, was that Lalmohan Ghose, the so-called 'lamentable goose', actually ran in a general election in England. Given the recent electoral context in England, this was quite fascinating.

The political landscape of Britain in 2022 was nothing short of tumultuous. The country saw three Prime Ministers in one year. Each resignation shocked the political system. During this time, one person gained global attention: Rishi Sunak. His election to 10 Downing Street made waves in India. People celebrated with pride. News channels, social media, and public discussions buzzed with excitement. Sunak's win was more than just a political event. It was a symbol of history, representation and retribution.

However, Rishi Sunak was definitely not the first Indian to run in a British election. Over a century before him, an Indian did the unthinkable. His name was Lalmohan Ghose. This is the story of a man who, while India was still under British rule, dared to enter the empire's political system—and he almost made it.

Discovering democracy and hypocrisy

The year was 1885. Deptford was a small but busy industrial town located in southeast London. One day, an Indian lawyer began a bold political campaign in the town. Lalmohan Ghose became the first Indian to run for a seat in the British Parliament. His campaign made waves. His banner, 'Vote for Ghose!' was everywhere. It was a remarkable achievement at a time when India was under British rule. Just to put it in context, Indians had little to no political power, even in their own country. Ghose's decision to contest the election in England was a direct challenge to the very system that kept Indians out of governance.

Lalmohan Ghose was born in 1849 in Krishnanagar, Bengal, to an intellectual family. From a young age, he understood the importance of justice and advocacy. He chose a career in law, following his brother. Ghose became one of the first Indians to qualify as a barrister in England. He strongly believed that India's progress depended on education, empowerment and active political participation.

In 1869, when he was just twenty, Ghose set sail for England to study law. In London, he was gradually drawn into the city's lively political scene. The structured legal system appealed to him. The heated parliamentary debates and, above all, the strong democratic institutions fascinated young Ghose. Like many reformers of his time, he saw Western education as an important tool for India's progress and future self-rule.

However, his time in England also exposed him to the deep dichotomies of the British Empire. He noticed how Britain took great pride in democracy, freedom and justice for its own people, albeit for men; women in Britain had no vote. At the same time, it denied these same rights to millions of Indians living under its rule. He was especially disturbed by the severe lack of education for Indians and strongly argued for a comprehensive national policy to provide primary education for all.

To Ghose, an informed and educated populace was not merely a necessity—it was an inalienable right and the very foundation of self-rule.

Chosen to fight from within

While Ghose was establishing himself as a prominent barrister in England, back in India, the Indian Association—one of the earliest political organizations advocating for Indian rights—was seeking ways to push for greater representation in British governance. They needed a voice in the British Parliament, someone who could articulate India's struggles and aspirations on an international stage.

Lalmohan Ghose emerged as the ideal candidate for this historic mission.

His oratory skills were exceptional, and his speeches resonated deeply with audiences. His fluency in English and mastery of political rhetoric earned him admiration, even among the British elite. John Bright, the esteemed Liberal British statesman, was left in awe after witnessing Lalmohan Ghose speak at Willis's Rooms on 23 July 1879. In his diary, he recorded:

> 3 o'clock, to Willis's Rooms, a crowded meeting, of which I was Chairman. Lalmohun Ghose spoke for an hour—admirably. I think no Englishman could have spoken better in language, matter, clearness and beauty of expression or force.

For Bright, this was no ordinary speech. The eloquence of his Calcutta friend, as he affectionately called him, along with his precision and force of argument, shattered colonial prejudices, proving that an Indian could match—if not surpass—Britain's finest orators.

His growing reputation eventually caught the attention of the Liberal Party, which recognized his potential and nominated him as their candidate for the 1885 general election from the Deptford constituency.

This moment was unprecedented in British electoral history. For the first time, an Indian was running for a seat in Parliament. The Indian diaspora in Britain was elated. For the first time, it seemed possible that their voices might be represented in the corridors of power.

Disappointed, yet determined

Despite running a formidable campaign, Ghose confronted the harsh realities of British electoral politics. Though he secured an impressive 47.5 per cent of the vote, he narrowly lost to the Conservative candidate, William John Evelyn, by a margin of just 367 votes. It was a bitter defeat, but Ghose refused to be deterred.

Determined to give it another shot, he ran for election again in 1886. This time, his campaign gained even more momentum. Deptford was buzzing with energy. Banners waved in the streets once again, and crowds at rallies grew bigger every day. On election day, Ghose rode through the city in a carriage with his daughter. Supporters cheered as they passed by. The excitement in the air was impossible to miss.

But once again, luck was not on his side. The Liberal factions were divided. The split in votes hurt his chances significantly. His opponent, William John Evelyn, won again—this time with a slightly bigger lead of 627 votes.

Sketches from the day

Thanks to Caroline Derry's beautiful blog on Deptford, we found a lovely engraving in the archive of Bridgeman Images. The illustrations were created by an anonymous artist for

> *The Graphic*, 10 July 1886. Two illustrations captured the contrasting election day scene at Deptford. In one, Mr W.J. Evelyn, the successful candidate, is greeted triumphantly as he rides in a horse-drawn carriage. In the other, an Indian man raises his hat to thank his voters in front of the central committee room. The big banner on the building still reads 'Vote for Ghose'.

It was a tough loss, but Ghose had already made history. He proved that Indians, too, could stand for Parliament. Until then, most people believed only white men could run for such a position. Ghose had challenged that belief in the boldest way possible.

Though his bid for a seat in the British Parliament ultimately ended in defeat, Lalmohan Ghose did not fade into obscurity. Returning to India, he remained a steadfast advocate for political and educational reforms. His bold attempt to enter British politics paved the way for future Indian leaders. Just a few years later, in 1892, Dadabhai Naoroji succeeded where Ghose had come close—becoming the first Indian elected to the House of Commons.

Home to a hero's welcome

When Lalmohan Ghose returned to Krishnanagar in 1886, the *Hong Kong Daily Press* published a small but noteworthy report about his welcome. The town greeted him with great enthusiasm. A grand procession escorted him home in a horse-drawn carriage, with people cheering along the way, including women who rarely joined such public events. Around 3,000–4,000 people from all backgrounds gathered. They stood in two neat rows patiently and kept waving flags. Ghose spoke to the crowd in Bengali. He didn't forget to thank the people of England for their support. He stressed the importance of education and the need to build public awareness. Only an informed society, he said, could truly understand and fight for its rights. And how true that is!

Although history books have largely overlooked him, Lalmohan Ghose was a trailblazer. His story is not merely one of electoral defeats. He was a man who dared to challenge an empire at a time when the very idea of an Indian in British politics was almost unthinkable. His obituary in the *Daily News* (London) paid tribute to his exceptional political acumen, describing him as 'the most accomplished political speaker that India has sent to this country. A man of remarkable gifts, Mr Lalmohan Ghose, in happier circumstances, would have carved out a greater career for himself'.

36

Emerging from His Brother's Shadow

If you have seen Satyajit Ray's *Sonar Kella*, featuring his sleuth Feluda, you can never forget the character of Mandar Bose—the fake globetrotter played brilliantly by Kamu Mukherjee. But not all globetrotters are fake. The story that we tell you here features a hero from real life, who became a thorn in the side of the English rulers of India, then travelled across various parts of the world like the USA, Germany and Russia—leaving his indelible mark everywhere before returning home and again devoting his life to the cause of the motherland.

There is a famous old English idiom—chip off the old block, meaning an offspring turning out to be very similar to the parents. In the case of our hero, Bhupendranath Datta, this did prove very true, although in his case, the old block was his eldest brother. Born in September 1880, Bhupendra was the third and youngest son of Viswanath and Bhuvaneswari Datta of north Calcutta. But his early claim to fame was his eldest brother: Narendranath, whom the world knows as the great spiritual thinker Swami Vivekananda.

Stellar elder brother

Apart from his role in bringing Hinduism to the global spotlight, Vivekananda had a profound impact on the rise of Bengali nationalism in the late years of the nineteenth century.[1] His speeches roused the fire of patriotism in the minds of countless youth, who plunged into reclaiming their national identity—some through spirituality, some through sports and physical activities, while others went more extreme, embracing arms to bring about a revolution.[2]

Due to the age gap (Bhupendra was seventeen years younger than his eldest brother) and the loss of his father while still a young boy, for Bhupendra, his borda (Bengali for elder brother) became a father figure as well as a philosopher and guide. Moreover, born amidst the Bengal Renaissance, his early years were shaped, directly or indirectly, by some of the finest Bengali minds of the time. Bhupendra's early schooling was at the Metropolitan Institution, founded by Ishwar Chandra Vidyasagar. In his early youth, he joined the Brahma Samaj, where the great thinker and educationist Sivanath Shastri left an indelible impression on him.

Years later, in his book, *Swami Vivekananda: Patriot-Prophet*, Bhupendra wrote:

> It was a truism to say that there is a correlation between Swamiji's appeals to the young countrymen and the intensity of revolutionary urge in the minds of succeeding generations. His works, along with the writings of Mazzini and Garibaldi, were the mainspring of inspiration to the youth of India. In every gymnasium of the revolutionary networks, his work *Lectures from Colombo to Almora* was read. The youths were profoundly inspired by his saying, 'One is nearer to God through football than through the Gita. We want men with strong biceps.'

On the path of revolution

By the time Swamiji died in 1902, young Bhupendra was already deeply immersed in the nationalist movement and was in close contact with Aurobindo Ghosh's Anushilan Samiti (Chapter 15). At the turn of the century, inspired by words and writings of icons like Swami Vivekananda, Rashtraguru Surendranath Banerjee and Bankim Chandra Chattopadhyay, the Bengali race was discovering the meaning of patriotism. And soon, an English aristocrat's actions would add fuel to a smouldering fire.

In January 1899, George Nathaniel, first Marquess Curzon of Kedleston, better known as Lord Curzon, arrived in Calcutta to take over as the viceroy and governor-general of Her Majesty's Indian Empire. At the start, he made a fairly good impression, with his efforts at addressing mistreatment of Indian emigrants to South Africa earning him words of praise from a certain Mohandas Karamchand Gandhi. But one action of Curzon in 1905 turned him into the biggest villain of the land. That year, it was announced that the Bengal Presidency, which comprised the present-day Indian states of West Bengal, Assam, Bihar, Jharkhand, parts of Odisha and Chhattisgarh, and East Bengal (now the nation of Bangladesh) was to be divided into two parts: Hindu-majority western Bengal and Muslim-majority eastern Bengal.

Although the rationale given was administrative convenience, most Bengalis saw it as an attempt to create a divide on religious lines. Bengali society immediately exploded in anger, resentment and protest. The announcement of this partition fired up the passionate Bhupendra. He helped set up Anushilan's party mouthpiece: *Jugantar Patrika*, and became its first editor. The name of the magazine was a tribute to his mentor, Sivanath Shastri, who had written a political novel of the same name.

Jugantar Patrika aimed at spreading the revolutionary thoughts of the main leaders of Anushilan, such as Aurobindo Ghose, Barin Ghose and Abinash Bhattacharya, to name a few. It called for the youth of the nation to rise up in arms and end colonial oppression. Under the stewardship of Bhupendra, *Jugantar* did not hold back, expressing its views most vigorously, and its growing popularity soon became a cause for concern for the administration. Finally, in 1907, Bhupendra was arrested and charged with sedition against His Majesty's Indian government.

Bhupendra's trial became the talk of the town. His fiery courtroom speech turned him into a hero. He said:

I am solely responsible for all the articles in question. I have done what I have considered in good faith to be my duty to my country. I do not wish the prosecution to be put to the trouble and expense of proving what I have no intention to deny. I do not wish to make any other statement or to take any further action in the trial.

While his trial was in progress, rallies were out on the streets hailing Bhupendra's heroism. He was eventually sentenced to one year of rigorous imprisonment.

By the time he was out, the Anushilan Samiti was in turmoil. In the aftermath of the failed assassination attempt on Magistrate Kingsford by Khudiram Bose and Prafulla Chaki (Chapter 15), most of the Anushilan leaders, including the Ghose brothers, had been arrested. Sister Nivedita and Sister Christine, two of Swami Vivekananda's most earnest disciples, were worried that Bhupendra, due to his past associations and his defiant stance during the trial, would be arrested soon. Bhupendra was smuggled out of Calcutta and remained in hiding briefly at the Ramakrishna Mission ashram in Belur, before setting sail for the New World.

Travels abroad

He arrived in New York in late 1908 and was put up at the India House and enrolled at Brown University to pursue post-graduation. At Brown, Bhupendra found a mentor in Prof. Lester Ward, his sociology professor and a well-known proponent of socialism. Encouraged by Ward, Bhupendranath joined the Bronx Park Socialist Club and attended lectures and sessions by renowned American socialist thinkers. A new horizon was opening up for him.

In 1914, Bhupendra completed his studies at Brown and was contemplating his doctoral studies when geopolitical twists across the Atlantic changed his life again. By this time, the clouds of war were hovering over Europe, and the major players were looking to checkmate the opposition. Imperial Germany was actively championing the cause of India's independence right from the highest level, and plans were afoot to trigger a revolution across India and other British interests in Southeast Asia, supported by German arms and ammunition. It was a cause that appealed to the revolutionary spirit in Bhupendra. He went and met the German consul in New York City with the offer of raising an Indian volunteer corps in the USA and other countries that would support imperial Germany in any military conflict against the British.

Around this time, convergence of his socialistic and nationalistic views also brought Bhupendra in close contact with the Sikh Ghadar Party. He realized soon that the action was in Germany and sailed for Berlin. There, Bhupendra joined the Berlin Committee, later named the Indian Independence Committee, and by 1916, was the organization's secretary. One of the major initiatives of this period was the 1915 Christmas Day Plot that planned to realize the revolutionary dream of ending British colonial rule in India and Singapore (Chapter 19). Unfortunately, the plans were leaked at the last minute and the uprising failed, culminating in the Indian revolutionary leader Jatindranath Mukherjee's death fighting the British forces.

In 1917, waves of revolution ended the Tsarist rule in Russia. The communist Soviet Union was established by Vladimir Lenin. Bhupendra had been following the developments in Moscow keenly, and with World War I ending in German defeat and disarray, he realized that German support was now a thing of the past and a new ally was needed. And when an invitation from Soviet leaders arrived in 1921, Bhupendra was more than ready and willing to look for a fresh start.

A major hallmark of Bhupendranath was his open mind. While he was a socialist thinker and communism naturally appealed to him, he had simultaneously been following the emergence of Mahatma Gandhi as the leading face of the nationalist movement back home. Gandhi's focus on the upliftment of the weakest classes impressed and appealed to him.

At the 1921 Comintern in Moscow, Bhupendra presented his thesis to Lenin himself who responded extremely positively and recommended the Indian revolutionary leaders to focus on the farmer/peasant class and plan any activity around them. The Moscow years further broadened Bhupendra's horizons. Two years later, he received his PhD in anthropology from the University of Hamburg, and decided time had come for the prodigal son's return home.

Fighting for the people

After a sixteen-year exile, Bhupendranath Datta finally returned to India and immediately threw himself into the cause of the Indian farmer and labour classes. He joined the Indian National Congress, becoming the voice of the working classes within the party. He found support from a fast-emerging young leader of the INC: Jawaharlal Nehru. At the Karachi Congress of 1930, Nehru supported Bhupendra in incorporating points on the fundamental rights of the farmers in the final resolution.

Over the years, he travelled extensively across the Bengal Presidency, urging the working classes—farmers, labourers, and artisans—to seek freedom from foreign rule and economic bondage. When the British government cracked down on mill workers who were increasingly vocal against their rampant exploitation, Bhupendra persuaded Nehru and INC to provide financial support to the arrested individuals. He kept toiling for the cause of the voiceless, establishing the Calcutta Tram Workers' Union and also a union for Calcutta's street vendors/hawkers. Wherever the working class staged a protest, despite his advancing years, Bhupendra stood in solidarity with them. And amidst all this, he also found time to take active part in the Salt Satyagraha and other such programmes, courting arrest multiple times, and wrote several books and articles on these topics.

Bhupendra's open mind made him try and play peacemaker between the INC and the Indian communists. Despite always being a sympathizer for the communist cause, he did not shy away from opposing some of their stances, most famously the decision to oppose the Quit India Movement. He ended up being criticized by both sides for his efforts at finding a middle path.

After Independence, Bhupendranath Datta refused the freedom fighter's pension offered by the government, devoting himself to writing and a life away from the spotlight. Here, it would be interesting to mention the middle Datta brother—Mahendranath, a globetrotter of repute, who in the late nineteenth century, left for London and then travelled extensively across Europe, North Africa, Middle East and West Asia for six years. The two brothers, lifelong bachelors, spent their final years together in their ancestral home in north Calcutta.

Bhupendranath Datta not only visualized an India free from British rule but, more importantly, an India where every person would have a right to an honourable life and not face exploitation. How far his dream came true, we leave it to you, dear reader, to contemplate.

37

A Nightclub in Mexico City

We landed in Mexico City in August 2017, expecting to make a short visit. But Mexico City isn't the kind of place that lets you leave so easily. It pulls you in with all its energy. What was supposed to be a brief stay stretched longer and longer, as the city revealed more of itself, layer by layer.

Before we even left the airport, we found our first surprise. It was a small store, and the banner read 'Librerías Gandhi'. It was a bookstore named after Mahatma Gandhi. At first, it seemed like a coincidence. But we soon realized the influence of the Indian freedom movement in Mexico ran deeper than we thought.

Back in our university days in Miami, we had seen Hispanic students celebrating something called the 'Traditional Gandhi Day of Service'. They wore white shirts with bold green lettering and a picture of Gandhi, spending the day volunteering in their communities. It was quite a fascinating cultural overlap that goes back in time. In fact, a month before his assassination, Gandhi had sent an autographed portrait to the President of Mexico. A Mexican world traveller personally delivered it.

Mexico City was everything at once—grand and chaotic, historic yet modern, overwhelming but irresistible. The streets were alive with the aroma of tacos and the sound of music from open windows. And then there were the colours. The pink cabs caught our eye immediately. But this wasn't just any pink—it was Mexican pink.

For centuries, it had appeared in textiles and murals. And more recently, if you watched *Barbie* (yes, the one with Margot Robbie and Ryan Gosling), you've seen the very Mexican pink in action.

Ice cream and an unexpected discovery

We stayed in Hotel MX Roma, in Roma Norte, a trendy, historic neighbourhood that felt like it had stories hidden around every corner. Its dramatic streets, historic mansions and indie cafés gave it a charm that was both old-world and effortlessly modern.

A few blocks from our hotel, we spotted a tiny ice cream shop painted in that same unmistakable Mexican pink. It was a cheerful little place, standing out against the subdued tones of the old buildings around it. But what we didn't know yet was that just beyond that shop, something even more surprising was waiting for us—a hidden story that would add yet another unexpected chapter to our Mexico City experience.

It was the third day of our visit and it was quite late at night. While waiting in line for our ice cream, something else caught our attention. Just a few steps away, a long queue stretched outside what looked like an old, unassuming residence. It wasn't the kind of place you'd expect to see a crowd gathering at night. Yet, there they were—people dressed in their finest, trying to talk their way past a stony-faced bouncer.

What made it even more intriguing was the music. A soft, hypnotic disco beat was drifting out from behind those partially closed doors. It was very subtle but impossible to ignore. With our ice creams in hand, we edged closer, watching as the bouncer turned people away one by one. Just beside the entrance, a sleek plaque read:

CLUB PRIVADO M.N. ROY.
SOLO SE PERMITE EL ACCESO A MIEMBROS DEL LUGAR
(M.N. ROY PRIVATE CLUB. MEMBERS ONLY)

A secret club, strict entry, an air of exclusivity—this was clearly no ordinary venue.

We had heard whispers about this place before. Apparently, M.N. Roy was one of the most exclusive clubs in Mexico City, notoriously difficult to get into. But luckily, we had a friend who knew how to navigate the city's underground scene. And, as it turned out, there was a little loophole—foreigners, or gringos, sometimes had a better shot at entry. A quick passport check, a hefty payment for cover charges, a nod from the bouncer, and we were in. What we stepped into was beyond anything we had imagined.

At first, the entrance seemed normal—a dim hallway. But as we walked in, the music got louder. The walls were covered in black tiles, lit from below. Then, suddenly, we saw a huge wooden pyramid stood before us, glowing in warm light. Time seemed to stop as we took it in. Below, a busy dance floor pulsed with energy. The DJ booth was high above, surrounded by walls made of wood, leather, and shiny copper. Everything glowed, with deep colours reflecting off glass and metal.

It wasn't just a nightclub. It was an experience.

The night unfolded in a blur of Latin EDM trap beats, hypnotic nu-disco rhythms, and overpriced cocktails. The crowd was a mix of artists, socialites and those who had simply managed to slip past the club's velvet rope. The food? Overhyped. The drinks? Ridiculously expensive. But the sheer atmosphere of the place? Unmatched.

It should have occurred to us earlier, but it was only later that we discovered the story behind the name—M.N. Roy. What had seemed like just another cryptic club moniker was actually a tribute to an Indian revolutionary, a Bengali man named Manabendra Nath Roy, who had founded the Communist Party of Mexico nearly a century ago.

In a city full of unexpected connections, this one felt like the most surreal of them all.

Once home to revolutionary thinker M.N. Roy, this building in Mexico City's fashionable Roma district is today a sought-after club—an irresistible stop on our walk. (Photo courtesy: Kanishka Dam)

A revolutionary goes westwards

Manabendra Nath Roy was no ordinary figure. To us, he is one of the most fascinating personalities India has ever produced. And there is no way we can pack his life story into a single chapter. But then, this book isn't for that, either.

Still, let's take a short trip through time—back to the early twentieth century, into the home of a young man named Narendra

Nath Bhattacharya. Narendra Nath was born into a priestly family in West Bengal.

> **A temple to visit**
>
> If you ever find yourself in Kheput village in the Midnapore district, do not miss the mesmerizing Kheputeswari temple that has been standing tall for almost three centuries. Once upon a time, Narendra's grandfather was its head priest.

Bengal, at the turn of the twentieth century, was a seething cauldron of revolution. Educated young men were being drawn into a firestorm of nationalist fervour, convinced that the British Raj could only be ousted by force. Narendra Nath was no exception.

Under the mentorship of Bagha Jatin (Chapters 17 and 19), the great anti-British revolutionary, he quickly proved himself a natural leader. By the age of twenty, he had already made his mark. In November 1908, he gunned down Nandalal Banerjee, the notorious police officer who had arrested Khudiram Bose (Chapters 15 and 19), one of India's youngest martyrs. The British now had their sights fixed on him.

As World War I had begun, the rival empires were eager to weaken Britain. Indian revolutionaries saw their chance. If they could secure weapons and funding from Germany, they could overthrow British rule. Narendra Nath volunteered for this mission.

Between 1915 and 1916, he travelled through Java, Malaya, Philippines, Japan, Korea and China, trying to procure arms. Every attempt failed. Finally, in June 1916, he landed in San Francisco.

That was when things took a wild turn.

The American press had already heard of him. The newspapers screamed: 'Mysterious Alien Reaches America—Famous Brahmin Revolutionary or Dangerous German Spy?' Narendra had no choice. He had to vanish. He fled to Palo Alto, California, took on a new name—Manabendra Nath Roy, or M.N. Roy—and started over.

Love and a life in Mexico

California, surprisingly, now opened new doors. One of them was to Evelyn Trent. In 1916, at the home of the president of Stanford University, Roy met Evelyn, a brilliant graduate student at the institution. Their connection was instant, and it was Evelyn who influenced Roy to study Marxism. He found himself drawn not just to nationalism but to Marxism. His beliefs evolved. Their bond grew stronger, and in 1917, Roy married Evelyn.

Roy, like many other Indian anti-colonial activists, soon came under suspicion of being a potential German agent in the US. Facing increasing scrutiny, the Roys fled to neutral Mexico to escape the growing threat.

In Mexico City, Roy found a second home. It was surprising to see how an Indian revolutionary, so far from home, became deeply connected to the city's intellectual life. Mexico City welcomed him in unexpected ways. Roy fully embraced Mexico's intellectual environment. He formed ties with key figures from the Mexican Revolution movements. He gradually refined his beliefs, especially his understanding of Marxism and revolutionary theory. Mexico's history of resistance against imperialism resonated with him. He grew more dedicated to international solidarity as the way to break colonial chains.

During this time, the Roys lived in modest circumstances. He wrote often, contributing to journals and newspapers, spreading his message of anti-colonial struggle. In Mexico, he met exiled figures from around the world, including Germans, with whom he discussed raising funds for the independence movement.

As he reflected in his memoirs, Roy lived in a small house on the outskirts of Mexico City, nestled amidst maize fields with the towering, snow-capped Iztaccíhuatl mountains in the distance. The local people called the range 'Sleeping Woman' because, when viewed from east to west, the mountains resembled the figure of a reclining woman. This tranquil setting was a far cry from the struggles he faced, yet it was here that he felt most alive. With a pair of Mauser pistols by his side and his loyal Alsatian dog, Roy felt connected to the revolutionary spirit of the land. He used to ride Silver King, a trusted white Mexican horse, exploring the vast countryside and the slopes of the Sierra Nevada every morning.

Roy's boundless intellect, sharp writing, and captivating charm placed him at the heart of Mexican politics. He was mingling with the who's who of the political elite—both liberal and socialist—including Venustiano Carranza, the President of Mexico. In 1919, Roy did something historic. He founded the Communist Party of Mexico—the first Communist Party outside Russia.

Roy later moved to the Roma neighbourhood for the convenience of his work. As he recalled in his memoir, his new residence—a house in the affluent Colonia Roma, furnished with green-satin-covered Louis XV furniture—felt almost ironic for a revolutionary like him. By then, meeting in cafés was no longer an option, and the two-storey house became the centre of his intellectual and political engagements. It had eight rooms, all filled with furniture, and was run smoothly by Maria, an excellent cook, along with a young boy who assisted with household tasks. This very house would later become the foundation for today's M.N. Roy Club, remodelled and built upon—right where the pink ice cream shop also stands.

However, one might have expected a club named after M.N. Roy to be more inclusive rather than positioned as an exclusive private space. But at the end of the day, it remains a private club. Would he have liked a nightclub as a tribute to his legacy? There's a certain quirkiness to the whole idea.

M.N. Roy was a man of many talents, with a vivid and varied outlook on life—part rebel, part bohemian. He wasn't just a revolutionary; he was a true Renaissance man who embraced a range of passions. He learned wrestling, mastered horseback riding and even took tennis lessons from a Mexican national player. His love for chess led him to train under his Spanish teacher who was a champion in Mexico, and later, in Russia, he even managed to draw a match against Alexander Alekhine, who would go on to become the world champion. Incidentally, Kolkata's famous Alekhine Chess Club was named after the same chess maestro.

Beyond politics and intellectual pursuits, Roy was a man of culture. As J.B.H. Wadia recounted in *M.N. Roy: The Man*, after India's independence, Roy celebrated 15 August by hosting parties at his Dehradun residence. He personally cooked for his guests and took great pleasure in preparing a special cocktail. It was served in a large bowl, made with fine wine—likely his own twist on sangria—blended with delicate flourishes that reflected his passion for refinement.

His friends affectionately called it 'Roy's cocktail'.

Now, there's something for you to try at home. And on second thoughts, maybe M.N. Roy *would* have loved to have a nightclub named after him.

38

From Rosario to Revolution

The bus journey from Buenos Aires to Rosario took a little more than four hours. The journey was exciting, with the anticipation of meeting one of the co-founders of the Iglesia Maradoniana.

The Iglesia Maradoniana, or Church of Maradona, is a quirky parody religion founded by passionate fans of the legendary Argentine footballer Diego Maradona. To them, Maradona is not just a player; he is the greatest of all time. The church was created as a tribute to his extraordinary legacy, blending reverence with humour, as its followers consider him nothing short of a football deity.

After an incredible conversation with Alejandro Veron, one of the co-founders of Iglesia Maradoniana, we set out to explore more of Rosario—but not before being baptized in the name of D10S. In Spanish, Dios means 'God'. It is a term used to refer to the divine being in various religions, including Christianity. In the context of D10S, it's a playful reference to Diego Maradona's shirt number, 10. Rosario had a rich history of legends; it was the birthplace of Che Guevara, as well as football stars like Lionel Messi and Angel Di Maria, among others. But there was one particular address that caught our attention and drew us in: Avenida Alberdi 26, Rosario, Santa Fe, Argentina.

This was the residence of Baba Bujha Singh when he moved to Argentina.

Who was Bujha Singh, you may ask. According to the records held at the British Library in London, his passport indicates that he was a British Indian national. His profession was listed as 'day labour', and his physical characteristics were noted as follows: height: 172 cm, build: medium, complexion: wheatish, hair: black, and he was clean-shaven.

A disappointing son: Bujha turns baba

Born in the village of Chak Mai Dass, located in what was Jalandhar district (now part of the Shaheed Bhagat Singh Nagar district) in Punjab, Bujha Singh was the eldest son of Dharam Singh and Jai Kaur. Dharam Singh was a hard-working farmer.

Jai Kaur passed away when Bujha Singh was only fifteen years old. The grief of losing his mother may have drawn him closer to the monastery where he received his education. As time passed, his father Dharam Singh was getting older and wished that his eldest son, Bujha Singh, would take on the responsibility of managing the household and attend to his worldly duties. However, there were no indications that his son would oblige—Bujha Singh considered God and his messengers his utmost priority. Nothing Dharam Singh did or said would make Bujha Singh change his ways. At last, Dharam Singh arranged a marriage for his son, hoping that would help him settle down.

By that time, the first Ghadar uprising of 1915 had occurred. A man named Labh Singh, a leader of the Ghadar Party, frequently visited Bujha Singh's home in Chak Mai Dass. Upon hearing Bujha Singh's religious discourses, Labh Singh recognized his oratory skills and believed that he could become an effective evangelist for the Ghadar Party. The struggle for freedom initiated by the Ghadar Party was about to escalate further, requiring more fighters. Labh Singh began motivating Bujha Singh to take on the work of promoting the cause of freedom.

Until then, Bujha Singh had no involvement in the freedom movement. However, he was motivated by a deep desire to help those in need and began to serve the cause with fervour. His father was left to manage the family's affairs, and he was drowning in debt and overwhelmed by hardships. Bujha Singh's wife and their two daughters were also under his care. Since this could not go on, Dharam Singh requested his friend Maha Singh to give Bujha some life advice.

Sent away to seek his fortune

Maha Singh consulted with Labh Singh, and they advised Bujha to go to America. Bujha readily agreed in the hope of alleviating his family's hardship. However, they needed to arrange funds for his travel. Dharam Singh was doubtful about the venture, and remarked, 'Let's see if he becomes successful by going abroad. He has never done any work here. What can he possibly achieve abroad?'

Maha Singh secured a loan of Rs 30 from a commission agent in Phagwara to help Bujha get started. Before leaving, he entrusted his Granth to Maha Singh, and left his drum and cymbals at home. He took only his kamandal (an ascetic's water pot), a religious book, and other necessary items with him and departed for China. Nobody in the extended family was aware that he had left the country.

This was 1929. At that time, a passport was not required to travel to China. After landing on the southern coast, Bujha Singh walked for several months along unfamiliar paths, till he reached Shanghai. In September 1930, the Chinese government eventually issued him a passport to visit the British Empire, Japan and Panama. He travelled to Panama and, finally, made his way to Argentina from there.

Argentina: Learning and labour

He applied for immigration status in Argentina and was granted permission to reside there until 2 September 1934. The Punjabi immigrant community in Argentina had a custom of providing free food and accommodation to newly arrived individuals until they found work. Bujha Singh didn't find any work for two months due to the prevailing economic recession and rising unemployment. His fellow Punjabis supported him while he spent his days reading both new and old issues of the *Ghadar* and *Kirti* magazines, which were actively campaigning to promote the struggle for freedom and the ideology of socialism.

Then came the harvest season for the maize crop, which demanded hard labour from the workers. Many labourers would avoid this season and seek other work, leaving only those who had no other option to work in the fields. Bujha Singh was also forced to take up this job. Though he found it difficult and considered running away, he persevered and continued working despite the challenges.

Whenever he felt overwhelmed, his father's words echoed in his mind: 'Let's see if he becomes successful!'

He put in his best effort and worked tirelessly throughout the entire season. When the season for harvesting corncobs ended, their jobs were assessed. The results were surprising. Bujha Singh was thrilled to learn that he had come out on top and was declared the champion among the workers.

He went on to make a better life for himself and moved to a house on Alberdi Avenue in Rosario.

Now, it was our turn to go there. We stopped for lunch and had Lionel Messi's favourite food, milanesa napolitana. This dish is often called Argentina's unofficial national dish. It's a simple but tasty meal made of a breaded slice of prime beef, fried in hot oil until it curls up.

After lunch, we arrived at Alberdi Avenue. A short drive away from Messi's childhood football club, Newell's Old Boys, is the avenue, named in honour of the distinguished liberal politician and economist Juan Bautista Alberdi, who had penned the Argentine Constitution of 1853. The residence of Bujha Singh, located at Alberdi Avenue 26, Rosario, served as the formal address for the Ghadar Party in Argentina.

Baba turns rebel leader

In the early 1930s, a group of young individuals, including Naina Singh Dhoot, Rattan Singh and Teja Singh Sutantar, began advocating for an armed revolution as a means to achieve India's independence. They subsequently established a military training course in Rosario for the Indian youth residing there. Baba Bujha Singh emerged as a prominent leader in the founding and promotion of the Ghadar, Kirti and other mass movements within Argentina.

In the meantime, Argentina went through a coup. The British ambassador to Argentina exploited this political upheaval to instigate an attack on the Ghadar Party headquarters in Rosario. Despite the aggression, the Ghadarites and the local populace resisted, preventing any arrests of Ghadar Party members. However, the attackers were able to wreak havoc throughout the entire office.

Teja Singh and Bujha Singh went travelling in the south, establishing party committees in various areas and gathering funds. In Buenos Aires and Cordoba, they successfully organized state committees, recruited new members and provided guerrilla training.

Committees were also established within the railways union. All Ghadar Party delegates from Argentina convened in Rosario for a three-day conference to discuss the political situation in India. However, the government had declared martial law in Rosario, and Teja was arrested. But his release was secured soon through mass protests.

By then, Bujha Singh had risen to the central committee of the Ghadar Party. Following an extended debate and discussion at the conference, the central committee put forth a proposal suggesting that the Indian Ghadarites should travel to the Eastern University in Moscow to study Marxism. Upon completion of their training and the acquisition of a political ideology, they were expected to return to India.

The Ghadar and Kirti movements played a pivotal role in the Indian independence movement, acting as both cherished legacy and beacons of inspiration for future generations. The Ghadar Movement stood out as the first to advocate for complete independence. Demonstrating selflessness and unity, the leaders and workers of the Ghadar Party, disregarding religious and caste differences, made the ultimate sacrifice in the pursuit of liberating the Indian people from British colonial rule.

Bujha Singh led the first cohort of Ghadarites to receive an education in Marxist theory at the Eastern University in Moscow, in the then USSR. As a result, he became a roaming encyclopaedia of Marxist theory and revolutionary movements.

Upon returning to India via Moscow, Bujha Singh found himself arrested on three separate occasions by the Banga and Jalandhar Police in 1935. He endured severe torture for two consecutive months. In December 1935, he was eventually released but was subsequently declared a prisoner of war.

Despite not spending an extensive period behind bars during his life, Baba Bujha Singh remained a dedicated revolutionary. His rich political legacy embodies the combined and invaluable treasure of the Ghadar Movement, the Kirti Movement and the Tenant Struggle.

For us, it was a memorable day to explore a quiet corner of Argentina, not far from the birthplace of revolutionary leader Che Guevara and football legend Lionel Messi, from where a group of Sikh rebels clandestinely charted their course for the next daring move in their struggle for Indian independence, setting the stage for an unexpected collision of worlds.

39

The One-Armed Patriot: Sacrifice in Shiraz

'Every bottle tells a story,' a friend once said as he raised his glass. We were savouring our time together, aided by a bottle of Shiraz wine.

Shiraz wine, known for its rich, bold flavour, is famous worldwide. But its history is as fascinating as its taste. The wine takes its name from Shiraz, an ancient city in Iran, known for its poets, gardens and, once upon a time, its wine. Well, that's not entirely true—but we'll come back to that. Although alcohol has been banned for Muslim Iranian citizens since 1979, Iran has a long and rich history of winemaking, especially around the area of Shiraz.

But here's where it gets interesting: the Shiraz wine we drink today is not directly tied to the city of Shiraz in Iran. The grapes used in modern Shiraz wines, known as Syrah grapes, are grown elsewhere, primarily in France. Yet, the history of Shiraz wines remains inseparably intertwined with the ancient city of Shiraz— well, it's more legend than history. What we can't deny, however, is that a bottle of Shiraz wine introduced us to the fascinating history of Shiraz.

Now, you might be wondering, why are we talking about Shiraz, a city in Iran, and what does it have to do with India's freedom movement? Well, here's where the story takes a fascinating turn. In the early twentieth century, a few thousand kilometres from the

Indian subcontinent, in the city of Shiraz, a school was founded by a man who had come from India. But this was no ordinary school, and this was no ordinary man. The founder of this school had only one hand. His name was Sufi Amba Prasad, and he was an Indian revolutionary in exile.

A scholar, Sufi and activist

His journey, however, didn't start in Shiraz. It began in the quiet streets of Moradabad, a town in what is now the state of Uttar Pradesh. Amba Prasad was born there in 1858, a year that marked the aftermath of the Great Indian Rebellion of 1857. From the very beginning, Amba Prasad was different. He was born without his right hand.

Amba Prasad had a wry sense of humour about his missing limb too. He would often joke, 'In my previous birth, I must have lost my right arm fighting against the British in 1857. I was reborn without it to remind me of the unfinished fight.'

He had a natural talent for languages and was proficient in Hindi, Urdu, English and Persian. A great scholar, he was well-respected for his knowledge. After the loss of his young wife, he turned to spirituality and became known as Sufi Amba Prasad. His wisdom and compassion earned him the love and respect of both Hindus and Muslims alike.

As a young man, Amba Prasad became a journalist in Moradabad. He was the editor of a newspaper called *The Peshwa*. His articles were sharp and bold, openly criticizing British policies in Punjab. By the early twentieth century, he had been jailed twice for his fiery writings. For instance, Amba Prasad translated and published pamphlets like *Bandar Bant* (The Monkey's Arbitration) and *Ungli Pakarte Pah Uncha Pakra* (Grasping a Finger, Grasp the Whole Hand) in Urdu. These pamphlets criticized British colonial rule, comparing the British to the monkey in the fable, pretending to arbitrate while exploiting disputants. Another pamphlet, *Baghi Masih* (Christ the Rebel), argued that Jesus Christ was persecuted not for blasphemy but for challenging Roman authority.

The *Bharat Mitra* (Calcutta) reported the harsh punishment inflicted on Sufi Amba Prasad for a defamation charge. He was sentenced to seven years of rigorous imprisonment—under Section 500 (defamation), Section 506 (criminal intimidation), Section 471 (using a forged document), among others—a punishment the paper criticized as extraordinary and disproportionate.

In the early 1900s, Amba Prasad joined the growing movement against British rule. In Punjab, farmers were struggling under heavy taxes and unfair laws. Amba Prasad stood with them, working alongside leaders like Lala Lajpat Rai and Sardar Ajit Singh, the uncle of Bhagat Singh. Together, they founded the Bharat Mata Society, a group dedicated to freeing India from colonial rule.

They flee to Iran

Soon, Amba Prasad's activism made him a target. Eventually, he was forced to flee India in 1907 along with Sardar Ajit Singh (Chapter 18) and a few other associates. His journey eventually took him to Persia (modern-day Iran). Persia, with its vibrant anti-imperialist circles, became a hidden base for Indian revolutionaries in exile.

In Iran, they first arrived at Bushire, travelling by boat from Karachi. Today known as Bushehr, this steamy port city in southwestern Iran is famous as the site of Iran's first nuclear reactor. Back then, it served as a gateway for revolutionaries seeking refuge and new alliances.

In Bushire, Ajit Singh and his comrades quickly established connections with Iranian revolutionaries who were fighting against their despotic king and resisting the growing interference of European powers. Ajit Singh forged close ties with influential leaders like Syed Asadullah Mujatubik and Zia-ud-Din Tabatabai— prominent liberal Mujtahids who supported the Persian Revolution. Historian Savinder Pal suggests that Syed Asadullah Mujatubik might be Sayyid Abdullah Bihbihani, a key religious figure who backed the revolutionary movement in Persia.

As Ajit Singh later recounted in his autobiography *Buried Alive*, from Bushire they embarked on a perilous journey to Shiraz, carefully avoiding British surveillance. The road to Shiraz was fraught with danger, but the stakes were too high to turn back.

Iranian nationalists had long expressed solidarity with the Indian struggle against British imperialism. During World War I, a small group of Indian revolutionaries in Iran joined forces with activists from the Iranian Democrat Party, sharing a vision of anti-imperialist resistance. While Ajit Singh left Iran in 1911, Sufi Amba Prasad chose to remain in Shiraz, continuing his revolutionary work.

Portrait of Sufi Amba Prasad, around 1909—his right arm is disabled, a subtle detail in the composition. (Photo courtesy: Jagdhali. Public Domain via Wikimedia Commons.)

Close bonds wrought in Shiraz

The bond between Iranian and Indian nationalists extended beyond politics and into the cultural sphere. This anti-imperialist solidarity found a unique expression when Sufi Amba Prasad, along with his Iranian supporter Shaykh Mohammad Rahim, established Anjuman-i-Sufieh—a Sufi society in Shiraz, influenced by the global theosophical movement. In Shiraz, Amba Prasad continued his fight for freedom. He worked with other exiled Indians, building networks and spreading revolutionary ideas.

Sufi Amba Prasad was able to easily blend in with Iranian culture, thanks to his proficiency in Persian. Iranian revolutionaries respected him for his fluency in Persian and his profound knowledge of the language. One notable ally he influenced was Mirza Jawad Mudirzadeh, who absorbed anti-British ideas from Amba Prasad and Ajit Singh during their time in Shiraz. Together, they collaborated to spread revolutionary propaganda, with Mudirzadeh publishing these ideas in his newspaper, *Hayat*. Amba Prasad himself became the editor of another publication, *Intiqam*, which was a vocal platform for anti-imperialist sentiment. His fearless writings and ideas led to his arrest. Despite the risks, Amba Prasad refused to stop.

In his brief stint in Iran, Amba Prasad even helped establish a school in Shiraz with a modern curriculum, and served as its principal, committed to blending progressive ideas with traditional values. It's fascinating, almost unbelievable, to think that a distant city like Shiraz in Iran—best known to many for its connection to wine—was quietly influenced by an Indian revolutionary from Moradabad.

The University of Tehran is one of Iran's most prestigious institutions. It was established in 1934, but its foundation began in a key meeting in 1933. At that meeting, Ali Asghar Hekmat, the minister of education, strongly argued for a world-class university. His vision made a lasting impact, leading to the creation of Iran's finest educational establishment. And here's where it connects back to Sufi Amba Prasad. Dr Hekmat, who also served as Iran's ambassador to India, hailed from Shiraz and received his early education under none other than Sufi Amba Prasad.

His last stand

When World War I began, Amba Prasad joined efforts with the Ghadarites, who sought to launch attacks on British forces stationed in Iran. Sufi Amba Prasad played a key role in organizing an army composed of Indian prisoners of war and soldiers from Turkey, Germany, and the Middle East. His aim was to rally the troops for the cause of Indian independence. However, the tides turned against their mission. Soon, Turkey was defeated, and Baghdad fell into British hands. With their supply lines cut off, Sufi Amba Prasad and his rebel forces retreated to Shiraz. The British, eager to crush the rebellion, launched a major attack on Shiraz in 1916. This led to the infamous Siege of Shiraz. Despite their efforts, the rebels were eventually defeated, and Sufi Amba Prasad was captured. It is reported that a day before his execution, Sufi Amba Prasad was found dead in his prison cell, presumably having committed suicide.

We may not know much about Shiraz beyond the legends of Shirazi wine, but there is a long-standing connection between Shiraz and India. For centuries, horse traders from Shiraz travelled to India, even before the Mughal rule, reaching various parts of the country, and some of them eventually settled here. One of the most famous of them was a sixteen-year-old boy who, in the early 1800s, left his home in Shiraz and moved to Bengaluru with his two brothers to sell horses. He eventually settled in Bengaluru, where he built several iconic heritage buildings. Today, if you walk down a short stretch of road between Infantry Road and Cunningham Road, you'll find 'Ali Asker Road', named after Aga Ali Asker, the horse trader from Shiraz.

But beyond such well-known figures, there are many lesser-known ones too. In Kishanganj, Bihar, there's a small hamlet called Irani Basti, where the descendants of horse traders from Shiraz still live as a small community.

They have remained a footnote in the shared history between Shiraz and India. And so does the story of Sufi Amba Prasad.

40

A Pepper Named Barrackpore

There are few places in the world as intoxicating as the Caribbean. The heady mix of history, cricket, music and cuisine makes it a paradise for the senses. Our journey to Trinidad had been driven by a singular obsession though—cricket. Our base was San Fernando, a quaint town almost an hour south of Port of Spain. The Windies might not be the indomitable force they once were, but here, cricket was more than just a game; it was a way of life, a religion that bound the islands together. And then, of course, there was Brian Lara.

He wasn't just a batsman; he was an artist, a magician. But beyond the records, beyond the memorable innings, what we admired most was his humility. We experienced this first-hand, as we were fortunate to meet him while watching a game in a pub at the Hyatt Regency in the heart of Port of Spain. He had an ease about him even in that dark bar, which made you forget you were in the presence of greatness.

But what surprised us even more was a type of pepper we found in the bustling markets of Trinidad. That evening, we went for a quick dinner—Trini roti—its unleavened flatbread filled with a savoury, slow-cooked meat curry. The shopkeeper asked the usual question about spice level—hot, medium or mild. Now, beware—at most places in Trinidad, or at least the one we visited, if you said 'hot', they had something special in store for you.

Because in Trinidad, 'hot' doesn't just mean spicy—it means a searing, merciless heat. We didn't have the courage to taste it, but from what we heard, the burn was unlike anything else. And when we finally asked what it was, the answer was as unexpected as the fire it carried: '7 Pot Barrackpore'.

A Trinidad pepper named after an Indian town?

The name was certainly very interesting, as Barrackpore is also the name of a town in West Bengal. Discovering how this fiery pepper from Trinidad came to bear that name led us to an unexpectedly fascinating chapter of history.

The 7 Pot Barrackpore was named after the place where it was originally discovered—the small hamlet of Barrackpore in Trinidad. Located in southern Trinidad and Tobago, about an hour's drive from Port of Spain and only thirty minutes from our hotel in San Fernando, this village has a rich history tied to sugarcane and oil fortunes.

Peppers, cricket and chutney music

This wrinkled, unassuming pepper from Trinidad and Tobago—the 7 Pot Barrackpore—is among the hottest chillies in the world. Its name is a testament to its potency—one pepper is enough to spice up seven pots of stew. If you plan to buy this wicked pepper, the warning is clear—wear gloves when handling these chillies, and even kitchen goggles to prevent chilli burn. With a Scoville Heat Unit (SHU) rating of up to 1.3 million, it leaves the humble jalapeño, which barely touches 10,000 SHU, far behind. To put its heat into perspective, the Barrackpore chilli is at least 100 times hotter than a jalapeño. Cricket enthusiasts might recognize Barrackpore as the hometown of Daren Ganga, the former West Indies top-order batsman turned commentator.

For music lovers, the village is even more significant—it was the birthplace of Sundar Popo, widely regarded as the father of chutney music. For the uninitiated, chutney music is a fusion of Indian folk traditions—especially Bhojpuri folk music—with Caribbean calypso and soca. It developed in Trinidad and Tobago before spreading to other Caribbean islands, shaped by the descendants of Indian immigrants from Bihar, Uttar Pradesh, Bengal and south India.

But why was this village in Trinidad named after a bustling town in West Bengal?

In fact, it's not very uncommon to find towns across the world that share names with towns from India. We've visited a little town called Delhi in Louisiana, stayed in an Airbnb in a small town named Golconda in Illinois, and even seen a Baroda in Michigan's wine country. There is also a town named Calcutta in Ohio, and Patna in Scotland. The legacy of Indian migration and colonial history has scattered these names across continents. To uncover the story of Barrackpore in Trinidad, we must first go back to the original Barrackpore in India.

Barrackpore. A small town fifteen miles north of Kolkata, known for its picturesque riverbanks, famous biryani joints and, most significantly, as the birthplace of India's First War of Independence. There are differing opinions on the origin of the name Barrackpore. Some believe it traces back to 'Barbuckpur' from the Mughal era, while others argue that it derives from the word 'barrack', as the area housed the oldest British barracks or cantonment in the country. Maria Graham, in her work *Journal of a Residence in India*, beautifully described Barrackpore:

Close to Calcutta, it is the busiest scene one can imagine; crowded with ships and boats of every form ... On one side the picturesque boats of the natives, with their floating huts; on the other, the bolios and pleasure-boats of the English ...

When we came to the port of Barrackpore, the tamarind, acacia and peepil trees, through whose branches the moon threw her flickering beams on the river, seemed to hang over our heads, and formed a strong contrast to the white buildings of Serampore, which shone on the opposite shore.

Indentured or escaping, sail for Trinidad

In March 1857, an ordinary sepoy in the 34th Regiment of the Bengal Native Infantry named Mangal Pandey (Chapters 27 and 29) turned Barrackpore into a symbol of rebellion when he raised his musket against the British officers of the East India Company. His act of defiance, sparked by the growing anger among Indian soldiers over the use of animal-fat-greased cartridges, was brutally crushed. He was court-martialled and executed, but his actions ignited a fire that spread across the subcontinent. The revolt of 1857 saw uprisings in Delhi, Kanpur, Lucknow, Jhansi and beyond—each one a desperate, courageous attempt to overthrow British rule. Though ultimately suppressed, it marked the beginning of a long and determined struggle for independence.

Now, to understand how the distant town in Trinidad came to be named after Barrackpore in India, we must journey back to 1845, when the British Raj, facing a labour crisis in its sugar colonies, turned to India for workers. That year, the first ship carrying indentured labourers set sail from Calcutta to Trinidad. Indentured labourers were individuals who, in exchange for passage to a foreign land, agreed to work for a specified number of years, often under harsh and exploitative conditions. The contracts often blurred the lines between indenture and slavery. While technically not slaves, the terms of their contracts were often brutally restrictive, with many subjected to gruelling hours of labour in plantations, most often sugar, under the watchful eye of their British overseers.

The historic ship was called *Fath Al Razack*—Arabic for 'Victory of God'—but, true to colonial tradition, the name was anglicized to the more Western-friendly *Fatel Razack*. Ralph Premdas, in his book *Trinidad and Tobago: Ethnic Conflict, Inequality and Public Sector Governance*, notes that between 1845 and 1917, some 143,939 indentured labourers arrived in Trinidad, with only 33,000 returning to India. Most of them were Hindus, along with some Muslims. The majority settled permanently in Trinidad, while the rest of the Indian migrants dispersed across various Caribbean islands. To this day, Trinidadians celebrate Indian Arrival Day to commemorate the date when the first ship arrived, marking the birth of the Indian diaspora in the country. The celebrations often feature miniature replicas of the ship, proudly bearing the name *Fatel Razack*.

Identity can have many names

J.C. Jha, in his article 'Indian Heritage in Trinidad' published in *India Quarterly*, notes that the vast majority of Indian immigrants to Trinidad came from north India via the port of Calcutta, because of which they were known as Kalkatiyas. Those who left from south India through the port of Madras were referred to as Madrasis in Trinidad. Interestingly, Kamla Susheila Persad-Bissessar, the Prime Minister of Trinidad and Tobago at the time of writing, is a descendant of Kalkatiyas, with ancestors from Bihar who boarded their ship from Calcutta.

As these migrants settled in Trinidad, they named their new settlements after familiar places from their homeland. Thus, Trinidad saw the emergence of villages named Calcutta, Fyzabad, Coromandel, Malabar, Madras and Patna, among others.

However, it wasn't only landless peasants from Uttar Pradesh and Bihar who made the journey to the Caribbean. The aftermath of the 1857 sepoy rebellion triggered a surge in emigration. Many sepoys from disbanded regiments who survived the uprising returned to their villages, only to face continued persecution. The British retaliated harshly, burning villages that had supported the rebels and imposing heavy punitive taxes.

Fearing execution, many Indian sepoys who had taken part in the uprising fled to Trinidad. Others were forcibly exiled as punishment, as the British Raj, eager to rid itself of these 'troublemakers', found an expedient solution—sending them off to distant colonies as indentured labourers. Consequently, emigration to Trinidad increased sharply in 1859, just after the suppression of the revolt, and the trend continued for several years.

Syed Reza Ahsan, in his dissertation 'East Indian Agricultural Settlements in Trinidad: A Study in Cultural Geography', highlights the significant role of Oudhis (residents of Oudh), who made up about 40 per cent of the Bengal Army, in the rebellion. Many of the uprising's key centres—Meerut, Kanpur, Lucknow and Jagdishpur (Arrah)—were precisely the areas from which most Indian migrants to Trinidad originated.

One of these settlements was Barrackpore, Trinidad. Given that the original Barrackpore in India was a hub of Bengal Army sepoys, it is no coincidence that a settlement in Trinidad, where many former sepoys and their families resided, carried the same name. Brinsley Samaroo, in *Indian Diaspora in the Caribbean: History, Culture, and Identity*, edited by Rattan Lal Hangloo, recounts how villagers in Barrackpore, southern Trinidad, passed down ancestral accounts stating that the village was so named because originally Indian sepoys and their descendants settled here.

We never imagined the Trinidad trip that started with cricket and meeting Brian Lara would lead us to a fiery local pepper, and tracing back its roots would take us back to the great uprising of 1857 in India and its connection to this tiny town in southern Trinidad. The town gave us chutney music, and if you ever wondered as a child why so many West Indies cricketers bore Indian names, this is the reason. This is yet another legacy of the First War of Independence, which led to the growth of the Indian diaspora in distant lands.

On our way back to Port of Spain, we passed by a school—Chandernagore Presbyterian Primary School. Chandernagore—another town in India, right next to Barrackpore. A quiet reminder of how history, migration and memory have woven invisible threads between distant lands. The world is vast, yet it is these small, unexpected connections that make it endlessly fascinating.

007
VOTE FOR GHOSE
CHICAGO RADIO
Underdogs

41

When Football Became a Part of the Freedom Movement

Sometime in the 1870s. A carriage bearing a rich Indian lady and her young son was passing through Red Road in British-ruled Calcutta. In an adjacent ground, European soldiers were playing a game of football. The boy was enthralled—he pleaded with his mother to stop the carriage so he could take a closer look. The lady finally relented. As the boy watched from the sidelines, the ball rolled out of play towards him and a soldier asked him to kick it back in play. That kick has been immortalized for posterity as the first time ever a Bengali kicked a football. The account is in all probability apocryphal. But the impact this boy would go on to have on the game of football and its spread across Bengal would be no less than legendary. Nagendra Prasad Sarbadhikari—that was his name—would absolutely fall in love with the game and, in time, come to be acknowledged as the 'founding father of Indian football'.

Father of football and social reform

In the 1880s, Sarbadhikari championed football in Calcutta, setting up several sporting clubs—Boys' Club, Friends' Club, Presidency Club—and later merging all three to form Wellington Club in 1884. Something else was happening in Calcutta and Bengal then. Inspired by the writings of Swami Vivekananda and Bankim Chandra Chattopadhyay, a wave of nationalism started surging through the land. Riding on this wave, football in Calcutta grew exponentially in the last decade-and-a-half of the nineteenth century. A race ridiculed for lacking in martial character suddenly discovered a medium to compete with their overlords as equals.

In 1887, after the inclusion of a low-caste player led to protests from other members, Sarbadhikari dissolved Wellington and formed Sovabazar Club; the Sovabazar and Cooch Behar royal families were patrons. The club was societal progress in action and 'offered open membership to sportsmen, irrespective of class, caste, community or religious affiliations'. Sarbadhikari's Sovabazar would become the first torchbearer of the Indian (Bengali) community's footballing aspirations, waging lone battles against the European hegemony of the city's footballscape. Gradually, more followed. Manmatha Ganguly's National Association, Sir Dookhiram Majumdar's Aryan Club, Kalicharan Mitter's Kumartuli Park and Mohun Bagan Athletic Club (formed by three aristocratic north Calcutta families) all came up, as football became a symbol of expression against the shackles of foreign rule (Chapter 45). Though success on the field was rare initially, owing to a combination of lack of experience, biased officiating, and poor infrastructure (most native teams played barefoot), it didn't deter their zeal.

Pride and identity on the football pitch

In 1891, Sovabazar became the first native club to take part in the Trades Cup—the first open football tournament held in India. A year later, led by Sarbadhikari, they pulled off the unthinkable—defeating East Surrey Regiment 2–1 in that year's Trades Cup. In 1893, the Fort William Arsenal—consisting entirely of Indian players—won the Cooch Behar Cup. It was the first trophy won by any native club/players against European opposition. In 1900, National Association raised the bar higher, becoming the first Indian side to win the Trades Cup, and repeated the success two years later.

As the nineteenth century gave way to the twentieth, the nationalistic fervour in Bengal kept rising. Lord Curzon's infamous

Bengal partition plans of 1905 added fuel to fire. It had a direct impact on the sport. From just being a format to contest sporting supremacy, football became an expression of protest of the Bengalis against what they saw as evil machinations by the British to divide their land and their society. In many cases, akhadas (gymnasiums) and sports/fitness clubs became a front for the armed insurgency movement. Success on the football field soon became a way for Bengali young men to level up with their colonial masters and their oppressive rule. The barefooted Bengali youth taking on the boot-wearing sahibs became a microcosm of the Indians' struggle against their richer, more powerful colonial rulers.

Sometimes, matters got out of hand. In a Trades Cup match played around this time (1907), Mohun Bagan was leading Dalhousie by 3 goals to 2. The European players of Dalhousie could not take this humiliation and, supported by a pliant official, started playing aggressively, committing serious fouls which the referee routinely ignored. Eventually, the assembled crowd had had enough. They raced onto the field and started raining punches and kicks on the Dalhousie players and officials, leading to the game being abandoned. The primacy of the Bengali team wasn't a one-off, either. The football field had increasingly become a platform for the Indians to compete with the British and reclaim pride. And from the reaction of the Dalhousie players, it was obvious that Indian clubs like Mohun Bagan were increasingly getting under their skin.

By the time 29 July 1911—a day that has now entered the annals of Indian football history—came around, football had become an integral and inseparable part of the Bengali milieu. That day, in the final of the Indian Football Association (IFA) Shield, Mohun Bagan squared off against East Yorkshire Regiment. With Sovabazar and National Association fading into the background, Mohun Bagan had become the focal point for all Bengalis in the struggle against the British, and had enjoyed a steady run of success in the preceding years. The crowning glory was a 6–1 drubbing of reigning Shield champions Dalhousie.

When the IFA Shield of 1911 began, no one gave Mohun Bagan much of a chance. However, it did not deter huge crowds at their matches. And as they took down one European opposition after the other, these crowds continued to swell in numbers. By the time the final came around on 29 July, support for Mohun Bagan had reached a fever pitch and estimates of the crowd that day were close to 100,000 people! Football had given the average Indian a way of avenging injustices of a century-and-a-half—from Clive's treachery with Siraj-ud-Daulah to Curzon's malevolent plans of bifurcating Bengal.

Mohun Bagan's historic 1911 IFA Shield-winning team, pictured by Hop Singh & Co., as featured in *Modern Review*, September 1911. (Photo author unknown. Public Domain via Wikimedia Commons.)

Incidentally, winning the IFA Shield wasn't important only for the Indians. The experience of Reverend Sudhir Chatterjee, one of the vital members of Mohun Bagan's backline, shows that the match was as much a prestige issue for the other side. Rev. Chatterjee was at the time engaged as a tutor at the London Missionary Society College, Bhowanipore. On the day of the match, his English superior kept delaying his departure for the ground on small pretexts. Chatterjee only just made it to the ground, and played a vital role in Mohun Bagan's historic triumph.

Football star but patriot first

Sudhir Chatterjee's football career came to an untimely end in 1914 due to an injury, and Mohun Bagan officials recruited a young man as his replacement. His name was Gostha Behari Paul and in addition to becoming a legend of the club and Indian football, Paul would also leave an indelible mark for his unparalleled patriotism. Although Mohun Bagan did win the IFA Shield in 1911, it was only after Paul's arrival that they started to consistently give the English sides a run for their money. His bone-crunching tackles put the fear of God in the opposition. Such was Gostha Paul's impact that an English journalist was compelled to write words of praise for him: 'Gostha is as impregnable as the Chinese Wall.' To avoid getting castigated by his brethren, the poor journalist was forced to use an alias while publishing his piece.[1]

Gostha Paul's fearless showing against European sides not only inspired his own teammates but also put hope in the hearts of the common Indian that they were in no way inferior to their colonial overlords. He became a rallying symbol for the natives' nationalistic aspirations. Once, even Subhas Chandra Bose came to the ground to watch Gostha Paul take on European opposition.

Incidentally, one of Gostha Paul's most celebrated 'performances' against the British came on the cricket field. Mohun Bagan had a heated rivalry with the Calcutta Cricket Club (CCC). In one of their league encounters to be played at CCC's home ground, Paul arrived at the last minute and did not have his cricket-playing kit. So he took to the field in his shirt and dhoti. The CCC players objected to the umpires, who asked Paul to either change or leave the ground. Paul refused, asking the officials to show him the exact rules which debarred him from playing in his normal clothes. A heated argument followed, with the Mohun Bagan players, led by Paul, staging a sit-in protest on the pitch itself. The match was abandoned and CCC suspended cricket matches with Mohun Bagan for the next few years.

The statue of footballer Gostha Paul is situated near the Salt Lake Stadium in Kolkata. Dubbed the 'Chinese Wall', Paul is widely regarded as one of India's greatest-ever defenders.

Paul's staunch nationalist pride eventually hastened the end of his football career. In 1935, Mohun Bagan was playing their arch-rivals Calcutta Football Club (CFC). As always, the English referee was being extremely biased against Mohun Bagan. After a particularly blatant call went in favour of CFC, Paul gathered his players and all of them lay down prostrate on the ground as a mark of protest. The governing body, Indian Football Association, dominated by the English, was left red-faced over this incident. Paul became a targeted man. Rather than compromise on his values and bow down to the ruling class, Gostha Paul decided to retire from football. But his legacy was forever secured.

Right from the inception of the twentieth century until Independence, Bengal remained one of the biggest headaches for the British Indian administration, and was mostly the vanguard of the freedom movement. The role of football in shaping this remains a unique aspect in the history of the game.

Acknowledgement: We are grateful to Shri Girbban Paul, grandson of the late Shri Gostha Paul, for sharing some anecdotes of his grandfather's life with us.

42

From Podiums to Protests

On 3 February 2021, a tweet from the 'Master Blaster' Sachin Tendulkar started a huge controversy across social media.[1] At that time, the farmers' protest against the controversial 'farm laws' was making headlines worldwide. While activists and global celebrities were rallying behind the farmers, Sachin's unexpected tweet supporting the Indian government caught millions of his followers off guard. The legendary cricketer, known for his powerful stance on the field, suddenly seemed to shift gears off it.

But in his defence, his stance made sense. It is never easy to take a stand against the ruling power in India as a popular public figure; not everyone has the stomach for it. Those who had done so, risked their legacy being thrust into oblivion. Let us give an example—the sport field hockey in India is associated with the legend Dhyan Chand—a name any follower of the game knows. But how many of them ever cared to celebrate Jaipal Singh Munda? The man who captained the Indian hockey team in the 1928 Summer Olympics in Amsterdam, won India its first gold medal[2] in the sport and paved the way for Dhyan Chand's ensuing success in the Olympics. There's a reason Munda remained lost in the shadows of history—or rather, multiple reasons.

Jaipal Singh Munda was a fearless leader. In pre-Independence India, he worked in a princely state and challenged the egos of many princes. He did this in front of thousands, even in the presence of the press. He could look powerful people in the eye and speak for the common, powerless and oppressed people.

From a tribal village to Oxford

Jaipal was born to Amru Pahan and Radhamuni, a priestly family of the Munda tribe in Pahantoli, a small hamlet in Tarka village in Khunti district of today's Jharkhand. His childhood name was Pramod until his father admitted him to St. Paul's School in Ranchi. There, the principal Canon Cosgrave took him under his wing, baptized him and probably gave him the name Jaipal Singh. In his autobiography *Lo Bir Sendra*, Jaipal mentioned: 'My name was Pramod Pahan, son of Amru Pahan. I don't know how it changed to Jaipal Singh when in 1911 my father took me to Saint Paul's School, Ranchi, on January 3rd. That [date] was taken as my birthday and it has stuck ever since.'[3]

The change of name wasn't only a minor identity modifier. Coincidentally, a whole new life was waiting for him. Fate intervened for Cosgrave when his superior, Bishop Westcott, told Cosgrave he was approaching retirement at St. Paul's. Cosgrave cabled Bishop Moule of Durham,[4] seeking help to find a new position. Bishop Moule swiftly responded, offering him an honourable position at the parish of Holy Trinity in Darlington.

As the canon prepared to bid farewell to the familiar grounds of the school, he made a decision that would not only alter the trajectory of a young life but also the destiny of an entire marginalized community. Jaipal was a brilliant student and a rising sports prodigy. Cosgrave, with the wisdom of a seasoned observer, saw something special in the fifteen-year-old boy, a potential that could turn into something great. He had Jaipal brought to England.

Jaipal's higher educational journey began at St. Augustine's College in Canterbury, England. But his intellectual trajectory took a significant turn when he transferred to St. John's College, Oxford. This move proved to be a pivotal point in his life. Immersed in the rigorous academic environment and vibrant campus life of Oxford, Jaipal truly flourished, realizing his full potential both as a scholar and an athlete.

St. John's Hockey Team, 1925. In the middle, Jaipal Singh—a student then, a national icon in the making. (St. John's College, Oxford, Archive PHOTO I.F.5. Reproduced by permission of the president and fellows of St. John's College, Oxford.)

Besides being a star hockey player—an Oxford 'Blue'—he was president of the Oxford Indian Majlis, a debating society and intellectual hub for Indians of the time (which included today's Bangladesh, India and Pakistan), and much more. A brilliant future lay before him.

In time, Jaipal would become the face of India's tribal landscape, just like his forerunner, the legendary Birsa Munda. Santosh Kiro's book *The Life and Times of Jaipal Singh Munda* is another biography and a detailed reflection into Jaipal Singh Munda's life, which painstakingly describes his transformation.

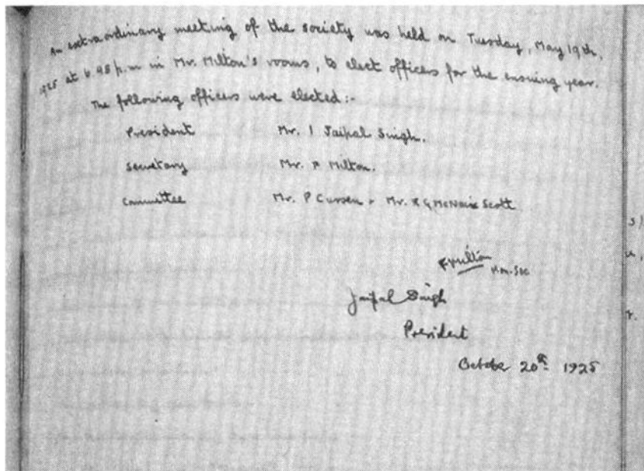

Historic minute book entry from the Debating Society, St. John's College, Oxford, signed by its president at the time, Ishwardas Jaipal Singh. (St. John's College, Oxford, Archive UGS V.4 f.110r. Reproduced by permission of the president and fellows of St. John's College, Oxford.)

In his childhood, the open fields of his village were his playground. Surrounded by other Munda children, he developed a natural athleticism. Hockey, played with makeshift bamboo sticks, became a natural part of their lives. He quickly rose above his peers, even those who were much older than him. Despite lacking formal training, Jaipal's childhood in the village probably laid the foundation for his exceptional hockey skills.

Career vs Team India

Jaipal's sporting odyssey in England began with the Oxfordshire team, where his exceptional talent quickly shone through. He soon became the captain. Hailed by the British as the 'finest fullback of the century',[5] Jaipal's hockey prowess captured the attention of the British press. News of his triumphs began to filter back to his homeland, creating a wave of excitement and admiration.

In 1928, India was set to compete in the Summer Olympics in Amsterdam, with the team scheduled to travel through England. Jaipal, deeply immersed in his Indian Civil Service (ICS) training at Oxford, remained blissfully unaware of this news. Two British Indian Army officers, Colonel Bruce Turnbull and Major Ricketts,[6] both members of his church club, broke the news, urging him to lead the team as captain. This presented a daunting dilemma: participating in the Olympics would require weeks of leave from his rigorous ICS training, a request that was strictly forbidden. Undeterred by the potential consequences, Jaipal defied orders, choosing national pride over his career aspirations.

Jaipal joined the national squad at Tilbury and was initially sceptical about their capabilities except for Shaukat Ali and a certain Dhyan Chand who had already made quite a name for himself playing for the Indian army in Australia. To assess the squad, Jaipal organized several practice matches and toured all over England with the team. He invited the Indian students in England to join the tour, just in case some positions could be strengthened further. Among the enthusiastic students was Iftikhar Ali Khan Pataudi, father of the former captain of the Indian cricket team Mansoor Ali Khan Pataudi and grandfather of Bollywood's iconic star Saif Ali Khan. According to sources,[7] Iftikhar did play a few practice matches but never made it to the final cut. As they say, morning shows the day—India's performance in these practice matches captured the attention of the French and British presses and they predicted that India would be the favourites to win the gold medal in Amsterdam. England, the then European champions, shockingly withdrew from the competition. This decision followed a humiliating 4–0 defeat to India in a practice match.[8]

The Indian team, led by Jaipal, did not disappoint the predictors. Although he did not play in the last group match and the final due to a dispute with the team management, the Indian hockey team made Olympic history, capturing the nation's maiden gold medal in hockey. The team's dominance was absolute, conceding no goals throughout the entire tournament.

Change of track

After guiding his nation to eternal glory, Jaipal returned to Oxford to resume his ICS probation, but Oxford remained rigid to their rules: a break in probation meant Jaipal had to re-do his probation for one more year. Jaipal disagreed and left his ICS dreams to start a new phase of his life in the corporate sector. He became the first Indian to be appointed as a covenanted mercantile assistant in the Royal Dutch-Shell Group. His job soon brought him a posting back to India. Despite the lucrative salary, Jaipal's corporate career proved short-lived. He yearned for academia, and accepted a position at Prince of Wales College in Ghana. Subsequently he joined Rajkumar College in Raipur, India, as principal. This prestigious institution catered to the pampered princes of various states, each with his own entourage, kitchen and private tutors. The princes were wrapped in royalty, and they all wanted an English principal instead of an Indian who only came from Britain. The pressure was mounting, and he knew he needed to find a new job soon. It was perhaps to teach his students a lesson and give them a reality check, that he landed upon a crazy idea.

Jaipal organized an exhibition football match for the princes against school students from Calcutta. During his brief stay at Calcutta as a Burmah-Shell employee, he had made friends in the local Mohun Bagan Club who readily agreed to arrange the match. A special train was arranged from Raipur to Calcutta for the match, as the princes rolled up their sleeves to showcase their royal sporting abilities. The result was disastrous: the princes suffered a humiliating defeat on the ground and the press was flooded with headlines like 'Princess Playing Football!'

The governor's unexpected advice

Despite the humiliating defeat inflicted upon the princes, Jaipal had impressed an unlikely observer: the maharaja of Bikaner. Recognizing his leadership qualities, the maharaja appointed Jaipal as the foreign secretary of Bikaner State. This unexpected turn of events thrust Jaipal into the world of national politics, a realm he initially viewed with some apprehension.

However, a chance encounter with Sir Maurice Hallett, the governor of Bihar, would soon ignite a newfound passion within him.

'Don't waste your time. Go to Ranchi ... You have wandered all over the world serving others. Now do something for your own people.'[9] Maurice Hallett's words were a revelation for Jaipal. They ignited a spark, rekindling the embers of his ancestral legacy—the legacy of Birsa Munda. It was time to embrace his true identity and chase the unfulfilled dreams of his forefathers.

Looking after Adivasi rights

The next day he drove to his village to see his recently widowed mother. When he told his mother about his future plans and asked about her opinion on it, she said, 'Do what you like, but you must not expect gratitude.'[10] That was the beginning of Jaipal's selfless journey as the face of the oppressed Adivasis of India.

Jaipal Singh, despite years spent far from his homeland, was immediately embraced by his people upon his return. He was crowned 'Marang Gomke'[11] (Great Leader) and elected president of the Adivasi Mahasabha. Education reform for his people became his burning crusade, a cause he felt uniquely equipped to champion. However, his pleas for support fell on deaf ears, repeatedly ignored by Bihar Congress president, Dr Rajendra Prasad.

The truth was, many in the Congress leadership were aware of Jaipal's brilliance back at the Oxford Majlis and saw him as a threat to the party's overall influence and goals. In their eyes, his concerns for the tribals were mere distractions from the paramount goal of national independence.

But Jaipal's popularity was exploding. In the 1939 district board elections, the Adivasi Mahasabha swept the polls, capturing sixteen out of twenty-five seats in Ranchi and a staggering twenty-two out of twenty-four in Singhbhum.[12]

Alarmed, the Congress party convened a crucial conference in Ramgarh, a village in Hazaribagh, on 19–20 March 1940, a massive gathering that would feature towering figures like Maulana Azad, Mahatma Gandhi, Jawaharlal Nehru and Sardar Patel.

Two days earlier, Subhas Chandra Bose, planning his own anti-compromise conference at the same venue, found his path blocked by the Congress, who used their influence to organize a blockage on the Ranchi–Ramgarh Road. Bose turned to Jaipal, who convinced 5,000 tribal men, armed with bows and arrows, to accompany Bose to navigate the treacherous jungle path and help him reach the anti-compromise conference. The anti-compromise camp was in place on time, across the Damodar River from the Congress camp. Jaipal ensured Bose's conference was a resounding success.[13]

However, the Congress party's luck ran out. Although Gandhi and others addressed the people on the first day of the conference,[14] on the second day, Ramgarh was washed away by torrential rains, bringing it to a hasty end. This was an additional blow for the Congress, following the electoral setback at the hands of the very people they had neglected for so long.

Jaipal's ever-growing fight for his people took him to the Constituent Assembly in 1946, where he demanded a separate

Jharkhand state for the Adivasis. During the debates, he would often refer to himself as 'Jungli'[15] and would continue to demand multiple safeguards and reservations for the marginalized tribals of India, right up to his death.

The voice of the oppressed everywhere

Jaipal Singh Munda was the voice of the Adivasi community in India's freedom movement. Later, he travelled to the USA to speak on Adivasi affairs at various universities. And there, something unthinkable happened. The Chickasaw tribe of Oklahoma, also known as the Spartans of the Lower Mississippi Valley, bestowed upon him the title of honorary chief and presented him with a traditional Native Indian headdress, a symbol of their deep respect.[16]

In his own words, as stated in his autobiography, *Lo Bir Sendra*:

The biggest surprise awaited me in Oklahoma City. At the airport there was a guard of honour. There were six motor bicycles escorting me to the hotel. All traffic was stopped. A lunch was given in the country club where I was presented with an expensive Red Indian headgear and made honorary pelichi (Chief) of the Chickasaw Nation. At Norman, eight miles away, I was given the freedom of the City by the woman mayor. The Americans can afford to be genuinely generous.

But, in India, his legacy remains largely forgotten. Perhaps it is because he dared to challenge the established order, to champion the cause of the marginalized, those deemed 'backward' and 'trivial' by the masses. His dreams, once considered utopian, found fruition in the creation of the state of Jharkhand thirty years after his death.

43

An Unusual Maharaja and His Swadeshi Avengers

'*Aur is aitihasik jeet ke baad bhi, Bhuvan aur uske saathiyo ka naam itihaas ke panno me kahin kho gaya.*' (And even after this historic victory, the names of Bhuvan and his comrades got lost somewhere in the pages of history.)

Anybody who has watched Ashutosh Gowarikar and Aamir Khan's 2001 magnum opus *Lagaan* can never forget the closing lines of the movie delivered by Amitabh Bachchan in his trademark deep baritone. A story about eleven villagers who take on the might of Queen Victoria's Empire at a game completely foreign to them, to pull off a remarkable win, *Lagaan* was India's official entry at the Academy Awards for 2001–02. Combining the country's biggest passions, cricket and cinema, the film became a rage at the box office and witnessed theatres across India turn into cricket stadiums.

Lagaan began with a standard disclaimer about the events and characters of the movie being fictitious. But what if we tell you that while *Lagaan*'s story may have been born out of fiction, not too many years after the times depicted in the film (early 1890s), a similar clash of unequals did happen where an assembly of Indians handed out a chastening defeat to their colonial masters at their own favourite game of the willow.

Remember Kulbhushan Kharbanda's Raja Puran Singh in the movie? A man whose heart was with his poor subjects but who could not muster the courage to stand up to the British Raj? A king also plays a central role in our story. But unlike Raja Puran Singh, this royal was not afraid to flaunt his Indianness. His name was Maharaja Jagadindra Nath of Natore in Rajshahi district (in present-day Bangladesh). At a time when almost all Indian royalty tried their best to cosy up to their colonial masters, Jagadindra Nath was a rare exception—an Indian royal imbued with nationalism. His proximity with one of the earliest nationalist leaders, Rashtraguru Surendranath Banerjee, had imbued him with a deep sense of patriotism and Indianness.

At the time, Europeans, especially the British, firmly believed that Indians were inferior to them when it came to matters physical. By the late 1880s, thinkers and writers like Swami Vivekananda, Rashtraguru Surendranath, Bankim Chandra Chattopadhyay and others had been vocal against this, exhorting their countrymen to prove the British wrong. Already, in the field of football, Nagendra Prasad Sarbadhikari's Sovabazar Club had set a benchmark, pulling off an upset win over an English side in the Trades Cup tournament in 1891.

Two rajas and their cricket rivalry

Raja Jagadindra had also chosen a sport to break the mental block Indians had against their white rulers. His choice of sport was a darling of India's ruling class and the pride of the Englishmen: cricket. But there was another more personal motivation for Jagadindra. At the time in Bengal, there was another king who also was a passionate lover of the game of willows. Maharaja Nripendra Narayan of Cooch Behar was a well-known patron of the game. He had built two exquisite cricket grounds: one in Cooch Behar and one in Alipore, Calcutta (Woodland Gardens). He would also invite top players to play for his Cooch Behar team in challenge contests against sides representing other Indian royals. However, Nripendra Narayan's teams consisted of European players or members of the aristocracy only. The common or average Indian had no entry to this prestigious lineup.

Raja Jagadindra naturally wanted to get one up on Nripendra Narayan. But unlike the Cooch Behar royal, he wanted to go the 'swadeshi' route. His Natore team would not include any Europeans but would consist only of Indian players of ordinary lineage. And just like Raja Nripendra Narayan, the Natore king also built a beautiful ground in the Ballygunge area of south Calcutta. The rivalry between the two cricket-loving kings went a long way in popularizing the game in late nineteenth century Calcutta and Bengal. But it was a cricket team other than Cooch Behar that became Jagadindra's bête noire.

Jagadindra's Avengers vs CCC

The Calcutta Cricket Club (CCC) was the premier cricketing club in Calcutta at the time. It was also the most snobbish. It became Raja Jagadindra's mission in life to defeat the Calcutta Cricket Club. He kept on attempting it, but the desired result continued to evade him. Eventually, Jagadindra hit upon an idea that Colonel Nick Fury would employ successfully in Marvel's Avengers movie a century later: to bring together a group of diverse superheroes and make a powerful team. So, the raja of Natore started putting together his own brand of Avengers from the best cricketing talent across India, from diverse backgrounds, to create a team that would fulfil his dream.

Joining the best of local talent were some of the finest players from all parts of the subcontinent: fast bowler H.L. Sempre from Karachi, acclaimed batter Kekashru Mistry from Poona, wicket-keeper K. Seshachari from Madras, and the Palwankar brothers, Baloo and Shivram, from western India. Jagadindra would have been well justified in claiming, like John Hammond did in Steven Spielberg's *Jurassic Park*: 'No expense spared!'

'Untouchable' star of the team

The inclusion of the Palwankar brothers was most groundbreaking. They belonged to the chamar caste that resided at the bottom of the orthodox Hindu caste hierarchy and were considered untouchables. When Baloo, a brilliant left-arm slow bowler, was first selected in the Poona Hindu Gymkhana, despite quickly establishing himself as the premier bowler in the side, he faced poor treatment from his teammates. They refused to eat meals with him, would not touch him in celebration and even refused to hand the ball to him—instead placing it on the ground and kicking it towards Baloo. The man tolerated this beastly behaviour with fortitude and in time, his talent would break down social taboos and he would be accepted as an equal. But for a member of the royalty to invite an 'untouchable' to play for his side must have sent shockwaves through the Hindu upper classes at the time. And it also showed what a large-hearted man Jagadindra was.

So, one fine winter day in the first decade of the twentieth century at the Eden Gardens of Calcutta, Natore's Hindustani Avengers lined up against the all-European Calcutta Cricket Club. Not surprisingly, it was Palwankar Baloo who emerged as the bowling star, mesmerizing the batters with his guile of flight and spin. Raja Jagadindra's dreams finally came true as his all-Indian side handed a chastening defeat to the Calcutta Cricket Club. But an even greater human story was scripted alongside.

An unlikely pairing wins the day

Wicketkeeper Seshachari was an Iyengar Brahmin from Madras: the highest of high castes. But in a classic display of the equalizing power of sports, this man combined with the untouchable Baloo to bring about the downfall of many a white batter that day. In his charming book, *A Corner of a Foreign Field: The Indian History of a British Sport*, historian Ramachandra Guha quotes Romesh Ganguly, who was present for the match, in describing this most unusual tango:

> The cricket colossus, Seshachari, dark and forbidding, in his stand in close vicinity behind the stumps. The fastest ball would not remove him from his place of operation so near to the batsman's citadel. He crouched low and I wondered if the bails would not be disturbed from their cradle on top of

the stumps by the volume of air let out by his lungs which I thought had the capacity of bellows. He reminded me of the sinister hill that hangs over the edge of a plain. I noticed some of his fingertips were somewhat crooked. What made them so? The question intrigues me even today!

Some off-the-field sledging

The raja of Natore may have won the match but the other side was never going to be a gracious loser. Enter the scene: Calcutta Cricket Club's captain, ironically named Major White. As the raja joined the CCC players for refreshments, White, smarting from the defeat, could not resist a dirty shot. He sarcastically applauded Raja Jagadindra and asked him how many 'gentlemen' were there in his playing eleven, obliquely indicating that the raja had hired paid professionals to achieve the win, which was, therefore, tainted.

But that day, nothing was going White's way. Former Bengal captain Raju Mukherji writes in his book, *Eden Gardens: Legend and Romance*, that the raja smiled and gave a reply akin to a ravishing cricket drive: '[Only] myself as I have nothing else to do but play cricket. All the other players are my invitees, who out of love for cricket, honour me by playing for my team.' Major White was badly 'stumped' and decided to beat a retreat.

Raja Jagadindra Roy and his Indian Avengers scripted history that day—smashing the British arrogance and proving that Indians were more than an equal match for them in any walk of life.

But like Bhuvan's men in *Lagaan*, this rather unusual king and the historic win achieved by his merry band of Avengers also got lost somewhere in the pages of history.

<h1 style="text-align:center">44</h1>

Assassination on a Football Field

If you are not an avid football follower, Mohammedan Sporting Club might not immediately ring a bell. But the reality is that it was once a formidable name in Indian football. Usually, when people think of Kolkata football, their minds drift to the two towering giants—Mohun Bagan and East Bengal. Yet, Mohammedan Sporting was once as dominant as the other two. Mohammedan became the first Indian team to win the coveted Calcutta Football League in 1934, and in 1938, the first to win it five times in a row.

However, this is where history takes an odd, somewhat cinematic turn: Mohammedan Sporting Club became inadvertently linked to a deadly chapter of India's freedom struggle. It was a regular afternoon in British India, and a football match was underway. A group of young revolutionaries walked onto the field. And their presence changed everything. Football has often been a stage for passion, drama and rivalries, but rarely does it cross into such a degree of political tension. Yet, on 2 September 1933, in this game, India witnessed the most extraordinary scene.

This was no ordinary game, and certainly no ordinary day for the people of Midnapore (now Medinipur). And as unlikely as it sounds, the football match provided the perfect cover for one of the most daring acts of rebellion in colonial India. If you're unfamiliar with Midnapore, it's a historic town located in the current West Medinipur district of West Bengal. Nestled on the banks of the Kangsabati River, this town was once a hotbed of resistance and revolution. The busy

294

Medinipur railway station offers an unassuming starting point for a journey into history. The historic St. John's Church is a peaceful yet eerily important monument that is only a short stroll from the station.

Visit to an old church

Since 1770, the church has stood as a mute reminder of a time of colonial oppression and imperial rule. Its details in architecture are distinctly European. The tall, slender spire still has a weathercock on top of it. There is only a basic crucifix and a lectern (Bible stand) within the church, where the vicar would have delivered sermons to the devout, rather than any elaborate decorations or large statues. Facing these, the old wooden pews from the British era stand quietly. The church has a large cemetery all around it. Numerous weathered gravestones stand on this site, most of them vandalized. This site was previously designated for the British officers, their loved ones and important members of the district administration.

Medinipur's St. John's Church, West Bengal—resting place of Bernard E.J. Burge, killed during a local football match in 1933. (Photo courtesy: Archan Chakraborty)

The tombstones are typically made of slate and marble. They feature brief epitaphs, each telling its own story. Among them, three graves stand out, each sharing one chilling story in common.

These graves belong to James Peddie, Robert Douglas and Bernard E.J. Burge, three consecutive district magistrates of Midnapore.

Medinipur's St. John's Church, West Bengal. (Photography: Archan Chakraborty)

Each of these men was a high-ranking officer in the British Indian Civil Service. All three were killed by revolutionaries from the Bengal Volunteers in this very town. The killings were meticulously planned and occurred over a span of three years. These events were so shocking but also daring that they ignited a wave of resistance that spread far beyond this small town.

Midnapore's triple assassinations

The year 1931 was pivotal for Midnapore and, indeed, for the entire subcontinent. While Gandhi's Salt March was galvanizing millions into civil disobedience, the youth of Bengal were taking a more direct approach to challenge British authority. Amidst this backdrop, James Peddie, Midnapore's district magistrate, became the first target of the revolutionaries.

On 7 April 1931, during an exhibition fair at the Midnapore Collegiate School, two young revolutionaries, Jyoti Jiban Ghosh and Bimal Dasgupta, struck with precision. Skilfully evading his security cordon of trained police dogs and vigilant bodyguards, they entered the hall and fired five rounds from their Webley top-break revolver, leaving him fatally wounded. Peddie's assassination sent shockwaves through British administrative circles, but it was only the beginning.

Both the young revolutionaries were members of the Bengal Volunteers group, an underground revolutionary organization in Bengal opposing British rule in India. The group was first organized by Netaji Subhas Chandra Bose during the Calcutta session of the Congress in 1928 and remained active until India's independence.

Peddie was succeeded as district magistrate by Robert Douglas, who took on an extremely hazardous role. However, the course of his tenure was identical to that of his predecessor. Two young men who were members of the Bengal Volunteers, Pradyot Bhattacharya and Probhanshu Pal, carried out their audacious plot on 30 April 1932, at a district board meeting. They made sure that Douglas would not escape by firing at him at close range.

Tension between the local population and the British government grew as a result of the cycle of murders and retaliation. It was also an unsettling reminder that British civil servants could no longer feel safe in Midnapore.

By the time Bernard E.J. Burge was appointed district magistrate in 1932, Midnapore had become a veritable deathtrap for British officials. Burge's wife, Barbara, vehemently opposed his posting, but her objections fell on deaf ears. The family took residence in a heavily guarded bungalow in what is still known as Burge Town. The bungalow's sentries were always alert. Bodyguards accompanied Mr Burge during the day and slept nearby at night. Sentries patrolled constantly. It was an almost wartime situation in the daily life of a civil official. Bernard Burge, also known as Bobby Burge, was a man of routine, but he also had a passion for sports. This, ultimately, would lead to his death.

Bobby Burge was not just a skilled administrator, but also a well-known figure in the local community. He earned a fair share of praise for his talent as a cricketer, playing for the Stragglers of Asia Cricket Club and leading the Ballygunge Cricket Club in Calcutta. Burge was no minor figure in the sporting community.

The Stragglers of Asia had a fascinating history. Originally formed by officers and civil servants on leave in India in the early 1920s, they would gather in the Simla hills during summer to play cricket. They were often invited by the maharaja of Patiala, and the games were made even more enjoyable with a few Patiala pegs along the way.

On the other hand, Ballygunge Cricket Club was the predecessor of the Calcutta Cricket and Football Club (CCFC), a place famous for hosting the Merchants' Cup. It's also home to the oldest rugby institution founded outside the United Kingdom—something anyone who grew up in Kolkata would recognize.

It was the peak football season in Midnapore, and the Bradley-Birt Trophy was in full swing. This local tournament was named after Francis Bradley Bradley-Birt, a British diplomat, writer and former district magistrate of Midnapore. Back in 1912, Babu Ramcharan Sinha, the athletics instructor at Midnapore College, instituted the cup in honour of the magistrate.

Bobby Burge, though he had long given up football, recognized the value of connecting with the local community through sports. So, he laced up his boots again, occasionally starting to play for the local Town Club. This rekindling of his football-playing days created an opening the Bengal Volunteers had been waiting for. They began planning his assassination during one of these football matches.

To participate in the Bradley-Birt Trophy, football powerhouses from Calcutta frequently travelled to Midnapore to face local teams. Burge had watched and even played a few matches, including one featuring Mohun Bagan, but the heavy security around him thwarted any attempts by the rebels to strike. August passed without success, and as the football season neared its end, the Bengal Volunteers grew desperate. Their window was closing.

Finally, on 2 September 1933, they got a chance. A match was scheduled at the Midnapore Central Jail grounds between Calcutta's famous Mohammedan Sporting Club and Midnapore Town Football Club. According to case files from the Calcutta High Court, this match was part of the Corners Shield Competition, not the Bradley-Birt Trophy.

Burge had to play for the Town Club to put up a fight against a strong Calcutta team. The game attracted a large crowd, including the revolutionaries, who had meticulously planned their move. Among them were a few brave young members of the Bengal Volunteers—

Nirmal Jibon Ghosh, Anath Bondhu Panja, Mrigendranath Dutta, Ram Krishna Roy and Brojo Kishore Chakravarty. Most of them were students—young and fearless. It's said that they drew lots to determine who would take on the mission, such was their eagerness to participate.

As players from Mohammedan Sporting warmed up near the southern goal, Anath and Mrigendranath mingled on the field, posing as players, while Ram Krishna and Brojo Kishore stood watch near the southeast corner. The revolutionaries blended seamlessly into the crowd as Burge arrived in his car, surrounded by armed guards.

At around 5 p.m., as Burge stepped on to the grounds, gunshots rang out. Four bullets struck him, and he collapsed instantly. Chaos ensued, but Anath Bondhu and Mrigendranath did not flee. They ensured their mission was complete, firing their last bullets into Burge before being overpowered.

Anath Bondhu Panja was killed on the spot, while Mrigendranath Dutta succumbed to injuries the next day. The other conspirators—Nirmal Jibon Ghosh, Brojo Kishore Chakravarty and Ram Krishna Roy—were arrested, and all three were executed in October 1934.

45

Banians, Akhadas and a Bhadromohila[1]

Just a stone's throw from Kolkata's Eden Gardens stands the iconic Mohun Bagan Football Club. On 29 July 1911, during the Indian Football Association (IFA) Shield final, Mohun Bagan faced the East Yorkshire Regiment of the British army (Chapter 41). The stakes were high as eleven barefoot Indian players took on eleven British soldiers in a match that became a symbol of national pride. In a historic win, Mohun Bagan defeated the British team, marking India's first major football victory over a colonial power. The 1911 win remains a historic moment in Indian history.

A few days after Mohun Bagan's historic win, the *Manchester Guardian* reported, 'There is one person in Calcutta to whom the remarkable win of a Bengali football team over a crack British regiment will bring a lively satisfaction. This is Miss Tagore.' The newspaper believed that without Miss Tagore's influence, Bengali men wouldn't have competed against the strong British players, and they were right.

But who was Miss Tagore, and why was the *Manchester Guardian* highlighting her?

The article continued, 'A team of Bengalees won the Football Association Shield in India after defeating the crack teams of three British regiments amidst the applause of 80 thousand of their countrymen. There is no reason, of course, of being surprised. Victory of Association goes to the side with the greatest physical fitness, the quickest eye, and the keenest wit.'

The patron saint of Bengali athletics

Surprisingly, the strength and resilience of Bengali athletes in that era traced back to one remarkable woman. She was the driving force behind Bengal's athletic movement in the late nineteenth and early twentieth centuries, shaping sports into a platform for nationalism and anti-colonial resistance.

Miss Tagore, however, was not her real name. The journalist at the *Manchester Guardian* mistakenly assumed so due to her close ties with the Tagore family. In reality, she was Sarala Ghoshal, the niece of Rabindranath Tagore!

Sarala was a trailblazer—a social reformer, writer, educationist, feminist and freedom fighter. While her role in the Non-Cooperation Movement is well documented, her impact on Bengal's athletic movement has largely been forgotten. Despite coming from an illustrious literary family, privilege didn't make her complacent—it fuelled her drive. She became the first female gold medallist in English Literature from her college at a time when women graduates were rare. After a brief teaching stint in Mysore, she dedicated herself to the freedom struggle and women's rights.

During the days of the Empire, sports became more than just a game—it was a form of resistance. But when facing British opponents, something was missing. Even Punjab's mighty wrestlers, known for their strength, struggled against British challengers. Sarala saw this fear and made it her mission to erase the awe of white skin from the Indian psyche.

We spoke with Sayantani Adhikary, an independent scholar and assistant professor in the history department at Sadhan Chandra Mahavidyalaya. She has studied this subject in depth. She explained, 'The Bengali male, especially the middle-class Hindu male, was seen as weak, lacking physical strength and emasculated.' To illustrate this perception, she was kind enough to show us several Kalighat paintings (patachitra) featuring caricatures of cowardly Calcutta babus, highlighting the stereotype of cowardice associated with this class. She added, 'The race was considered "non-martial" and pleasure-loving, almost like a dandy. This perception appears in colonial accounts and even in Bengali writings, such as *Hutom Pyanchar Naksha*.'

Sarala Devi—a visionary whose voice, actions and dedication to physical fitness and the akhada tradition transformed the social fabric of Bengal. (Photo author unknown. Public Domain via Wikimedia Commons.)

When outrage led to constructive action

Sarala's turning point came when she read Rudyard Kipling's 'The Head of the District', a story that depicted a Bengali man as too weak to govern a northern Indian district. Outraged, she wrote to Kipling, challenging him to have one of her brothers wrestle him within five years. But beyond this challenge, she began to think—how could she truly change this perception?

She realized the issue wasn't lack of skill but deep-seated fear. Indians weren't losing because they were weak but because they had been conditioned to see the British as superior. To change this, Sarala focused on building both physical and mental strength. Sarala's solution was akhadas—homegrown gymnasiums where strength, confidence and resilience could be forged.

An akhada was a place similar to modern gyms, but without any heavy equipment. It was a space where athletes could train, refine their skills and perfect their techniques. More importantly, it focused on building mental strength alongside physical fitness. Sarala understood that it wasn't just the body but the mind that needed strengthening. She aimed to use sports to transform her people into a powerful and confident race, one that would never see itself as inferior.

In her own words, Sarala described her efforts to bring her mission to life, as noted in *The Many Worlds of Sarala Devi: A Diary* (translated from the Bengali *Jeevaner Jharapata* by Sukhendu Ray):

Returning to Calcutta, my search for an expert coach to train our boys in the art of wielding swords, clubs, etc., eventually led me to Professor Murtaza, a Muslim gentleman. I engaged him on terms of a generous remuneration to train our boys at a club that I had founded at our home. This club was later shifted to No. 26 Ballygunge Circular Road to which we had moved. It was a big house with a sizeable lawn in front and a water tank at the back. Behind the tank was a sort of square plot which was used by the boys to practise with their weapons and equipment. I personally funded the expenses of the club, which included not only Professor Murtaza's remuneration but also the cost of equipment, such as boxing gloves, clubs, swords and daggers, shields, rods and poles.

The fitness phenomenon called Sandow

In this context, we must mention Eugen Sandow, the Prussian bodybuilder who had a surprising influence on India in the early twentieth century. He became the original 'strongman' and the father of modern bodybuilding, captivating audiences across Europe and America as the ultimate symbol of strength. If you're a Sherlock Holmes fan, you'll be interested to know that Sir Arthur Conan Doyle himself followed the intense muscle-conditioning regimen of Eugen Sandow. Sandow's fame eventually reached India.

From 1904 to 1905, Sandow toured Calcutta, Madras and Bombay, drawing huge crowds wherever he went. When his train arrived at Howrah Station in Calcutta, excitement filled the air, and the crowd erupted in cheers as he stepped onto the platform, looking every bit as powerful as his photos. His India tour became a sensation, as detailed in Carey A. Watt's renowned work, 'Cultural Exchange, Appropriation and Physical Culture: Strongman Eugen Sandow in Colonial India, 1904–1905'.

A message of empowerment

However, his shows weren't just about muscles; they carried a deeper message. Sandow told Indians that, with discipline, they too could be as strong as the British. His words ignited a sense of national pride, encouraging young Indians, especially Bengalis and Parsis, to embrace fitness as a means of empowerment. For example, Gobar Guha, the first Asian to win the US World Wrestling Championship, and his friend were regulars at Sandow's shows.

Eugen Sandow, renowned Prussian bodybuilder, whose signature style influenced the Indian Sandow vest. (Public Domain via Wikimedia Commons.)

> **The Sandow legacy**
>
> Sandow eventually became part of a forgotten subculture. The pioneer of the silent film era, P.K. Nagalingam earned the nickname P.K. Raja Sandow for his physique and gymnastics skills. M.M.A. Chinnappa Thevar, the writer and producer of *Haathi Mere Saathi*, was known as Sandow Chinnappa Thevar for his strong build, fighting skills, and fitness dedication. Sandow even appeared in one of Sukumar Roy's classic poems.

Inspired by Sandow's iconic look in early images, young men across Calcutta and India began wearing vests similar to their Prussian idol and headed to their local akhadas. This is how the 'Sandow vest' or 'Sando banian' is believed to have gained its name. The busy streets of Calcutta also witnessed a rise in akhadas. This surge, attributed in part to Sandow and in part to Sarala Devi, not only boosted a fitness culture but also played a key role in fuelling the Swadeshi Movement and igniting a cultural revival.

An unstoppable force

Sarala, meanwhile, continued her work like a force of nature. In *The Many Worlds of Sarala Devi: A Diary*, she recounted her efforts to inspire the youth with ideals of heroism through various festivals she created, including the Birashtami Utsav, Pratapaditya Utsav and the Udayaditya Utsav. For example, during the Birashtami Utsav (started in 1902, the eighth day of the Durga Puja celebrations),[2] she described how young men gathered around a sword, chanting a poem with the names of heroic figures, starting with Krishna. As each name was called, the participants showered the sword with flowers. After the ritual, there were demonstrations of physical training and competitive games. Interestingly, the prizes were awarded by a Muslim woman, the wife of Sujatali Beg, while the teacher of physical exercises was Professor Murtaza, also a Muslim. Sarala's efforts were an attempt to build unity between Hindus and Muslims while introducing Bengali youth to the philosophy of armed revolution.

Sarala's work had a far-reaching impact. Her efforts quickly spread beyond Calcutta, inspiring the creation of more clubs and gymnasiums across Bengal. These spaces, once dedicated to sports, became significant in the freedom movement. Her actions made her a prominent figure, drawing both praise and criticism. The British police closely monitored her, but Sarala was never one to back down. By blending physical strength with mental resilience, she created a powerful platform for nationalism.

Samuel Kerkham Ratcliffe, editor of *The Statesman*, had noticed Sarala's efforts to boost local athletes' morale against the British. Later, as a writer for the *Manchester Guardian*, he acknowledged her impact. When Mohun Bagan won in July 1911, with 80,000 spectators celebrating, Ratcliffe recognized that Sarala's unyielding spirit had driven Bengal's athletic movement. He knew 'Miss Tagore' would be proud of that victory.

007
CHICAGO RADIO
VOTE FOR GHOSE
The
Makers of
Tomorrow

46

The Widow Who Dared and the
Pioneers of Uttarpara

Nanibala Devi was a widow who broke out of the place dictated by the society of her time (which was to pretend you don't exist) to throw herself wholly into the freedom struggle. She was clever and brave and loyal, successful in her assignment, and took the consequences like a real hero. Her mission was to trace a German Mauser pistol, and she successfully outwitted British intelligence, besides becoming a social pariah, to do it. To top it off, she even slapped a British police superintendent in his own office.

To discover her roots, we had to go back to a neighbourhood in Bengal. That's where we discovered the legacy of a pioneering family, and gradually, the true extent of her heritage began to unfold.

Uttarpara's zamindar who cared

Uttarpara, a quaint town nestled on the banks of the Hooghly River in West Bengal, intrigued us for many reasons. One of the most captivating stories was how Aurobindo Ghose, after his release from prison in 1909, found his way to Uttarpara to deliver his famous speech. Netaji Subhas Chandra Bose too had given a speech there, though, despite the tales we had heard, we could hardly find any documented evidence of it before we decided to take the plunge and explore further.

We hopped on to a local train at the iconic Howrah Station, and headed to Uttarpara. We alighted from the train, and went to the rickshaw stand next to the station. At the head of the queue was Ganesh Babu, a seasoned rickshaw-puller, who was excited to take us on our adventure to Jaykrishna Library.

India's first free public library, the Uttarpara Jaykrishna Public Library, still carries the overlooked legacy of the freedom movement. (Photo courtesy: Debasish Mukherjee)

Ganesh Babu turned out to be a veteran of Uttarpara, well-versed in its history. When we asked him about the library, his face fell as he spoke about the current state of the once-renowned institution. He recalled how the library, which had proudly held the title of Asia's first free public library, had lost much of its former glory. Originally known as the Uttarpara Public Library, it had begun as a private collection of books, journals and documents owned by Jaykrishna Mukherjee. In 1851, Mukherjee had generously opened his collection to researchers, as a valuable resource for the community, and he built a library to house the collection, on the banks of the Hooghly.

The inspiration behind the library was Dwarkanath Tagore and a law passed in Britain in 1850 promoting local public libraries. Jaykrishna Mukherjee wanted to promote education and knowledge in Bengal. In August 1854, he proposed a public library for Uttarpara to the Burdwan divisional commissioner. He also offered monetary contributions. However, the proposal was rejected. So, he decided to fund the entire library on his own. The library was finally built and opened to the public in 1859. Today, it has been recognized as a Group 'A' library by the West Bengal state government. Work is being done to get it recognized as an institution of national importance.

This wasn't the first time that Jaykrishna took on the responsibility of setting up an institution. The son of a government employee, Jaykrishna had the privilege of attending a British army school and even served in the British Indian Army, and learnt to be very disciplined and punctual. At twenty-two, he started working in the land records department of Hooghly and married into a zamindari family. Thereafter he started buying estates and became a zamindar in his own right—a benevolent one.

During his lifetime Jaykrishna Mukherjee set up thirty-five schools, a college, seven health centres and the Uttarpara municipality. He was a true patron of education and health for the empowerment of the people.

The quiet fight for freedom

Jaykrishna was a close ally of Ishwar Chandra Vidyasagar, and his signature was the first on Vidyasagar's petition for widow remarriage. Through Vidyasagar and his other allies, Jaykrishna also financially supported the freedom movement, which had gained momentum after the First War of Independence of 1857. Mukherjee family's historian, Debasish Mukherjee, corroborated this, adding that Raja Peary Mohan Mukherjee, Manohar Mukherjee and others too regularly helped the freedom fighters financially. In fact, Jaykrishna had proposed Dadabhai Naoroji for president at the second session of the Indian National Congress.

Jaykrishna's middle son, Peary Mohan Mukherjee, continued his legacy of philanthropy and actively invested in education, healthcare and social reforms.

Kaushik Mukherjee, a current descendant of the family, told us:

'We have looked at India's independence from only a single dimension—great men fighting the Brits with arms and ammunition, getting caught and hanged, making supreme sacrifices. In pure corporate terms, that'll be operations. But a working organization cannot function with just ops. It requires strategy and finance. That's where the Mukherjees come into the picture—giving the movement a platform and direction. The Mukherjees of Uttarpara pumped in lakhs of rupees in building the infrastructure for education—close to 560 schools and colleges; holding positions in the power centres, influencing policies and laws; and, finally, buying arms from Germany. Biren Roy[1] met with Hitler in 1936 to smuggle in arms through Thailand and Batavia. This was six years before Netaji's meeting with Hitler.'

A photograph of Netaji Subhas Chandra Bose at his family home in Uttarpara, where he spoke on 17 July 1938, was recovered and shared by Kaushik Mukherjee. It had lain forgotten in the Jaykrishna Library basement for decades. (Photo courtesy: Jaykrishna Library and Uttarpara-Kotrung Municipality)

The significant role played by the members of the Uttarpara zamindar family in establishing the infrastructure for education, healthcare and other powerful centres of influence is rarely mentioned when we discuss free India. Their contributions often go unnoticed in the broader narrative of the nation's development.

Major General A.C. Chatterjee was an important leader in the Indian National Army (INA). Subhas Chandra Bose appointed him governor and finance minister of Azad Hind, a temporary Indian government set up in Japanese-occupied Singapore in 1943. A.C. Chatterjee was married to Sabitri Mukherjee, granddaughter of Rajmohan Mukherjee, Jaykrishna's youngest son.

Another shining star of Uttarpara's Mukherjee clan, Amarendranath Chatterjee, was at the forefront of the freedom movement and raised funds for the Jugantar movement, one of the two primary clandestine revolutionary movements advocating for Indian independence in Bengal.

Now, let us circle back to the beginning of this story: about Nanibala Devi.

The woman who broke bounds for azadi

Women in colonized India made huge sacrifices that have not been recognized for a long time. One of them was Nanibala Devi, aunt of Amarendranath Chatterjee, who also played an important role in the freedom movement.

Born in 1888 in Bally, a small town in Howrah, 4.5 kilometres from Uttarpara, Nanibala Devi came from a modest Brahmin family. Raised with basic education at home, her life followed a traditional path—marriage at eleven, widowhood at sixteen. Like many women in colonial Bengal, she faced isolation and suffering. But Nanibala defied expectations. She chose education as her escape, returning to her paternal home to continue her studies. A nearby missionary school offered her the chance to learn English.

She found a mentor in her nephew, Amarendranath Chatterjee from Uttarpara, who introduced her to the world of secret revolutionary operations. She was also trained as a spy. Nanibala Devi was his beloved 'shejo pishima' (paternal aunt), and that's how she was known in revolutionary circles.

In Bengal, she became a crucial link in the underground resistance, providing safe houses and logistical support to rebels fleeing the police. A few years later, Ramchandra Majumdar of the Jugantar party was arrested by the British in 1915 in their search for information on Amarendranath Chatterjee, Aurobindo Ghose and Jatin Mukherjee (Bagha Jatin). He was placed in solitary confinement at Alipore jail. Ramchandra Majumdar had hidden a Mauser pistol from the Rodda heist (Chapter 17), which Jatin needed for deployment. So, Amarendranath Chatterjee needed to know where it was hidden. Nanibala Devi was sent to the prison disguised as Ramchandra Majumdar's wife.

It was a mission that could have come straight out of a Hollywood spy thriller. This was a bold act in an era when women were expected to remain behind the veil. For her, being a widow and daring to disguise herself as someone else's wife was an extraordinary act of courage. Upon seeing her, Ramchandra immediately grasped the purpose of her visit. Without directly mentioning the pistol, he told Nanibala that there was a particular scripture located in a specific place. If she were to obtain it, he could read it in jail. Nanibala left the meeting with the precise location of the weapons, and it was retrieved.

Flight, capture, torture—and a slap back

When the British police suspected her involvement, they issued a lookout notice. Nanibala Devi subsequently fled to Peshawar, where she was eventually arrested and brought back to Benares (Kashi). She underwent unimaginable torture under the direction of the superintendent of CID, Jiten Banerjee. But she didn't break!

As described in the book *Swadhinata Sangramer Manche Bharater Nari* by Krishnakali Biswas, there were interrogations after interrogations, accompanied by obscene insults. When the police couldn't get Nanibala Devi to speak, they ordered extreme torture. The jailer took her to a separate cell, where she was forcibly stripped and had chilli paste inserted inside her body. Even after such brutality, when they could not extract any secrets from her, she was moved to the punishment cell, a place of further torment.

The conditions in the cell were horrific, with only a small locked door for light and no ventilation. Nanibala Devi was kept in this dark, cramped cell for three days. When the door opened, she was found unconscious but still refused to divulge any information upon regaining consciousness. She was later moved from Kashi to the Presidency Jail in Kolkata. She was Bengal's first female state prisoner in India.

There, every day she would be taken at 9 a.m. to the British police officer Goldie's office for interrogation till 5 p.m. Nanibala Devi eventually agreed to provide a written confession regarding the whereabouts of the freedom fighters. However, all she wrote was a terse line: 'I want to go to Bagbazar to meet Maa Sarada (Sri Ramakrishna's wife).' Goldie was furious and angrily tore the paper and threw it at Nanibala Devi. This insult infuriated Nanibala Devi, and she stood up and slapped Goldie in front of his entire staff.

Another heroine left alone

Nanibala Devi was eventually released in 1919 but she was rejected by her family and most of her revolutionary colleagues were gone. Subsequently she became a hermit and disappeared from public view and memory.

According to Satyendranath Gangopadhyay in an article in *Saptahik Basumati* (28 January 1965), Nanibala spent the rest of her life in a narrow bylane in Bose Para, Calcutta, living alone in a rented place for decades. She was known as 'Sadhu Ma' in the neighbourhood. In an interview with the writer in 1964, she remarked, 'The freedom for which we sacrificed our lives—seeing its form now fills my heart with disdain.'

47

A Dream of Freedom Woven in Romance

Boy moves into a new place. Boy meets girl. They become friends. Soon romance blossoms. They come from very different backgrounds. Girl's family likes the boy but only until they find out about the budding romance. Then they turn into strident antagonists. Meanwhile, as news trickles back home, the boy's father blows a fuse and orders him to return home immediately.

Sounds like the script of a Bollywood potboiler? What if we tell you now that this happened in real life? And not just to anyone, but two stalwarts of our independence movement. Surprised? Shocked? Intrigued? Lend your ears to the story of two lovebirds who became thorns in the flesh for the British.

Today, Barama is in Chittagong, Bangladesh. In 1885, when our story begins 140 years ago, it was a part of the undivided Bengal Presidency in British India. The Senguptas were a prominent family of Barama. The head of the family was Jatra Mohan Sengupta, a renowned lawyer of Chittagong, who was also well known for his philanthropic activities and for being an early nationalist voice.

Born to privilege, raised to serve the underprivileged

On 22 February 1885, Jatra Mohan's wife Binodini Devi gave birth to a boy, the couple's third child. He was named Jatindra Mohan. A girl child, born after Jatindra, died as an infant. As a result, as the youngest child, Jatindra grew up cossetted by his mother and other female relatives, enjoying a largely sheltered childhood. But his father Jatra Mohan had quietly made his plans. He was determined to ensure his son followed in his legal footsteps so that Jatindra could fight battles for those who couldn't fight their own.

And so progressed Jatindra's life. After a few initial years of schooling in Chittagong, Jatindra was moved to Calcutta where he finished school and finally graduated from the famed Presidency College. Jatra Mohan's plan was proceeding smoothly as his son now sailed for Britain to pursue his legal studies at Downing College in Cambridge University. The year was 1904. Young Jatindra had come a long way from Barama.

The sudden change in terms of weather, culture, language, cuisine and way of life must have been drastic for Jatindra. But he coped as well as he could, devoting time to his studies, but also enthusiastically participating in sports: he earned University 'Blues' in cricket and tennis besides making a name as a rower. The discussions and debates at the famed Cambridge Majlis drew Jatindra's attention, and soon, he was a star there, eventually becoming the Majlis president in 1908. Meanwhile, one of his English friends persuaded him to appear for the prestigious Indian Civil Service Examination. But his father Jatra Mohan immediately quashed such plans—he was determined that his son would be independent and work for the betterment of his country and countrymen.

And then something happened that would not only change Jatindra's life but even help save the Indian freedom movement at a time of crisis.

An unexpected storm

Frederick William and Edith Henrietta Gray were a popular couple in Cambridge who often rented out a part of their residences to young Cambridge students. The Grays were warm, friendly and sympathetic to students from the colonies and didn't hold any prejudice. It made their home a popular destination for Indian students. Boarders could always bring along a few friends and count on Mrs Gray for a pleasant evening.

That was how Jatindra first visited the Gray house. From the beginning, the Grays liked the soft-spoken and polite Jatindra. The young man in turn enjoyed the Grays' company and frequented their place. Soon, it emerged that Cupid was at play.

Born in 1886, Edith Ellen Gray was the only daughter of the Grays. She had inherited her parents' friendly nature and was always pleasant to the students visiting their house. However, one particular student clearly made a special impression on Edith.

When it came to light that Jatindra and Edith were madly in love with each other, the Grays were horrified. As much as they liked Jatindra, they couldn't envisage their only daughter getting married to an Indian and living the rest of her life in the colonies far away from them. Meanwhile, when Jatindra informed his father back home, the formidable Jatra Mohan sent a sharp reprimand in response. The senior Sengupta also shot off a missive to Mrs Gray, discouraging any marital alliance between the two young people.

Jatindra received another letter from Jatra Mohan, along with money for the fare to India. By this time, Jatindra had qualified as a barrister and had been called to the Bar in England. However, having never disobeyed his father in his life, he decided to quit his practice in England and return to India. After bidding what must have been a tearful and heart-rending goodbye to his beloved Edith, Jatindra boarded the ship for India. But as they say, there is no greater force than the power of love.

Every day spent in the solitude of the high seas further increased the longing in Jatindra's heart for Edith. Eventually, at Port Said in Egypt, Jatindra disembarked from his ship and caught another vessel travelling to England.

A heartbroken Edith was overjoyed when Jatindra made his unannounced appearance at her doorstep. Despite his best efforts, though, Mrs Gray would not allow them to get married. Inevitably, the young couple had to quietly get their marriage registered at Royston. When the news broke, Mrs Gray gave in and even threw a magnificent party to celebrate the happy union. Jatindra and his new bride now began the long journey back to Chittagong.

Portrait of Jatindra Mohan and Nellie Sengupta, photographed by the Central News Photographic Agency in Paris, circa 1930, from the archive of the Bibliothèque nationale de France. (Photo courtesy: Central News. Public Domain via Wikimedia Commons.)

Indian nationalist couple

When the couple turned up at the Sengupta house, everyone was astounded. Edith, who had now assumed the name of 'Nellie', was dressed demurely in a saree just like a Bengali bride and greeted all the elders by touching their feet. Even the quietly fuming Jatra Mohan's heart melted and sounds of joy and laughter rang through the Sengupta house. The young couple settled in Calcutta, where Jatindra began his legal career. But it was not long before the country came calling.

Inspired by Deshbandhu Chittaranjan Das, Jatindra started taking an active interest in the freedom movement. He was particularly concerned about protecting the rights of workers and labourers, often acting pro bono for their cause. Nellie, meanwhile, performed the role of a dutiful wife, taking care of her husband and three sons. But she was also a woman of independent spirit. Despite being English herself, the oppression of Indians at the hands of her own countrymen troubled her very much and she joined her husband in the freedom movement.

By the early 1920s, Jatindra had quit his legal practice and immersed himself full-time in nationalist politics, with Nellie standing like a pillar by his side. When Jatindra was arrested for organizing labour strikes at the Burmah Oil Company and the Assam-Bengal Railways, Nellie took over, leading protest rallies demanding the release of her husband. Both husband and wife immersed themselves in Gandhi's Non-Cooperation Movement. When Jatindra was arrested yet again, Nellie went from door to door, selling khadi clothes and visiting shops, asking the owners to stop stocking British-made goods.

More sacrifices, but soldiering on

After Deshbandhu's sudden death in 1925, Jatindra took over as the president of the Bengal Swaraj Party, which had splintered from the INC. In the coming years, he held many important roles, such as president of the Bengal Provincial Congress Committee and mayor of Calcutta. In 1931, Jatindra travelled to London to attend the Round Table Conference where he produced pictures of police atrocities at Chittagong following the failed rebellion there (Chapter 22). It was a daring exposé that put egg on the face of India's colonial rulers.

The regime struck back with vengeance, repeatedly throwing Jatindra into prison. The recurrent prison stays in unhealthy conditions had an impact on Jatindra's health and on 23 July 1933, while incarcerated in Ranchi prison, Jatindra breathed his last. He was only forty-eight. Jatindra's deep devotion to the nation's cause had earned him the sobriquet 'Deshapriya'—favourite of the nation—from his countrymen.

The loss of her beloved companion of nearly three decades must have left Nellie devastated. But she was made of stern stuff.

With renewed determination, she immersed herself into the freedom movement. At the forty-seventh annual session of the INC in Calcutta, Nellie Sengupta was elected the Congress working committee president. She also served as an alderman of Calcutta Municipality in 1933 and 1936, and was elected to the Bengal Legislative Assembly twice.

All the while, Nellie continued to rally the troops to ensure that the cry for a free India did not die down. This became vital during the 1942 Quit India Movement, when almost all frontline INC leaders were imprisoned. After Independence, Nellie's responsibility didn't end. Alarmed at the reports of mistreatment of Hindu minorities in the new East Pakistan, India's first Prime Minister Pandit Jawaharlal Nehru requested Nellie Sengupta to stay back in Chittagong.

Nellie Sengupta became a champion of minority religious groups in East Pakistan while also immersing herself in social work. When she contested for the East Pakistan Legislative Assembly in 1954, she was elected unopposed—a mark of the respect she commanded. After an accident in 1970 left her with a fractured hip bone, Indian Prime Minister Mrs Indira Gandhi took the lead to bring Nellie

Busts of Jatindra Mohan and Nellie Sengupta at Deshapriya Park, often overlooked by passersby, still guard the memory of sacrifice and love. Nellie Sengupta's inscription reads: '...belongs to the select band of foreigners who made India their home and fought selflessly for the cause of India's freedom.'

Sengupta to Calcutta for treatment. The rest of her life was spent in Calcutta. In 1973, shortly before her death, Nellie Sengupta's immense contribution to India's freedom movement was recognized by awarding her the Padma Vibhushan.

In the compound of the sprawling Deshapriya Park in south Kolkata, named after Jatindra, two marble busts stand as a mute testimony to the couple whom love brought together and who gave everything to the cause of the nation. Thousands pass by every day, most of them oblivious of the Senguptas' glorious service to our nation.

48

Das & Company

Grand Master Oogway from Kung Fu Panda is a dear character for many of us here at Paperclip. He is one of the best and most revered movie characters not just for his martial prowess, but for his calm demeanour, his optimistic outlook and, above all, his deeply insightful yet simple lines. His words of wisdom transcend the screen and remain etched in our hearts, our favourite being, 'There are no accidents,' told to a rather sceptical Master Shifu. These simple words are a testament to enduring positivity, of purpose even amidst uncertainty.

When we were working on this story, the above line by Master Oogway kept recurring in our minds. For this is the story of a family that, for more than a century, through their karma, helped shape our society and nation into what it is today. All of this may have never happened but for an accidental choice. And yet, as we know, there are no accidents.

It was 1857, the year that saw large swathes of the Indian subcontinent light up in the fires of the First War of Independence and nearly ended the British presence almost a century before it eventually terminated. While the main acts of the rebellion took place across northern India, the embers spread far and wide. In this case, as far as the eastern extremities of our land.

The boy who lived

Sylhet, now a part of Bangladesh, was then a part of the eastern division of the Bengal Presidency. On 17 December, a rebellion broke out in Latu.[1] When the British authorities advised their civilian staff to evacuate immediately, many families sailed out on country boats. On one of the boats was Swarup Chandra Das aka Dewan Swarup Chand, a dewan in the Sylhet Collectorate and his six-months-pregnant wife. Mid-river, the lady started having labour pains, eventually giving birth to a baby boy, very premature. Sadly, the baby was found to be stillborn. This was the moment where destiny intervened.

The common practice in such events would have been to immerse the baby's corpse in the river. But for reasons unclear, it was decided to wrap up the inert newborn in clothes and keep him in the boat. Immeasurable must have been the joy of the couple when several hours later, the baby suddenly started crying and kicking! He was named Sundari Mohan.[2] With an eventful birth like that, everyone told the Das couple that their son was surely destined for great things. But possibly none of those making such prophecies of greatness had any inkling of the massive impact 'the boy who lived' would go on to have. Let's begin our story, then.

A brilliant doctor, an ardent activist

From a young age, Sundari Mohan excelled in his studies, and until he graduated he earned every merit scholarship. Over the years, he became the first man in Sylhet district to qualify as a doctor from Calcutta Medical College. Having graduated in gynaecology and midwifery, a young Sundari Mohan was appalled by the poor and unhygienic practices of childbirth prevalent in our country. He travelled far and wide, especially in the Sylhet district, to create awareness about following hygienic practices to reduce infant mortality. He penned two books: *Dhratri Bidya* (*Midwifery Techniques*) and *Briddha Dhratri'r Rojnamcha* (*Diary of an Old Midwife*) to further educate his countrymen on this matter.

Two significant events influenced young Sundari Mohan during his student days in Calcutta. Around this time (the 1870s, that is), the reformist Brahma Samaj movement had become very popular with the young, educated sections of Bengali society. Sundari Mohan was also attracted to the modernistic and progressive ideas of Brahma Samaj and became a member.[3] He helped establish a branch of the Samaj in Sylhet town and married the widowed niece of Sansar Chandra Sen, a minister of Jaipur state. His defiance of social norms earned Sundari Mohan his family's wrath. He was disowned and disinherited from the family property. Undeterred, he stuck to his path and made female education his life motto. He worked hard to establish girls' schools across Bengal.

Dr Sundari Mohan Das, founder principal of Calcutta National Medical College and prominent Swadeshi leader in Bengal, in a rare photograph from the family archive. (Photo courtesy: Sri Amit Das)

The other event was his joining the Chaitra Mela, later renamed Hindu Mela.[4] Sundari Mohan became adept in bodybuilding, kushti (freestyle wrestling) and lathi-khela (stick-fighting—fighting with light bamboo poles). Back then, the British, especially sailors, often harassed common Indians in the business district of Chowringhee and Dalhousie Square. Sundari Mohan and a few of his friends formed a vigilante group that roamed the area and protected Indians from such harassment, meting out a healthy dose of physical tonic to errant white men.

Swadeshi ultra: A medical school

A pivotal moment came in Sundari Mohan's life in 1905. After Lord Curzon's announcement of the partition of Bengal, a wave of nationalism swept the land. While the armed resistance to the plan was spearheaded by Aurobindo Ghose (later Sri Aurobindo), the leader of the civil resistance such as protest rallies, boycott of foreign-made goods and services, and propagation of 'swadeshi' replacements was none other than Sundari Mohan's closest friend and sworn blood brother, Bipin Chandra Pal.[5]

As anger against Lord Curzon's move grew, there were widespread calls for boycotting not only British-made goods and services but also all their institutions, which included the Calcutta Medical College. According to the Das family accounts, a large Swadeshi rally was held at Auckland Circus Park (present-day Muhammad Ali Park in central Calcutta) where Sundari Mohan was among the speakers. When he took the dais to give his speech, many medical college students, worried about their future, pleaded to him for help. Sundari Mohan apparently promised them that he would leave no stone unturned to establish a swadeshi-backed medical institution. This dream finally took shape when on 14 April 1921, Netaji Subhas Chandra Bose inaugurated the National Medical Institute at 11, Wellington Street.[6]

In keeping with his Brahma Samaj vows, Sundari Mohan contributed most of his income from private medical practice in establishing and running the National Medical Institute. He was also one of the main figures who founded the Bengal Technical Institute (forerunner of Jadavpur University) and taught for free at the Carmichael Medical College (present-day R.G. Kar Medical College and Hospital). Until his death at the age of ninety-two, Sundari Mohan Das served as the principal of the National Medical Institute without ever taking a penny as salary, accepting payment only for reimbursement of out-of-pocket expenses. We were treated to an interesting anecdote by Sundari Mohan's great-grandson Amit Das. When Sundari Mohan was ninety, doctors at National Medical were worried with a particularly complex pregnancy case and no one was daring enough to perform the delivery. On learning of this, Sundari Mohan scoffed at the assembly and successfully delivered the child himself, possibly the last of his illustrious career.

But Sundari Mohan's devotion to the Swadeshi cause was not limited to just his profession. He invested Rs 25,000 to set up a hosiery-manufacturing factory that churned out vests at his home. His other motive was to provide employment to poorer sections of society. Unfortunately, the business didn't really take off.[7]

He was also an active supporter of the armed revolutionary movement, providing it financial support. According to the Das family, revolutionary meetings regularly took place at Sundari Mohan's residence with Ullaskar Dutta being particularly close to Sundari Mohan. He also sponsored the opening of akhadas (gymnasiums) across Calcutta for the youth to get trained in physical exercises, as did Sarala Ghoshal (Chapter 45).

In 1924, after Deshbandhu Chittaranjan Das became the mayor of Calcutta, on his request, Sundari Mohan became the chairman of the public health committee, bringing his vast experience to the cause of better health for the common citizens of Calcutta.

Legacy of service

Sundari Mohan also ensured his legacy would live on beyond him. As recounted by Sundari Mohan's great grandson, Amit Das, his son Premananda Das carried on the flame of brilliance quite superbly. As a young man, Premananda was sent to the USA in 1908 to study pharmacology. It was part of Sundari Mohan's vision of cutting down India's dependence on imported medicine. Premananda had inherited his father's academic brilliance. In the US, he pursued a master of science (MS) followed by a PhC (pharmaceutical chemist) from Michigan State University. He thus became the first foreign-qualified Indian pharmaceutical chemist (along with S.N. Bal). Premananda also pursued diplomas in bacteriology and business administration from Harvard University during his five years' stay. Amit Das (Premananda's grandson) was kind enough to show us the business card of Premananda Das. Holding it in our hands and looking at it truly gave us goosebumps and yet provoked the question, why is this brilliant man largely forgotten today? We are extremely indebted to Amit Das for recounting to us in great detail, Premananda's career path after returning from the US.

Shortly after his return, Premananda moved to Rangoon where he started working as chief chemist with Jamal Brothers, one of Burma's largest business houses. He soon found himself in the cross hairs of the British government. Premananda was arrested on false sedition charges of delivering anti-British speeches during his stay in America.

Premananda was extradited to India and spent some time in prison, before Sundari Mohan used his considerable influence to get his son released. Sadly, he was banned from ever entering Burma again. Premananda focused on fulfilling his father's dream, and started a drugs-manufacturing business, the Standard Pharmaceutical Company. Premananda Das's Standard Pharma became the first Indian company to make tablets for influenza and with the Spanish flu pandemic ravaging the world, the English pharmacist Frank Ross bought off almost their entire first batch of output to be exported to the war fronts of WWI.

Das & Sons had achieved the impossible—making the British dependent on an Indian company!

Under Premananda's leadership and with Sundari Mohan as mentor, Standard Pharma was reconstituted as a limited company—Standard Drug & Pharma Co. Ltd. Besides being trained in Western medicine, Sundari Mohan was also an expert in indigenous drugs and remedies, a knowledge he passed on to his son, who used it to formulate new drugs. Sadly, their bank collapsed and Standard Drug & Pharma ceased to exist. But not quite.

From the archives: Premananda Das, son of Dr Sundari Mohan Das.
(Photo courtesy: Sri Amit Das)

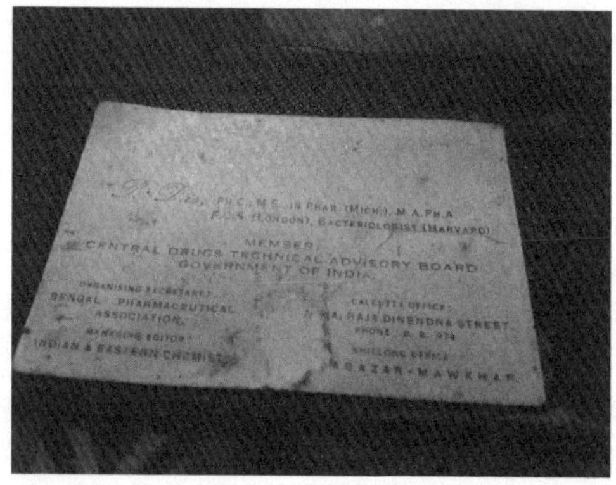

From the archives: Premananda Das's personal visiting card, preserved from the
past. (Photo courtesy: Sri Amit Das)

Ranajit Das, Premananda's eldest son, a chemical engineering graduate from Jadavpur University, underwent training in drug manufacturing from his illustrious father and set up a new business: the Universal Drug House, just a year before Independence.

The business is still around, although much reduced in size and scope now.

As India won her independence, Sundari Mohan Das's dreams of a nationalist medical institution of the highest quality and a swadeshi drugs business were both alive and kicking. When the curtain came down on his illustrious life in 1950, he must have been a contented man.

Not all the Das men trod the straight and narrow path indicated by their family. In the late nineteenth and first half of the twentieth century, there was a growing trend of young Bengali boys fleeing the staid confines of their homes to seek adventure in the world outside. The first and most dazzling was perhaps Colonel Suresh Biswas[8] (no relation of the Das clan) who was the ultimate swashbuckling adventurer who travelled the world and ended up an officer of the Brazilian army. The Das family also has a hero on similar lines.

Ajoy Das, Sundari Mohan's grandson and Premananda's younger son, vanished one day in 1937.[9] Barely twenty, he somehow made his way to China,[10] where he joined the ambulance corps and took an active part in the Sino–Japanese War. Some years later, Ajoy made his way to Southeast Asia, and signed up in Netaji Subhas Chandra Bose's Indian National Army. He was made the head of publicity, press and propaganda and handled broadcasting responsibilities. Among the broadcasts he handled was also Netaji's iconic 'Chalo Delhi' (Let's go to Delhi) clarion call. Ajoy later returned and joined his family business.

But it is not just the men of this family who made a mark in history. Premananda Das's three daughters, Arati, Kalyani and Anjali, were all inspirational people. All three sisters were active in the students' movements. Arati was involved in the people's theatre movement while Kalyani became a prominent figure in the communist movement of India. Kalyani also established a charitable medical institute in Silchar named after her grandfather: Sundari Mohan Seva Bhawan. The institution was later handed over to the Red Cross and is still active today.

'Mother of the World'

But possibly the most fascinating of the trio was Anjali Das. A firebrand communist in her youth who spent more than a year in jail, she became a legend during the 1971 Bangladesh Liberation War. Appalled by the pathetic conditions of the refugees streaming in from East Pakistan,[11] Anjali, then based out of Shillong, worked tirelessly to ease their suffering. She regularly visited refugee camps around Cherapunjee, Dawki and adjacent areas, providing financial aid, medicines, clothes and home-cooked food for hundreds of people. Anjali also helped many refugees secure livelihoods and organized a cultural function in Sunamgunj, the proceeds of which went to the Liberation War fund.

Her husband, Niren Lahiri, worked as a legal advisor to the refugees. The Lahiris' residence also became a shelter for injured and ailing freedom fighters of the Mukti Bahini. Her tireless efforts led to the muktijoddhas (freedom fighters) hailing her as 'Jagat Ma' (Mother of the World). She was later honoured by the Bangladesh government for her contributions.

While penning this chapter, we couldn't help but become a little reflective. No great achievement is ever done by only one or even a few individuals. It takes a concerted and collective effort to bring about a major change, whether social or political. Yet, many of the names and faces, who made such momentous events possible, vanish from popular history, slipping through the gaps between pages of history books.

Through chronicling the life and times of the Das family, we express our humblest gratitude to each and every such individual who fought against tyrannical rulers, social dogmas and oppressive traditions, to secure a better life for their countrymen.

49

When an Indian Boy Gave His Green Turban to Stitch the Pakistani Flag

In the vastly complex political landscape of India and Pakistan, there is an obscure story of an unforgettable day in 1947, when a group of young boys from the twin nations unfurled their national flags in the most bizarre of circumstances.

Before delving into this gripping account, one must understand the meaning and importance of 'jamboree'. Jamboree is a word with a fairly complex etymology. Based on the most popular belief, it traces its root to the Swahili word 'jumbo', meaning 'hello', but it is not verified. In the world of scouting, 'a jamboree is a large gathering of Scouts, at a national or international level'. The Scouting programme garnered global fame after Robert Baden-Powell founded it in 1908. The first World Scout Jamboree was held in 1920 in the United Kingdom and the twenty-fifth edition was celebrated in South Korea in 2023—the latest, as we write in 2025.

Jamboree on the eve of Independence

The sixth World Scout Jamboree was held in 1947 and was hosted by France at Moisson, a village on the outskirts of Paris. It was a former shooting range of the World War II era, located on the bank of the Seine. This was the first jamboree held after the devastating World War II and was aptly named the Jamboree of Peace (*Jamboree Mondial de la Paix*).

331

The Boy Scout movement had already gained momentum across undivided British India by then. After 1911, the programme was opened to native Indians and had started gaining prominence in Calcutta, Mysore, Jabalpur, Allahabad, Simla and Madras. In the province of Western Punjab, the scouting programme was introduced in the towns of Lahore and Ghora Gali. For the Jamboree Mondial de la Paix in 1947, 165 Boy Scouts were selected from all parts of undivided India with Danmal Mathur of Mayo College as the scoutmaster, and the leader was G.T.J. Thaddeus, a staunch Christian from Kerala.

The group of youngsters embarked upon their voyage from Bombay to Paris via Southampton on a ship named SS *Alcantara*. It took them eighteen days to reach England via the Suez Canal. The boys experienced massive seasickness. They struggled with sleeping, walking around and even eating, especially as the food on the ship was too bland. When they stopped at Aden and were taken to visit Cairo, they recovered their appetites and were thrilled to be served curry—but it had beef in it. The Hindus would not eat it and, in solidarity, the Muslim boys too rejected the food. Endearingly, the Hindu boys persuaded their Muslim friends to eat both shares! Eventually, the boys reached Moisson.

It was a true amalgamation of cultures of the world. About 40,000 Scouts[1] from twenty-four different nations joined the opening ceremony on 9 August 1947, six days before India gained independence. The first week went by celebrating brotherhood, but things changed suddenly when the camp received the news of India's Independence and the resultant Partition.

A flag born of unity

It was just before 15 August 1947. The Boy Scouts suddenly realized that they did not belong to the same nation anymore. Scoutmasters of the respective groups decided to hoist two different flags representing the separate nations, with the Scout flag in the middle. The Indian High Commission at London sent them boxes of sweets to celebrate

Independence with an Indian Tiranga (tricolour) flag. Unfortunately, there was no Pakistani flag available, as it was only on 11 August 1947 that the Constituent Assembly of Pakistan approved the design of the Pakistan national flag. The Muslim Boy Scouts of Pakistan had only seen a picture of the proposed Pakistani flag in a local newspaper. Meanwhile, Kurushid Abbas Gardezi, a boy from Multan, and his Scout buddy Iqbal Qureshi, along with the Punjab and Rajasthan contingent, were given the task of organizing the Pakistani flag, a day before the flag-hoisting ceremony. These boys then came up with a brilliant idea!

Gardezi donated his white shirt and Madan Mohan, an Indian boy from Simla, offered his green turban to provide the fabric for the flag of Pakistan. Two French Girl Guides worked all night to stitch the fabrics together and make the flag, and what they produced was the handmade Pakistani flag, *Parcam-i sitārah o-hilāl*, or the flag of the crescent and star. Meanwhile, back home at about the same time, the Indian subcontinent was witnessing the largest and most traumatic human migration in world history, with people from the two religions mass-murdering each other. In this backdrop, the story of a Pakistani flag made from an Indian boy's green turban bears special significance.

It was a riveting historic moment. Gardezi, Qureshi and their friends were the first ones to raise the Pakistan flag on foreign soil, far away from their homeland, on the day of liberation. During the flag-hoisting ceremony, the Indians sang '*Jana gana mana*' as their national anthem, but Pakistan was yet to decide on theirs, so all the Boy Scouts decided to sing '*Saare jahan se achcha*'. That remarkable day witnessed for the first time, the two independent dominions, India and Pakistan, unfurling their new flags one beside the other, at an international gathering.

The Boy Scouts soon after started their sixteen-day-long return voyage to Bombay on RMS *Strathmore*, the historic ship that had carried Don Bradman's Australia team to England for the Ashes in 1938. It is the same ship that took the 1936 Olympics gold medallist,

Dhyan Chand, and the Indian hockey team home from Berlin, accompanied by the nawab of Pataudi and the maharajkumar of Vizianagaram. This was no ordinary journey either! All the Scouts, who had travelled to Paris as the inhabitants of one nation, were returning as the citizens of two separate countries.

The situation was grave. They heard the news of Partition and the ongoing violence in the name of religion back home. Thadeus, fearing violence on board the ship, advised the boys to guard the deck in turns to ensure nobody was pushed into the water. The sleepless and frightening journey came to an end when the *Strathmore* docked at the port of Bombay. Back then, Bombay was burning with religious tension and riots. The Boy Scouts bid farewell to each other and the officials escorted the Muslim boys to Lahore and Karachi.

Post-Partition stories

For some of them, the world had turned upside down in a matter of a few weeks. Swaran Singh, a Punjabi boy from an opulent family of western Punjab, was one of the unfortunate boys. He came back only to find his parents waiting homeless at a railway station. Aftab, a Muslim boy from Ajmer, stayed in India on a quest to find his parents. His Hindu friends accompanied Aftab, gave him a Hindu name, hid him in a first-class train compartment, protected him from the rioting mob and escorted him to his parents in Ajmer.

The 1947 World Jamboree was a historic journey of smiles, tears and harmony. The boys returned home unharmed. Ranbir Singh of the Rajasthan contingent grew up to be a celebrated polymath. His fellow compatriot Jasdev Singh became a popular commentator for Doordarshan[4] and All India Radio. Later in life, he covered nine Olympics, and was also the iconic voice for India's Republic Day parade. The Pakistan Boy Scouts Association later honoured Kurushid Abbas Gardezi by presenting him with the Lifetime Achievement Award.

The future, however, was a stark contrast for a few; perhaps a tragic testimony of the hostile future of the two nations. One of the Boy Scouts from India at the jamboree grew up to be Colonel Narendra Kumar (also known as the Bull), a famous mountaineer who climbed the Himalayas and the Karakorams. He was also an Indian soldier, who played a key role in Operation Meghdoot to reclaim the Siachen glacier in 1984. Sarfaraz Ahmed Rafiqui was Narendra's good friend who had hoisted the Jamboree Organization flag in 1947, and later joined the Pakistan Air Force. During a siege of IAF Halwara Air Base in 1965, he made the supreme personal sacrifice.

The Hindu and Muslim youngsters, who together unfurled the flags of the two new dominions for the first time on foreign soil, could have little imagined that it was only the beginning of a bloodthirsty rivalry that would last for years to come.

50

India after Independence: Following Gandhi's Footsteps

'Injustice anywhere is a threat to justice everywhere.'

—Martin Luther King Jr

The great American civil rights crusader wrote these lines on 16 April 1963, while imprisoned at the Alabama jail. In many ways, we find an echo of Mahatma Gandhi's thoughts in the quote and it is hardly surprising. After all, Dr King was an ardent follower of Gandhian thought, studying the legendary Indian's writings very closely in his formative years. In Martin Luther King Jr's iconic 'I Have a Dream' speech, many of his followers standing behind him can be seen wearing Gandhi caps. In 1959, he also made a trip to India to learn more about Gandhi. During his visit to India, Dr King was pleasantly surprised to find that many in India were aware of the Montgomery bus boycott incident.[1]

But maybe he shouldn't have been surprised. When India achieved its freedom, our founding fathers were clear (as was Kamaladevi Chattopadhyay, Chapter 31) that the new nation had to chart a course of honour, justice and truth, and that was not to be limited to just Indian affairs. Even before Independence, in 1946, Jawaharlal Nehru was among the first global leaders to actively back Indonesian independence efforts. And this trend continued in the coming years not just in politics but in other walks of life as well, as we shall see soon.

Incidentally, talking of Gandhi, the importance of South Africa in shaping the man cannot be overemphasized. It is possibly fair to state that the two decades he spent in that country went a long way into the transformation of a young lawyer named Mohandas Gandhi into the Mahatma. His earliest experiments with the path of non-violent resistance bore fruit here.

The shocking mistreatment of Indians and native Africans in South Africa left a young Gandhi disturbed and he cancelled his originally planned return in 1894 to fight for the rights of the Indians living in the African country. It would be 1914 before a transformed man, burning with passion to secure freedom for his countrymen, returned to India. South Africa's marginalized communities did not forget him, though. In 1994, when black South Africans were finally granted the right to vote, Gandhi was remembered with fond reverence.

Talking of South Africa, it is ironic that the very year (1948) the Mahatma's life was cut short by a hate-filled assassin's bullet, the South African authorities introduced a racial segregation-driven governance that was reminiscent of what had been done in Nazi Germany in the 1930s. That year, the D.F. Malan-led Herenigde Nasionale Party emerged as the single largest party and formed the government in alliance with the Afrikaner Party, ushering in an era of state-sponsored racist oppression—apartheid. While South African society was already racially segregated, now, it bore an official stamp. From segregated residential areas to the disenfranchisement of black and 'coloured' citizens, it was one of the worst examples set by modern humanity, and over time it became more draconian.

Standing firm for principles

Having been at the receiving end of the worst excesses of colonial rule, it was but natural that India was at the forefront of resistance to the South African apartheid system. Even before apartheid was systematically legalized, India was the first country to bring attention to the widespread racism in South African society and institutions, when the Jawaharlal Nehru-led interim government raised the issue of the poor treatment of Indian-origin people in that country at the first session of the UN General Assembly in 1946.

The same year, India withdrew its high commissioner from South Africa in protest of racial segregationist policies, becoming the first nation to sever formal ties with South Africa. Even as the British Commonwealth and the USA continued a mildly reproachful approach towards South Africa, Nehru's India continued to abide by Gandhi's legacy by remaining at the forefront of putting international spotlight and pressure on the South African government.

India's persistent efforts finally bore fruit in 1960 when the UN Council for the first time officially denounced South Africa's racist policies. By this time, India had almost completely severed all ties with South Africa in all walks of life. There was a full boycott of South African goods; ships and planes from the country were not allowed to dock or land at Indian ports and India even refused fly-bys to South African aircrafts.

As a matter of fact, from 1946 to 1964 when Jawaharlal Nehru breathed his last, India tabled twenty-four resolutions at the UN, condemning South African government policies. Nehru also aided African National Congress (ANC) leaders Oliver Tambo and Yusuf Dadoo in their escape bid from South Africa to London. Such a thorn in the flesh was India and PM Nehru that South African minister Oswald Pirow called the latter a 'coolie' in 1953.[2]

Even after Prime Minister Nehru's death, India's stance towards South African apartheid policies remained as firmly opposed as ever. And as the decade of the seventies rolled in, matters reached a flashpoint.

The year 1971 was an iconic and memorable year for Indian cricket and for the nation as a whole. It was the year that saw Indian cricket coming of age, pulling off an unthinkable win against the Sir Garfield Sobers-led West Indies on their home turf, and then follow it up with another historic first victory on English soil. And yet, the first of those momentous wins almost didn't materialize. And it was the man hailed as the greatest cricketer of all time who was at the centre of the storm.

A misstep by Garry Sobers

In the summer of 1970, Sobers was invited to participate in a double-wicket invitational cricket tournament in Salisbury, Rhodesia (present-day Zimbabwe). Five years earlier, Rhodesia had become the first country to have UN sanctions imposed on it for racial discrimination against its own citizens. Sobers had his doubts but on being assured that there was no discrimination in team selection and participation, he went ahead and played the tournament. He earned a pay cheque of £600 and also had dinner with the Rhodesian premier Ian Smith. As he flew out of Rhodesia, Sobers had no inkling that he had triggered a diplomatic storm.

Back home, Sobers was criticized brutally for playing in an apartheid-country, with demands to strip him of the West Indian captaincy emanating strongly across the Caribbean. The Prime Minister of Guyana, Forbes Burnham, even warned that Sobers would not be allowed to enter his country unless he tendered an unconditional apology. While this was ongoing, the matter ceased to be just a Caribbean affair. India's Prime Minister Indira Gandhi sent out a firm message that her government would seriously consider cancelling the proposed trip to the West Indies in 1971 if Sobers was retained as captain. Mrs Gandhi was unequivocal in her message: India would not compromise one bit when it came to apartheid.

Eventually, the matter was resolved amicably thanks to the efforts of the Trinidadian premier Eric Williams, who drafted a suitable apology letter and got Sobers to sign and submit it to the West Indian board. The way was clear for the Indian team to embark on their historic voyage. But while one Indian sports team had a lucky breakthrough in time, another would meet a different fate.

Noble step back from glory

From its inception in 1900, the Davis Cup, the premier international tennis contest, had remained a privilege of the big four: USA, Great Britain, Australia and France. Till 1973, no other nation had won the Cup and at least one of the big four had featured in every final. But that changed in 1974.

In a major upset, the Amritraj brothers inspired the Indian team to a historic win over defending champions Australia in the eastern zone final. The contest produced 327 games—a record even now in Davis Cup annals. India followed it up with a resounding win over the Soviet Union in the world group semi-finals to be just one step away from glory. But there was only one problem: their opponents in the finals.

In 1970, the International Cricket Council (ICC) and the International Olympic Committee (IOC) expelled South Africa. But the International Tennis Federation (ITF) did not take any such steps, thus highlighting the inconsistency of the approach to South Africa by different sports bodies. And in 1974, South Africa made it to the Davis Cup finals against India. Worse, they were to be the hosts for the occasion.

Even before the official declaration came, the Indian Davis Cup team knew that the final wouldn't take place. Mrs Gandhi's stance on apartheid was clear. And in a way, it was just as well, since the Indian team's fans and supporters would have been forced to sit in the 'coloured' section of the gallery. For the players, it was a colossal disappointment—especially since South Africa weren't exactly fancied as winners and it was possibly the best chance India ever had of clinching the Davis Cup. But Vijay Amritraj, India's best player, put it in perspective most poignantly in an interview with the *New York Times*: 'As a sportsman, I was disappointed, but as an individual, I took pride in the fact that my government made the right call.'

South Africa was awarded the Davis Cup by forfeit, but India's commitment to the cause of equality and justice and its continued devotion to the Gandhian legacy earned it international plaudits, while also putting a renewed spotlight on the apartheid regime in South Africa.

But it was not just in the field of sports that India's anti-apartheid stance shone through. In 1976 and 1977, the Indian representatives at the Miss World contest, Naina Balsaver and Veena Prakash, were asked to stand down by the Indian government as there were two South African contestants: a white official Miss South Africa and a token black representative who was not allowed to call herself Miss South Africa. It was hypocrisy of the highest order, and India was among a handful of third-world countries that refused to be a part of it.

In the world that we inhabit today, with rising inequalities and injustice, the lessons from visionary leaders like Mahatma Gandhi and Martin Luther King Jr are more important than ever before. And a country like ours, which has been at the forefront in fighting for the rights of the oppressed everywhere, must realign its Gandhian roots with global geopolitical realities to chart a course that does justice to the vision of its founding fathers.

Acknowledgements

This book began almost by chance—almost because we had been toying with the idea for some time. It was at that moment that HarperCollins India reached out to us, and the project began to take concrete shape. We cannot thank Ridhima Kumar, our commissioning editor, and the entire HarperCollins India team enough for believing in us, and creating this opportunity to present history in the quirkiest possible way.

In our preface we mentioned: We've been fortunate to travel a lot over the years and lucky to meet some truly fascinating people along the way. This book is a collective effort shaped by the extraordinary contributions of many of them, our friends and their network, the historians and journalists who documented the anecdotes of our freedom struggle.

We would like to extend our heartfelt gratitude to all those who helped us with our research. Abhijit Lahiri, Arnab Jan Deka, Ashmita Lahiri, Girbban Paul, Imran Ahmed, Kaushik Mukherjee, M. Ansari, Sayantani Adhikary, Shahin Rahmani, Sujit Saraf and Vikas Kumar (Library and Information Officer, PMML) for sharing their knowledge and all relevant resources.

We are indebted to Amit Das, great-grandson of Dr Sundari Mohan Das, Uttarpara Mukherjee, family historian Debasish Mukherjee, and Manzilat Fatima, Irfan Ali Mirza and Kamran Ali Mirza, direct descendants of Begum Hazrat Mahal, for opening up their homes, and providing us access to invaluable family archives that shaped these forgotten narratives even better and brought them to life.

Our deepest thanks to film historian Avijit Ghosh, film and music expert Pavan Jha, and National Award-winning author, Balaji Vittal, for their sharp insights on all things Bollywood, cricket historian and author Gulu Ezekiel and Madhumita Dutta for being her usual resourceful self as a journalist.

To all the kind souls who went above and beyond to connect us with the right people or helped us to source rare information and photographs that enriched the book, we are so grateful to you: Aditya Bhattacharya, Amrita Chaudhuri, Anindya Dasgupta, Anirban Kundu, Aratrika Ganguly, Archan Chakraborty, Debajyoti Moitra, Jaydeep Guha, Kanishka Dam, Michael Riordan (archivist, St. John's and The Queen's Colleges, Oxford University), Md Kaisar Hossain, Proma Sanyal, Ram Badrinathan, Santanu Basu, Shreyashi Bhattacharya, Somsubhra Ghosh and Tanuka Ghoshal.

Jayasree Roy of *Desh* magazine and Praveen Das and the Wikimedia Foundation team—thank you for the visuals that add to the charm of this book.

As we said in the beginning, we went down a rabbit hole while researching topics and often took a detour to craft a more intriguing story. Joseph John, our journalist friend, ensured we didn't get carried away by fact-checking each story meticulously and always kept the stories authentic. Thank you, Joseph!

Two people who are more than just our friends and an integral part of Paperclip deserve special mention here: Banshori Bhattacharya and Tamas Sinha.

While we have tried to acknowledge everyone we have spoken to, in case we missed naming any of you, it would be an entirely unintentional oversight. We remain thankful to each of you who made this book possible. If these pages have sparked even a moment of wonder, pride and inquiry, then our journey has been worthwhile. This book is a shared legacy, a tribute to all the people whose lives are the fabric of our freedom.

Notes and References

Scan this QR code to access the notes.

About the Authors

Founded on 15 August 2021, The Paperclip is an avant-garde digital media platform dedicated to authentic storytelling, binding together stories from India and beyond. In this age of social media when fake content spreads at the speed of light, The Paperclip has become a trusted voice that informs the audience about India's rich social, cultural and democratic diversity. Known for its signature content that is widely shared on social media and featured in leading print and news media, The Paperclip is also the creator of the Audible Original podcast *Long Story Short*, and continues to bring India's most compelling stories to life through its regular contributions to several major digital media platforms.

The Paperclip team

Abhinaba Maitra, the quiet worker, juggles his time between reading voraciously, gorging on biryani and hoarding stories. He scribbles what he reads and what he sees, and chases forgotten tales down until they agree to be written.

Indranath Mukherjee, a die-hard quizzer with a passion for everything music, Bollywood, pop culture and sports, spins fascinating stories from his eclectic mix of interests.

Priyadarshini Basu, a grammar purist and journalist at heart, looks at stories from an inverted pyramid structure and makes sure Wren and Martin get their due respect.

Saumyajit Ray, deeply versed in the nuances of Indian politics and governance, combines sharp strategic thinking with a storyteller's instinct. An Arsenal enthusiast and perpetual devil's advocate, he brings both intellect and edge to every story he tells.

Srinwantu Dey, a knowledge powerhouse and keen observer of Indian democracy, loves to transform obscure histories into gripping, thought-provoking stories.

Subhajit Sengupta is a seasoned storyteller who has a penchant to deep dive into any topic and come up with the most well-researched stories tempered with wordplay. Off the page, he's equally committed—to football and a good whisky.

Trinanjan Chakraborty, the scholar and author, is a walking, talking encyclopaedia on history, cricket, football and many things in between.

HarperCollins *Publishers* India

At HarperCollins India, we believe in telling the best stories and finding the widest readership for our books in every format possible. We started publishing in 1992; a great deal has changed since then, but what has remained constant is the passion with which our authors write their books, the love with which readers receive them, and the sheer joy and excitement that we as publishers feel in being a part of the publishing process.

Over the years, we've had the pleasure of publishing some of the finest writing from the subcontinent and around the world, including several award-winning titles and some of the biggest bestsellers in India's publishing history. But nothing has meant more to us than the fact that millions of people have read the books we published, and that somewhere, a book of ours might have made a difference.

As we look to the future, we go back to that one word—a word which has been a driving force for us all these years.

Read.

Harper Collins

Harper Sport

HARPER FICTION

HARPER NON-FICTION

हार्पर हिन्दी

HARPER LEARNING

HARPER VANTAGE

HCCB HARPERCOLLINS CHILDREN'S BOOKS

4th

HARPER PERENNIAL

HARPER DESIGN

BOOKTOPUS

HARPER BUSINESS